S0-BYD-449

Electronic
Resumes

Other Books by James Gonyea

On-Line Job Search Companion: A Complete Guide to Hundreds of Career Planning and Job Hunting Resources Available Via Your Computer

Selling on the Internet

Career Selector 2001

Working for America

Electronic Resumes

A Complete Guide to Putting Your Resume On-Line

James C. Gonyea

Wayne M. Gonyea

McGraw-Hill

New York   San Francisco   Washington, D.C.   Auckland   Bogotá
Caracas   Lisbon   London   Madrid   Mexico City   Milan
Montreal   New Delhi   San Juan   Singapore
Sydney   Tokyo   Toronto

Library of Congress cataloging card number: 96-76534

McGraw-Hill

A Division of The McGraw·Hill Companies

Copyright © 1996 by James C. Gonyea. All rights reserved. Printed in the United States of America. Except as permitted under the United States Copyright Act of 1976, no part of this publication may be reproduced or distributed in any form or by any means, or stored in a data base or retrieval system, without the prior written permission of the author.

2 3 4 5 6 7 8 9 0   DOC/DOC   9 0 1 0 9 8 7 6

Resumes Online—Copyright © 1995 by James C. Gonyea and Wayne M. Gonyea. All rights reserved.

Resumaker—Copyright © 1995 by Techno-Marketing, Inc. All rights reserved.

P/N 024188-0
PART OF
ISBN 0-07-912166-7

The sponsoring editor for this book was Betsy Brown, the editing supervisor was Fred Dahl, and the production supervisor was Pamela Pelton. It was set in Palatino by Inkwell Publishing Services.

Printed and bound by R. R. Donnelley & Sons Company.

While every effort possible has been taken by the authors and publisher to ensure that the resources listed in this book are available to the general public, and that the information contained herein about each resource is accurate and up to date, neither the authors, nor the publisher, shall be liable for any errors or omissions in data, nor shall the authors or publisher be liable for any damages, financial or otherwise, that may occur from the use of any resource contained in this book by the reader, regardless of whether the authors and/or publisher were forewarned of any potential damage by any third party.

MCGRAW-HILL MAKES NO REPRESENTATIONS OR WARRANTIES WITH RESPECT TO THE *RESUMES ONLINE* AND *RESUMAKER* SOFTWARE MATERIALS THAT ARE INCLUDED IN THE WORK, INCLUDING BUT NOT LIMITED TO THE DISK AND ITS CONTENTS. Accordingly, all questions and problems relating to the enclosed software materials should be directed to the appropriate source below:

Questions regarding *Resumes Online*: Gonyea and Associates, Inc., 1151 Maravista Drive, New Port Richey, Florida 34655, 813/372-1333

Questions regarding *Resumaker*: Techno-Marketing, Inc., 5170 West 76th Street, Edina, MN 55435, 612/830-1984

Gender Policy

The words "he," "his," "him" as used is this book are intended to refer to both men and women, and are used solely to reduce confusion and reading difficulty as often encountered when the broader terms of "he/she," "his/hers," and "him/her" are used.

 This book is printed on recycled, acid-free paper containing a minimum of 50% recycled de-inked fiber.

To all job seekers who wish to express their uniqueness and talents in a manner appropriate for communication with today's high-tech, computer online and multimedia culture.

And especially to Pam for her continued support during the times when I'm off writing another book. And to Korie, who has inspired me since her birth with a simple smile.

James C. Gonyea

To Leslie, Tony, Lisa, and Mike for a never ending well of encouragement, love, and support. Especially to Kassie for making the world a better place.

Wayne M. Gonyea

Contents

Acknowledgments   **xi**

1. Job Hunting on the Information Superhighway   **1**
Resumes in Cyberspace   1
A Guide for 21st Century Resumes   3

2. What Is an Electronic Resume?   **5**
Electronic vs. Traditional Resumes   5
Text File Resumes   6
Multimedia Resumes   7
Electronic Power Tools   7

3. The Purpose of *Electronic Resumes*   **9**
Not Another Resume Writing Book   9
Upgrading Your Traditional Resume to an Electronic
    Resume   10

Keywords—What Potential Employers Are
Scanning For   16

Upgrading to a Multimedia Resume   18

4. The Advantages of Electronic Resumes   21

A Win, Win, Win Situation ...   21

The Advantages for Job Seekers   21

The Advantages for Employers and Employment
Recruiters   23

5. Distributing Electronic Resumes Online   26

Click—and Your Resume Is in Paris!   26

How Are Electronic Resumes Distributed Online?   27

A Word About Email Addresses   29

6. Electronic Resume Checklist   32

7. Necessary Equipment   36

PCs Are Still King   36

What Other Equipment Do You Need?   36

Logging on to BBS Services   37

Logging on to Commercial Network Services   37

Logging on to the Internet   37

Other Equipment, Features, and Peripherals   37

8. Precautions to Keep in Mind   40

Have a Safe Trip   40

Create a Blind Resume   41

Posting on Bulletin Boards   42

Credit Card Information   42

Virus Infection   43

9. How to Create an Electronic Online Resume   45

Using *Resumes Online*   45

What Is *Resumes Online*?   46

Why Use *Resumes Online*?   46

Technical Help   47

System Requirements   47

Assumed Knowledge   47

Step 1: Install the *Resumes Online* Software Program   47

Starting the Program   48

Step 2: Create Your Electronic Resume   49

Categories   49

Automatic or Manual Options   50

Pace Yourself   50

Save Your Work   51

Built-in Help System   52

Special Keyboard Commands   52

Let's Begin   52

Step 3: Export Your Electronic Resume as a
Text File   88

10. How to Create a Multimedia Resume   90

Using *Resumaker*   90

Assumed Knowledge   91

Step 1: Install the *Resumaker* Software Program   92

Starting the Program   92

Step 2: Edit the *Resumaker* Multimedia
Display Area   93

Step 3: Prepare Your *Resumaker* Display and
Print Files   100

Decision #1: Number of Buttons   100

Decision #2: Button Labels   100

Decision #3: Text or Graphics   100

Setting the Number of Buttons   101

Setting the Format Characteristic of Each
Button   102

Editing the Button Labels   103

Preparing or Editing Text Files   104

Preparing or Editing Graphic Image Files   107

Preparing a Printed Copy of Your Resume   109

Step 4: Create Your Own Stand-Alone Resume   111

Compressing Files   112

11. Sample Resumes   114
Types of Resumes in This Chapter   115
Sample Resumes   118
Acknowledgments   201

12. Sample Cover Letters   203
Sample Cover Letters   205
Acknowledgments   224

APPENDIXES

Appendix A
Registering with the Worldwide
Resume/Talent Bank   227

Appendix B
Traditional Resume Resources   231

Appendix C
Electronic Resume Resources   233

Appendix D
Online Employment Advertising Services   248

Appendix E
Glossary   251

Index   255

Acknowledgments

The authors would like to thank the following individuals for their contributions to this book.

Joe Sherwood of Clear Mountain Designs and Rob Dachowski whose programming ability helped to create the *Resumes Online* software program.

Christopher Moon at Techno-Marketing for granting us permission to bundle a copy of the *Resumaker* software program with *Electronic Resumes*.

Theopholis J. Benderschwitz III for his pioneering vision of how electronic resumes can be used and for his guidance in shaping the content of this book.

The following individuals who agreed to act as our resource team of experts, and who graciously provided us with sample resumes and cover letters:

Gary Ames
R.L. Stevens & Associates, Inc.
630 Freedom Business Center
Suite 203
King of Prussia, PA 19406
610-962-1100

John Bakos
The Bakos Group
260 Worthington Street
Springfield, MA 01103
800-370-5627

Timothy Gibson
Professional Career Associates of Austin, Texas
9430 Research Blvd.
The Echelon II, Suite 140
Austin, TX 78759
512-338-9144

Tom Jackson
The Equinox Corporation
57 West 58th Street
Penthouse A
New York, NY 10019
212-832-5757

Kathryn Jordan
Employment Counseling Services
201 Church Street
Blacksburg, VA 24060
800-775-AJOB

Steven Provenzano
Advanced Resume Service
701 East Irving Park Road
Suite 201
Roselle, IL 60172
708-289-1999

Debarah Wilson
443 Waverly Street
Menlo Park, CA 94025
415-321-3275

And, of course, Betsy Brown at McGraw-Hill for her continued support and interest over the years in our professional activities, and for her wise and trusted guidance in preparing this publication.

1

Job Hunting on the Information Superhighway

Resumes in Cyberspace

By electing to purchase this book, or obtain it from your local library, you have made the decision to create your own *electronic* resume—or at least to explore this option.

Congratulations! You are about to learn how your resume, when converted to an electronic format, can be distributed worldwide using the power and reach of the Information Superhighway. Created by linking together commercial computer network services, private bulletin board services, and the Internet, the Information Superhighway is the world's largest information and communication network, interconnecting an estimated 40 to 60 million people around the globe! Your resume is about to travel down this grand-daddy of all information networks.

A new era of *electronic* job hunting has begun. Job seekers and employers communicate at the speed of light and are in touch day and night. They can meet online to chat in cyberspace—that invisible but nonetheless real part of our universe where information is stored or transferred electronically through the use of computers, modems, and phone lines. In cyberspace, people from any location on the globe and at any time of the day or night can meet and communicate in real time.

No longer dependent on the U.S. Postal Service, which is often slow and undependable, employers and job seekers can now communicate electronically from any location on the globe to any other location in only a matter of seconds. At the same blazing speed, they can distribute resumes, legal contracts, documents, and other materials using a variety of modern communication tools, such as email, file transfer, and online conferencing.

While distribution of printed resumes continues to be widely used and remains an appropriate job seeking strategy, it is no longer the only or main means of marketing yourself to potential employers. Job hunting electronically, while just recently grown from its infancy, is often far superior to the traditional methods of finding employment. With *Electronic Resumes*, the power of electronic job hunting is yours. All you need is your personal computer (equipped with a modem), the right kind of software (enclosed with this book), and access to an online computer network service.

Current research clearly reveals that for job seekers, the use of high-speed and instantaneous computer network services is widespread and growing. In finding and securing employment, speed of communication is a critical and deciding factor. In today's fast-paced society, if you fail to get your credentials into the hands of employers in time—ahead of the competition and before the hiring decision is made—your case for why you should be hired may never be heard.

Electronic computer network services have revolutionized how businesspeople communicate with each other. Whether you're communicating from one side of the globe to the other, from a satellite office downtown to your home office in the suburbs, from one end of the hall to the other, or even from your desk to your colleague's desk across the room, the time it takes to distribute information can often spell the difference between success and failure. As many business professionals know, the traditional means of communicating, such as first class mail (often referred to as *snail mail* due to its slow speed as compared to electronic mail), are just too slow in many situations today. In the business world, relying on such slow methods of communication can mean lost sales. For job seekers, relying on a slow method of distributing resumes, cover letters, and other job hunting documents can result in longer periods of unemployment, unnecessary rejections, and the loss of employment opportunities.

In the not-too-distant future, the majority of all communications, both personal and business, will be done electronically—if that day has not arrived already! Currently, millions of people have come to rely on the speed of electronic communication systems to satisfy their personal and professional needs. If you're searching for employment, or soon will be, and if you're not using the power of electronic communication networks to shine your light, then you're likely to miss out on many employment openings. But you don't have to!

By following the directions contained in *Electronic Resumes*, you can easily and quickly provide millions of people worldwide with access to your resume. By incorporating an electronic resume into your overall job search campaign, you can gain a considerable competitive edge over traditional job seekers who continue to distribute resumes the old-fashioned (slow) way—by mail. In short, you can find and land more jobs!

In less time than it takes most job hunters to prepare a printed copy of their resume and drop it in their home mailbox, you can, using electronic network services, actually have your resume in the hands of hundreds of employers worldwide.

As Bob Dylan is often quoted as saying, "The times they are a-changing." This has never been more true than now. How job seekers are finding and responding to employment opportunities is nothing short of revolutionary. If you are content with simply printing resumes and mailing them to employers you think may have an interest in hiring you, please think again!

Armed with computers, modems, special software programs with which to prepare electronic resumes, and subscriptions to online commercial network and BBS services, empowered by having access to the Internet, and enlightened by an understanding of how to job hunt electronically, millions of job seekers are beating out—actually crushing—the competitors who are job hunting the old-fashioned way.

Tom Jackson, a well-known author and leading expert in job hunting strategies, has for a long time been convinced that the best jobs do not necessarily go to the job seekers with the best qualifications. Often, the best jobs go to the job seekers who clearly understand the most effective job hunting strategies. If you expect to compete and to win in today's tight and constantly changing job market, you've got to have the proper tools and job hunting savvy. Otherwise you may find yourself constantly being passed over by employers who favor job seekers who have mastered today's job hunting secrets.

An essential tool that should be in every job hunter's bag of tools is an electronic resume. In a few short hours, using the special software enclosed with *Electronic Resumes* as your guide, you too will have the best job hunting tools available for your use.

With *Electronic Resumes* you can upgrade from your old, slow-moving, printed resume to today's leading-edge, turbo-charged, screechingly fast electronic resume, and cruise down the Information Superhighway to new and exciting career opportunities.

A Guide for 21st Century Resumes

In this book, you'll discover what electronic resumes are, how to create two kinds of electronic resumes (text and multimedia), how to get your electronic resumes posted online, and how to use your electronic resumes to find employment.

You do not have to have a resume already prepared to use this book. However, when you attempt to complete the chapters devoted to developing an electronic or multimedia resume, you should have a standard, printed resume on hand that you can use as a reference document. If you have already developed a resume, you can expect to complete these chapters fairly quickly. If not, please budget additional time since it will be necessary to develop your regular resume first and then convert it to an electronic format.

If you have never written a resume, or feel uncomfortable creating one, it is recommended that you first review one or two books on the subject before attempting to convert your resume to an electronic format (see Appendix B).

Electronic Resumes was written to help you increase your ability to quickly find and secure employment using today's most advanced communication technology: your personal computer and online network services. We will accomplish this goal by first guiding you step-by-step in the creation of an electronic and/or multimedia resume based on the information found in your current resume. Second, we'll help you secure employment by illustrating how you can distribute your electronic text or multimedia resume to employers and recruiters worldwide using the personal marketing power of today's leading commercial computer network services, such as America Online, CompuServe, Prodigy, or the Internet. These resources, when viewed as a whole, are often referred to as the Information Superhighway—a highway of information that can be used to distribute your electronic resume around the globe, all at the speed of light.

2

What Is an Electronic Resume?

Electronic vs. Traditional Resumes

Experts estimate that, on any given day, millions of printed resumes are being circulated by job seekers looking for employment. With the use of a resume, you are able to "tell your story." A resume provides you with a means of "shining your light," to convince a prospective employer that you can successfully handle the position for which you are applying. Your resume is your personal marketing tool, an important and central ingredient in your job search campaign.

An *electronic* resume has the same purpose as its traditional printed cousin: to advertise your employment value and availability to potential employers. However, the medium with which you tell your story is different. Rather than print your resume on paper and then distribute it by hand, by mail, or by fax, you gather your data with a personal computer and save it as an electronic document (or file), which can then be transferred electronically to other individuals worldwide using any number of computer online network services.

Another difference between conventional and electronic resumes is the speed at which they are distributed. Conventional printed resumes are usually distributed to employers via first class mail. Naturally, depending on the locations of the job seeker and the potential employer, this can take anywhere from a few days to several weeks for the resume to arrive at its intended location. Not so with electronic resumes. They can travel from any point on the globe to any other point in a matter of only seconds!

Electronic resumes can be created in a variety of formats, including text, audio, video, and multimedia. Audio resumes are usually produced on audio cassette tapes for listening by potential employers. Video resumes arrive on video cassettes, similar to the movie cassettes we are all so familiar with today. Audio and video resumes can range in price from inexpensive (if you record them yourself) to expensive (if produced by professional audio and/or video production services).

The most popular or common electronic formats are text (aka ASCII) files or multimedia programs. Because text file and multimedia resumes are the most popular, and the easiest and least expensive for the average job seeker to create, *Electronic Resumes* will guide you in creating just these two options. If you wish to explore the options of audio and/or video resumes, you might consider contacting a local audio/video production service. Check your *Yellow Pages* for a listing of local services. Also, see the upgrade option within the *Resumaker* program (Chap. 10) to add audio and video to your multimedia resume.

Text File Resumes

Most electronic resumes produced today use a computer and a word processing program. What you can create using a word processing program, such as a letter, memo, or a resume, is generically referred to as a *document* or *file*.

When you use a word processing program to create a document, you have the option of saving it in a format *native* to the word processing program that you used to created the document. For example, if you were to use Microsoft Word for Windows 6.0 to create a document, you could save the document as a file in Microsoft Word for Windows 6.0 format. Such a file can be read only by someone using either Microsoft Word for Windows 6.0 or a different word processing program that is equipped to read a Microsoft Word for Windows 6.0 document.

As an option, you could save your document as a *text* file. When you do so, your word processing program removes the special commands from your document that can be read only by the program that created it, leaving just the basic text in place. This procedure creates a generic document, one that can be read by just about any word processing program.

When you view a text document, all you see on your computer screen are words. No graphics, pictures, or other elements of any kind can be saved in a text file. Consider the text file format to be a universal computer language that all word processing programs can read. Therefore, if you wish to distribute your resume electronically to other people, you must first convert your resume into a format that can be read by any word processing program.

Fortunately, however, you don't have to worry about whether your word processing program can create a text file. The enclosed *Resumes Online* software program, which is discussed later in this chapter, is actually a special word processing program created to produce a text file version of your resume.

Multimedia Resumes

Unlike a text file, a multimedia resume can contain any or all of the following elements:

❏ Text (words on screen)
❏ Sound clips
❏ Graphic artwork (colored drawings and/or actual pictures)
❏ Animated scenes
❏ Live video scenes

Obviously, when all of these elements are combined, the overall effect can be more pleasant to our senses than simple text (words) on a screen. After all, the world is multimedia in design. When we view the world, we see colors and movement, we hear sounds, and we feel sensations. Therefore, any correctly done electronic resume that combines multimedia elements is much more likely to be seen and appreciated than one that includes only text. That's why multimedia resumes are becoming more and more popular.

Creating a multimedia resume that combines *all* of these elements requires a variety of sophisticated computer and audio/video recording equipment—more than what is available to the average job seeker. For this reason, we have elected to provide you with a software program called *Resumaker*, which is also covered later in this chapter, that will enable you to develop a resume that combines just text and graphics. Obviously, while not as appealing as a resume that combines all possible multimedia elements, it is nonetheless more visually appealing than a resume containing text alone. After mastering this first level of multimedia, you might then consider enhancing your knowledge, skills, and equipment to produce a higher-level multimedia resume.

Electronic Power Tools

Electronic Resumes comes bundled with two easy-to-use but powerful Windows-based software programs:

❏ *Resumes Online.* With your computer and this software program, you will be able to create an electronic resume for uploading to the Worldwide Resume/Talent Bank, a popular online resume database service. An electronic resume is a special storage medium whereby your resume is stored as a computer file, rather than as printed words on paper. *Resumes Online* can produce a text file format to allow your resume to be read by all modern computers.

❏ *Resumaker.* With your computer and this program, you will be able to create a basic multimedia resume. This type of electronic file format can contain both text and graphics (pictures and/or computer-generated artwork). Upon completion, you can distribute your multimedia resume online using electronic file transfer (FTP) or email, post it online as a downloadable file on any number of computer online network and BBS services, or distribute it on diskette. In addition, you can use *Resumaker* to create standard printed copies of your resume.

Refer to the following chart to identify which software program you should use to create an electronic resume, multimedia resume, or a printed resume.

If you wish to create …	*Use the following software program …*
An electronic resume for posting online in a searchable resume database	*Resumes Online*
A multimedia resume	*Resumaker*
A printed copy of your standard resume	*Resumaker*

3
The Purpose of *Electronic Resumes*

Not Another Resume Writing Book

Electronic Resumes is not another "how to write your resume" book, nor will you find a rehash of how to conduct a job search contained within these pages. What you will find is advice regarding how to create electronic resumes from two leading-edge and pioneering experts with more than 50 years of combined experience in guiding tens of thousands of job seekers in how to effectively secure employment, especially with the use of electronic resumes and online network services.

Electronic Resumes will not teach you how to use online services to find employment. To learn how to find and access over 100,000 employment listings on commercial computer network services, private bulletin board systems (BBS), and the Internet, please refer to our other book, *The Online Job Search Companion,* published by McGraw-Hill. Copies are available or may be ordered from most bookstores or by credit card by calling McGraw-Hill at 1-800-2-MCGRAW. For a brief list of online employment advertising services, please see Appendix D.

Electronic Resumes will not teach you the mechanics of how to write a resume. You will not be instructed in the development of the various categories of information that typically form a resume, or how these categories should be laid out on paper, nor will you learn how to word your resume to best advertise and promote your talents and expertise. There are plenty of resume writing books on the market today that do an excellent job of teaching you how to write a standard, printed resume (see Appendix B).

Upgrading Your Traditional Resume to an Electronic Resume

The computer revolution is changing some of the rules of resume writing. When comparing a traditional printed resume to today's electronic counterpart, some similarities and differences exist, depending on whether you are comparing a printed resume to an electronic text or multimedia resume.

When comparing a printed resume to an electronic text resume, the text resume can contain the same layout or style as found with conventional resumes. For example, most conventional resumes are written in a chronological, functional, or targeted format, depending on the work history and career aspirations of the job seeker.

An electronic text resume can be written in the same styles as a printed resume. Conventional resumes also contain special character formatting, such as:

Bold

Italic

<u>Underline</u>

        Centering

Superscript

Subscript

- Bulleting

Product Management

Name
Street Address
City, State, Zip
Telephone Number

OBJECTIVE: A position in *Product Management*, where proven technical skills would be utilized.

EXPERIENCE: DataLinkSystems, Inc., Scoreville, TX   10/87–Present
Product Manager
In charge of directing new product planning and development activities for this Fortune 500 firm, including the development and implementation of comprehensive marketing strategies and plans.
Administer budgets for media and product introduction materials.
Plan and conduct competitive product and market share analyses.
Research, produce, and update catalogs and price lists.
❑ Developed a detailed product cost and selling price spreadsheet.
❑ Provided full support in the training of sales personnel.

UNIX Corporation, Austin, TX   9/85–10/87
Product Line Manager—Payment Systems Division
Completely responsible for the preparation of marketing plans for new credit authorization terminals.
Designed innovative advertising/promotional literature, including slides and trade show exhibits.
❑ Wrote comprehensive system programming, installation, and operation manuals.
❑ Developed and successfully implemented customer training programs.
❑ Directly involved in the research and development of new products, including the planning, coordination, and testing of future software releases.

Motorola Corporation, Austin, TX   7/83–10/85
Peripheral Product Coordinator
Coordinated production of the NGC MultiSync monitor, including research of market potential and preparation of a comprehensive marketing plan.
Evaluated pre-production printers and monitors for performance and specification compliance.
❑ Researched and wrote detailed, annotated operational manuals.
❑ Established a product tracking system for the entire sales force.

EDUCATION: University of Texas, Austin, TX   Graduated 5/83
B.S. Degree: Marketing
❑ President of business administration student council.
❑ Elected as Honors Convocation Speaker and Emcee for the Business College.

ASSOCIATIONS: Member, Phi Chi Theta Professional Fraternity and the American Marketing Association.

Marketing and Promotions

Name • Street Address • City, State, Zip • Telephone Number

Entrepreneurial Skills
Self-starter with proven success in independently developing and marketing jewelry, golf accessories, and miscellaneous items to manufacturers. Manage new products from concept to patent work, promotion, manufacturing, and fulfillment. Utilize the ability to work with limited capital and resources while maximizing revenues and profits. A broad based decision maker with expertise in integrated organization management.

Marketing
Identified market opportunities; targeted product lines and calculated competitive pricing structure for MY OWN MERCHANDISE. Devised results-getting campaigns and promotions. Praised for creativity with production of a direct mail piece highlighting benefits for GREAT BUSINESS PRODUCTS boosting sales by 200% within 12 months.

Troubleshooter
Analytical with a track record for identifying complex problems related to product development, production, fulfillment, and contract administration. Resourceful and inventive in developing and implementing creative solutions resulting in increased profitability, sales, and client satisfaction. Significantly reduced delinquent orders for BIGCORP and regained a lost contract valued at $1,000,000.

Operations
Formulated policy, protocol, and captained all functions of MY OWN MERCHANDISE. Successfully coordinated logistics to meet contract demands for BIGCORP clients. Created effective performance measurements, cost control systems, and internal management tools integrating data from operations, administrative, and sales areas.

Human Resource Management
Recruited, trained, and provided motivation to employees with a record for inspiring a team commitment to organizational goals. Employed 575 on the UNIVERSITY OF ASTATE'S support staff. Instituted progressive hiring policies; developed wage and salary structures and selected benefits plans. Developed and maintained excellent employee relations.

EXPERIENCE

FOUNDER • PRESIDENT MY OWN MERCHANDISE—Somecity, TX   1986–Present
SERVICE MANAGER • CONTRACT COORDINATOR BIGCORP—Somecity, TX   1983–1984
SALES REPRESENTATIVE GREAT BUSINESS PRODUCTS—Somecity, TX   1981–1982
DIRECTOR, STUDENT STAFF UNIVERSITY OF ASTATE—Somecity, TX   1978–1980

EDUCATION

MASTER OF BUSINESS ADMINISTRATION IN MARKETING • MANAGEMENT, 1980
University of Astate—Somecity, Texas

BACHELOR OF SCIENCE IN BUSINESS ADMINISTRATION, 1978
Some College—Somecity, Texas

REFERENCES & FURTHER DATA AVAILABLE UPON REQUEST

Software Programming

Name
Street Address
City, State, Zip
Phone Number

JOB TARGET: Software Programmer

CAPABILITIES

❏ Program IBM PC and compatibles in DOS and Windows environments.
❏ Design user interface in software programs which incorporate easy-to-follow, logical progression of steps.
❏ Program software in C, C++, Visual BASIC, and Pascal.
❏ Design and produce computer generated graphics.
❏ Operate DOS machines and peripherals; diagnose and fix hardware problems.
❏ Operate a variety of software programs including most major authoring systems, word processors, data base programs, spreadsheet, and graphics packages.

ACCOMPLISHMENTS

❏ Designed and programmed an attendance/registration database program for the Ohio School of Electronics.
❏ Created six utility programs which have been distributed through the shareware network; received over two thousand registrations from satisfied users.
❏ Won Golden Disk Award (utilities category) for 1991.
❏ Established the Central Ohio PC User's Group; increased membership from 10 to 235 individuals in four years.
❏ Created and maintained an online, 24-hour bulletin board for the PC user's group.

WORK HISTORY

1989–present   WAYLAND PLASTICS, Inc.
                      Assistant Manager—Quality Control

1986–1989   OHIO SCHOOL OF ELECTRONICS
                      Registration Clerk (work-study)

EDUCATION

1989   OHIO SCHOOL OF ELECTRONICS

However, an electronic text resume cannot contain special character formatting. When a resume is converted to a text format, either by a word processing program, or by our *Resumes Online* program, all special character formatting is removed to enable the document to be read by a wide variety of word processing and text editor programs, as well as by most online resume database systems. A text resume is nothing fancy to look at, but it contains the same data displayed in a very similar format to conventional resumes.

Howard Ernst
1996 Stark Avenue
Portland, OR 97207
(503) 555-4487

Work Experience:

1990 - present J&R Catering, Portland, OR
Chief Caterer

>Developed business sales that exceeded $228,000 annually.
>Contracted catering services for parties; held a major account to provide catering for the Portland Civic Center.
>Catered many different events from picnics to formal dinners for one year.
>Managed catering services for the Vancouver Masonic Temple for one year.
>Managed staff of fifty persons; organized jobs; ordered, prepared food, and delivered food.

1986 - 1990 Inns Way Management, Inc., Seattle, WA
Night Chef

>Supervised 5 chefs during night shift for two area Radisson hotels.
>Received a four star rating by the American Automobile Association.
>Hired, trained, and supervised kitchen personnel; maintained payroll records; monitored performance.

1980 - 1985 The Grotto, Seattle, WA
Partner/Owner

>Took over a failing restaurant and in three years grossed over $2 million.
>Developed menu specializing in Cajun and Creole food.

Education:

1979 Portland Community College
Associate of Applied Science in Culinary Arts

Keywords—What Potential Employers Are Scanning For

Of particular importance when creating an electronic text resume is to make sure you have included all appropriate "keywords." *Keywords* are words that employers and/or recruiters most often use when searching an online resume database in an effort to find people with qualifications to meet their needs. Keywords in your resume could refer to the job titles associated with the positions that you have held or that you wish to secure. Keywords could also refer to your skills, experiences, special talents, characteristics, and affiliations that you have had. Whereas in a traditional resume you might pay attention to the verbs or action words you use, in an electronic resume the keywords or nouns take priority.

To ensure that your resume contains all the keywords appropriate to your background and that it will be selected when employers and recruiters search the online database in which you elected to enter your resume, examine your:

❏ Career objectives
❏ Work history
❏ Educational background
❏ Military background
❏ Community service
❏ Skills and knowledge
❏ Past affiliations
❏ Accomplishments

Identify all the words that are most often used by job seekers and employers in general when describing such information. Use as many of these words in your resume as possible when you are describing the preceding information. If you have additional or alternate words, create a special paragraph in your resume called "Keywords" and enter these words there.

Howard Ernst
1996 Stark Avenue
Portland, OR 97207
(503) 555-4487

Work Experience:

1990 - present J&R Catering, Portland, OR
Chief Caterer

>Developed business sales that exceeded $228,000 annually.
>Contracted catering services for parties; held a major account to provide catering for the Portland Civic Center.
>Catered many different events from picnics to formal dinners for one year.
>Managed catering services for the Vancover Masonic Temple for one year.
>Managed staff of fifty persons; organized jobs; ordered, prepared food, and delivered food.

1986 - 1990 Inns Way Management, Inc., Seattle, WA
Night Chef

>Supervised 5 chefs during night shift for two area Radisson hotels.
>Received a four star rating by the American Automobile Association.
>Hired, trained, and supervised kitchen personnel; maintained payroll records; monitored performance.

1980 - 1985 The Grotto, Seattle, WA
Partner/Owner

>Took over a failing restaurant and in three years grossed over $2 million.
>Developed menu specializing in Cajun and Creole food.

Education:

1979 Portland Community College
Associate of Applied Science in Culinary Arts

Keywords:

Head Chef
Senior Chef
Kitchen Management
Hotel/Motel Restaurant Management

An example of the value of keywords can be illustrated using the occupational titles of "secretary" and "administrative assistant." Both titles could apply to the same occupation and describe the same work tasks. If you use only the word "secretary" in your resume, and if an employer or recruiter is searching the database where your resume is stored using the words "administrative assistant," your resume will *not* be found, even though you might be well qualified for the position.

To avoid this situation, include the words "administrative assistant" in your keywords paragraph. In this way, regardless of which job titles employers and/or recruiters search for, your resume will be found.

Upgrading to a Multimedia Resume

Little similarity exists between a conventional printed resume and a multimedia resume.

Rather than presenting what many people consider to be boring printed text, a multimedia resume can bathe your senses in a variety of brilliant colors, images, animated sequences, sound, and even video.

The information contained in a multimedia resume is seldom laid out in the same manner as in a printed resume. Rather than presenting carefully crafted paragraphs of information, a multimedia resume attempts to capture attention first with color, sound, animation, and/or movement, and then presents brief "packets" of condensed information about the candidate as part of the multimedia elements. With a multimedia resume, the *medium* (i.e., the manner in which information is displayed for viewing) is actually as important as the *message* (i.e., the information about your employment history and qualifications).

The images presented with multimedia resumes can range considerably from basic formats that combine just text and graphics, to the more advanced versions that include sound, animation, and even live video clips. The factor that determines the level of multimedia sophistication is the skill level of the creator of the multimedia resume program. Most multimedia resumes are created by individuals skilled in computer programming or in the use of sophisticated computer graphic art and/or illustration programs. Until now, if you wanted to use a multimedia resume program, it had to be created specifically for you by a programmer experienced in multimedia development.

Not anymore! Now, with the use of *Resumaker*, you can create your own multimedia resume!

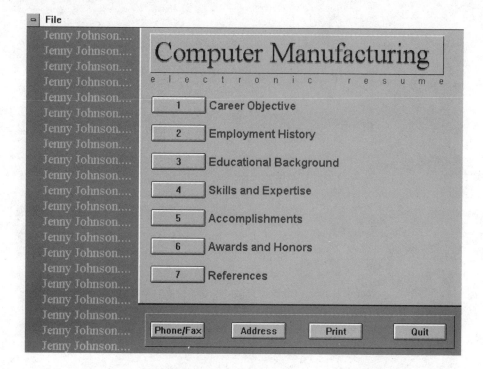

Since this is more than likely your first attempt at creating a multimedia resume, we have enclosed a version of the *Resumaker* program that will help you create a basic multimedia resume—one that can contain text and graphics. As you become more competent in creating multimedia resumes, you may wish to contact the developers of *Resumaker* to learn how their more advanced programs can be used to create even more sophisticated multimedia programs.

When you have completed the creation of your text and/or multimedia resumes, *Electronic Resumes* will show you how you can distribute them electronically around the world using various computer online network services, including the Internet.

4

The Advantages of Electronic Resumes

A Win, Win, Win Situation ...

Three groups of individuals can benefit from the use of electronic resumes: job seekers, employers, and employment recruiters. Here's how.

The Advantages for Job Seekers

As a job seeker, you should create and use an electronic resume, as compared to a standard printed resume, for at least five compelling and powerful reasons:

❏ *Speed of delivery.* Distributing your resume electronically, via a computer network service, is far faster than by mail. For example, a full three-page resume can be sent electronically from Los Angeles, California to New York City in only a few seconds. With today's postal service, it could easily take a week for mail delivery!

❏ *Cost savings.* Sending multiple copies of your electronic resume is much less expensive than sending multiple copies of your printed resume. For example, the average printed resume distributed by mail can cost about 62 cents. Here's the breakdown:

Paper (2 sheets of quality stock)	10 cents
Photocopy from your master copy	10 cents
Envelope	2 cents
Postage	40 cents
Total cost	62 cents

Assuming you mail out 500 copies of your resume over a period of one month (not an uncommon number in today's job market), your cost would be $310, not including the time it took you to print out your 500 copies, stuff them in envelopes, affix the postage stamps, and run them down to the post office. If you were to send a copy of your electronic resume via email to the same number of people using any of the most popular online network services, your cost would be approximately $1 (the time you would spend online prorated at the per-hour connect charge of your online service)!

❏ *Extended presence in the marketplace.* By depositing a copy of your electronic resume into any one of today's popular computer online resume database services, such as the Worldwide Resume/Talent Bank (see Appendix A), information about your employment history and qualifications could be available to tens of thousands of employers 24 hours a day, 7 days a week, 365 days a year!

Let's face it, no job seeker can reach all potential employers or maintain a constant presence in front of any single employer or group of employers for any extended period of time. However, the opportunity to have your resume accessible electronically by tens of thousands of employers at any given time, from any location on the globe, is a major resource that can be used to greatly enhance your job search. It is very unlikely that your printed resume, once distributed by mail, will remain in front of potential employers for as long a period of time as is the case with your electronic resume.

❏ *Global access.* For job seekers who wish to explore employment opportunities worldwide, the use of electronic resumes is almost mandatory. Attempting to identify employment openings overseas can require months of research work, contact with dozens of specialized employment placement agencies, and a countless number of dead-end leads—often at considerable cost to the job seeker. The world is a big place in which to search for employment. However, with the use of the Internet, employers worldwide can gain access to your resume if you first elect to store a copy of it in a recognized computer online resume database service.

In addition to enabling employers from all corners of the globe to more easily find you, you can use the medium of email to globally distribute your resume to dozens or hundreds of employers simultaneously in only a matter of minutes. In less than five minutes you can dial up a computer online service, such as America Online, CompuServe, or Prodigy, and email a copy of your electronic resume to potential employers in Moscow, Tokyo, London, Paris, and countless other destinations. Using the older method of mailing printed resumes could accomplish the same task, but it would take weeks for all of your resumes to arrive at their intended destinations—long after most job openings would be filled!

❏ *Powerful first impression.* In your attempt to convince employers that you're the right person for the job, how you present yourself is often as important as what you say about your qualifications. You only get one opportunity to make a first impression. If you come across as anything less than professional—even average—in today's competitive marketplace, your candidacy for the job can quickly evaporate.

Your use of an electronic resume, especially a multimedia format, says to employers that you are aware and capable of using today's leading-edge technology, that you understand its use and benefits, and that you know how to harness the power of technology for your personal and professional benefit. Surveys of employers have revealed that, next to occupational knowledge, the next most desired skill set they look for in new recruits is technical, computer-related knowledge. Creating and using electronic resumes as your "calling card" announces that you may be a higher-caliber candidate than your competitors.

In spite of the many advantages of the electronic resume over the traditional printed resume, the authors do not recommend that you abandon entirely the use of the printed resume. Rather, it is suggested that you incorporate the use of an electronic resume into your overall job search campaign. Continue doing what you have been to search for employment, but don't ignore the advantages of posting your resume online. You can take advantage of the best of both worlds—traditional and electronic resumes—since both combined can produce a more powerful job search strategy than either approach undertaken separately.

The Advantages for Employers and Employment Recruiters

In conversations with employers and employment agency recruiters who access electronic resumes looking for new employees, four reasons are often cited for the popularity of electronic resumes over printed resumes.

❏ *Higher caliber of candidates.* Because the use of electronic resumes requires a certain level of computer knowledge, employers and employment recruiters alike report that, as a group, individuals who use electronic resumes tend to possess a higher-level skill set than those who do not.

❏ *Access to a greater pool of candidates.* Various computer online resume database services, like the Worldwide Resume/Talent Bank (which at the time of this writing contained over 20,000 candidate resumes), provide employers and employment recruiters with immediate access to literally tens of thousands of resumes. Each employer and recruiter can therefore almost be assured of finding the right candidate at the right time. Such large numbers of resumes simply cannot be generated when employers and recruiters use conventional methods of finding candidates, such as when a classified help wanted ad is published in a local newspaper.

❏ *Faster turnaround time.* It is possible today, using an online classified help wanted posting service, for an employer to broadcast electronically at 8:00 AM that a new position is available, and actually start receiving resumes electronically from applicants within the same hour. If "time is money," then time spent looking for a new employee is time that is not being spent working for the employer—and that will cost the employer in lost revenue.

It is not uncommon for an employer to spend weeks, if not months, looking for the right candidate. All during this time, the yet to be discovered employee is making no contribution to the company's bottom line. And that loss of contribution means only one thing: the company is losing, not making, money!

For employment recruiters, the story is the same: Time spent looking for candidates to fill available positions is time for which they are not being compensated by their client companies. Many employment agencies are paid only when they find a qualified candidate, and only then when that candidate is actually hired by the employer who has contracted the services of the recruiting firm. The whole process often takes weeks to months to complete.

Clearly the time required for employers and employment recruiters to find appropriate candidates is a cost factor. The more this factor can be reduced, the less cost is involved in finding new employees. If your resume is available in an electronic format, you have the option of responding immediately to employment opportunities as they are posted online. See Appendix D for information on several electronic online employment advertising services where you can gain access daily to tens of thousands of current help wanted ads.

❏ *Less cost.* Because employers and employment recruiters are now able to immediately access tens of thousands of resumes online, the cost of finding new candidates is considerably less than with conventional methods, such as through the use of a newspaper classified ad. For example, the authors conducted a search of a well-known online resume database called the Talent Bank found in the Career Center forum area on the America Online service and found 389 resumes posted by people with a background in nursing. Few newspaper classified ads could draw this many resumes from a single posting. To obtain this many resumes from qualified applicants, an employer might easily spend weeks and hundreds or thousands of dollars in advertising fees.

Clearly, for employers and recruiters who wish to access a large pool of qualified candidates inexpensively, searching online resume databases is a wise business decision.

5
Distributing Electronic Resumes Online

Click—and Your Resume Is in Paris!

Imagine that you're a struggling young artist in Boston, trying to find the right job and employer where your talents can take root and flourish. Late one Friday evening, while you're reading the latest edition of the *Employment Review* newspaper, you discover that the Louvre Museum in Paris, France is advertising for a Restoration Artist—just the job you've been looking for! Without hesitation you draft a dynamic and powerful cover letter explaining why you would be a wise choice and then, with resume and portfolio enclosed, package your materials into an envelope for mailing on Saturday morning. You're excited about the possibilities that may come your way. You know you can handle the job and believe—hope—that you will hear back from the Louvre in a week or two. But nothing happens. No word arrives. Why?

This scenario is not uncommon to many of today's job hunters. While you may be well qualified for the position, you may have committed a fatal error: getting to the party too late, after it was already over.

By the time the Postal Service delivers your letter from Boston to Paris it is likely that the Louvre will have already received dozens, if not hundreds, of resumes sent electronically by job seekers worldwide who have spotted the same ad as you. More than likely, by the time your letter arrives in Paris, the Louvre will have already decided on a candidate—someone who forwarded a resume electronically, with a single click of the computer mouse. Rather than having an equal chance at employment, the only trace of you that can be found at the Louvre is in one of their waste-baskets.

How Are Electronic Resumes Distributed Online?

Electronic resumes are most often distributed online using two methods: being posted online in a searchable database for access by individuals at a later time on a need basis, or being distributed via email, file transfer, or on diskette.

For example, you could post your resume or find the resumes of others:

❏ *In an online resume database.* Resumes are stored in a computer database that may be searched directly or indirectly by employers and employment recruiters who are interested in finding individuals with various skills, experiences, and characteristics. Some companies offering such a resume review service allow employers and recruiters to "call up" their database (with the use of a computer and modem) and actually search the stored resumes while connected online. Some of these services operate automatically and may be accessed 24 hours a day.

The Worldwide Resume/Talent Bank service (see Appendix A) is a good example of an online resume database service.

Other online resume database services receive phone calls from employers and recruiters, and then through a question-and-answer process, identify the characteristics desired in an applicant. These services then conduct the search of their database at a later time and report back to the employer or recruiter with the names of candidates who may satisfy their personnel needs. With this option, the employer or recruiter does not directly search the resume database, but must rely on the ability of the service to identify appropriate candidates from its search of the database.

These online resume database services range in size from some containing only a few dozen resumes to others that contain tens of thousands. These services may be offered by an individual or small, private company that has installed a BBS (bulletin board system), or by a large commercial computer online network service. Some are accessed by only a few employers and recruiters, while others are used by thousands of employers and recruiters worldwide. Finally, some of these services allow only prequalified employers and recruiters to search their database, where prequalification can often require payment for access to the resume database. Other services make their resumes available to the general public at no cost.

See Appendix C for a listing of several online resume database services.

- *As an entry in an online file library.* Some commercial computer online network services, such as America Online, provide a means whereby job seekers may upload their resume to a file library location. If you are a member of a service that offers such an option, you may transfer (upload) a copy of your electronic resume (from your computer to the service's host computer), where it can then be downloaded by other members for viewing offline on their computers. These services usually impose no restrictions regarding who may upload or download a resume.

  If you are a member of America Online, CompuServe, Delphi, GEnie, or Prodigy, check the career and employment forum area online (if such an area exists) to see if a library is available where you can upload and post your electronic resume. On America Online, see the Career Center forum area.

  In addition, many private Bulletin Board System (BBS) services offer their members or visitors the opportunity to upload and download electronic resume files. If you are a member or visitor of a particular BBS service, contact the sysop (system operator) of the service to inquire if such a library area exists for the posting and downloading of electronic resumes.

  See Appendix C for information concerning how you can identify BBS services that might offer electronic resume posting.

- *File transfer.* If you have access either to a commercial computer network service that has an Internet gateway or to the Internet directly, you more than likely have the capability of sending and receiving files electronically using a function called File Transfer Protocol (FTP), or by using an email function called Attached File. Each day, thousands of files, many of them electronic resumes, are distributed around the world using these two options. Resumes that are distributed via file transfer or as attached email files can be viewed only after the file has actually been received and downloaded at the recipient's computer, and usually with a word processing program or text editor.

  If you are a member of a commercial computer network service, check with the user's manual that came with your network software, with the online Help system, or (if available) with an online customer service guide to learn more about how to transfer files using FTP or the email Attached File function. If you're using the Internet, check with the Internet access service that you have subscribed to if you have questions regarding how to use either of these two functions.

- *Email.* Now one of the most common and preferred means of electronic communication, email (short for electronic mail) allows an individual to send a message (letter, memo, report, or resume) electronically from one computer to another—anywhere in the world, as long as the two computers are connected by a phone line and both use the same network system. These messages are the equivalent of the printed page or written letter. The main differences are that they are distributed electronically rather than by hand or by the traditional mail system, and that they can be sent and received much faster than by traditional mail. Email messages can usually be read and responded to while online (i.e., while connected to the computer system used to receive the email message).

The difference between sending email with an Attached File and regular email is that, with regular email, the entire contents of your message is contained within the email itself. However, when you send email with an Attached File, both a message and a file are transferred at the same time. While you can usually view an email message while online, to read the contents of an Attached File, you first have to download the file to your computer.

❏ *On diskette.* Although it is the slowest of all the electronic options, many resumes are sent via diskette. Sometimes it is best to copy your resume from your computer to a floppy diskette (usually a 3.5-inch format) and mail or hand the disk to a potential employer or employment agency.

As you begin to travel the Information Superhighway, you will soon discover that there are many, many places to place your resume online (see Appendix C). However, some places are better than others. For example, you can post your resume at hundreds of places on the Internet and on BBS services. Unfortunately, few employers and employment recruiters visit each and every electronic site looking for new candidates. If you happen to have posted your resume on these sites, it may never see the light of day. How can you avoid this situation? Ask the owner or manager of the site for information regarding the number of people who visit the site each week or month. While we are not suggesting that you ignore the less visited locations, you should also post your resume in the more frequently visited sites, such as the Worldwide Resume/Talent Bank service (see Appendix A).

A Word about Email Addresses

People new to the world of online services sometimes have difficulty with the concept of an email address or screen name.

If you are a member of a commercial computer network service, then you have an email address (also referred to as a *screen name*). This email address (screen name) is either assigned to you or created by you when you first join the service. It identifies you from all the other members who use the same service, and it is your "electronic address" online for the purposes of sending and receiving email.

For example, the authors are members of America Online and have the following screen names:

James Gonyea = CareerDoc
Wayne Gonyea = CareerPro1

If James wants to send an email message to Wayne's America Online address, then email would be sent from CareerDoc to CareerPro1, and vice versa.

If you have access to the Internet, you also have an Internet email address, also for the purpose of sending and receiving email. Here are the authors' Internet addresses:

James Gonyea = careerdoc@aol.com

Wayne Gonyea = online@ns.cencom.net

You'll note that the route of James' Internet address (careerdoc) is the same as his America Online screen name. This is because James prefers to send and receive all his email using the America Online system. However, Wayne has both an America Online address and an Internet address. Therefore, if James wants to send an email message using his America Online account to Wayne's Internet address, the email would be sent from careerdoc to online@ns.cencom.net.

Now this is where it gets a little tricky.

Because commercial network services are linked to the Internet, it is possible to send email from a commercial network account to an Internet address (as just illustrated), and vice versa.

If Wayne Gonyea wants to send email from his Internet address to James' America Online account, the email would be sent by Online@ns.cencom.net to careerdoc@aol.com.

Note that, when you are sending email from a commercial network account to an Internet address, you have to indicate the recipient's Internet address (preceded by the @ symbol). If you're using an Internet account and wish to send email to another Internet address, or to a commercial network address, you must include the correct Internet addresses for both the sender and the recipient.

To reach a commercial account address from the Internet, all you have to do is add the appropriate Internet extension to the person's commercial address. For example:

If the commercial address is …	*To reach it from the Internet, add …*
FlyingHigh on America Online	flyinghigh@aol.com
12345.678 on CompuServe	12345.678@compuserve.com
CVT03A on Prodigy	cvt03a@prodigy.com

When sending email from one commercial account to another person on the same commercial account, the Internet extension is *not* necessary. For example, if James wants to send email on America Online to Wayne on America Online, the following should *not* be used:

CareerDoc@aol.com to CareerPro1@aol.com

While the email will get to the correct account, it is unnecessary to use the Internet extension, as the email will only go out into the Internet and then come right back into America Online in this case. The same is true when sending email on other commercial network services to someone on the same service.

The correct email addresses would be:

CareerDoc to CareerPro1

Finally (if you're not already totally confused), here's one more note. If you want to send an email message from one commercial account to another commercial account, you can do it since all commercial accounts are connected via the Internet. For example, if Wayne wants to send email from his America Online account to James' Prodigy account (CVTD03A), it would be sent from CareerPro1 to cvtd03a@prodigy.com.

6

Electronic Resume Checklist

As is the case with many new technologies, the subject matter of electronic resumes is foreign to many job seekers. Therefore, the authors have created a step-by-step *checklist of things to do* to guide you as you create your electronic resume and as you use various computer network services to distribute your resume electronically.

On the following pages you will find our suggestions regarding how best to proceed. Are there other ways to electronically distribute your resume? Yes. However, based on our experiences, we feel the following strategy will enable you to achieve a comprehensive distribution of your electronic resume without overwhelming you with details and facts, and without requiring you to become an expert in electronic job hunting.

Note: If you're new to the world of commercial online services, BBS services, or the Internet, please keep a detailed log of all the electronic online locations where you post (upload) your resume, and all the individuals who receive a copy of your resume. Also log information regarding the steps you take to get to each online location and how you can upload or download your resume. Your log will become indispensable when you attempt to return to the locations that you visited in the past, as well as in keeping track of who has received your resume and whom you should follow up with regarding employment.

_____ *Step 1:* If you haven't done so already, review Chapters 1–5 in *Electronic Resumes* to understand the purpose and use of electronic resumes, the advantages they can bring to your job search, and how to use the software programs included in this book.

Step 2: Chapters 7 and 8 detail what equipment you will need to distribute your resume electronically, as well as what precautions you should take to avoid the pitfalls that can occur when communicating in cyberspace. Set up your computer equipment as needed.

Step 3: If you do not already have a current copy of a resume developed in print format, create one. If you do have a printed resume, edit it, if necessary, to ensure that it contains all current and relevant information about yourself, your qualifications and experiences, and your career aspirations and goals.

If necessary, refer to Appendixes B and C to identify resources (books, software programs, etc.) that can help you create or edit your resume. Also review the sample resumes in Chapter 11 if you need suggestions regarding how to word and/or format your resume.

Step 4: Follow the directions in Chapter 9 to create an electronic text file resume using the enclosed _Resumes Online_ software program.

Step 5: Follow the directions in Chapter 10 to create an electronic multimedia resume using the enclosed _Resumaker_ software program.

Step 6: Decide to whom and how you want to distribute your resume(s) electronically. Your "to-whom" options include:

❑ Directly to employers.

❑ To employment recruiters or placement agencies.

❑ To people on your network list (friends, colleagues, business contacts, etc.) who may be able to help you identify employment opportunities.

Your to-whom list should be comprised of employers, employment agencies, and network contacts that (a) you already know or have identified and (b) you can identify from research.

For parties you already know, often a simple phone call is all that is needed to determine if they are online and able to receive resumes electronically. To find additional employers, employment agencies, and network contacts, spend some time "surfing" or roaming online to discover their electronic addresses or screen names.

Ideally, the best place to find employers online that can receive resumes electronically is to search employment advertising databases, such as the Help Wanted-USA service (see Appendix D). An excellent place to identify employment agencies online is within the Career Center on America Online. To find online contacts, search the membership directories of the commercial network services of which you are a member.

Your "how" options include:

❏ In a searchable online resume database.

❏ In an online file library.

❏ Via File Transfer Protocol (FTP).

❏ Via regular email.

❏ Via email with Attached File.

❏ Via diskette.

See Chapter 5 for more information regarding how to use these distribution options.

_____ *Step 7:* Follow the directions in Appendix A to upload (post) your electronic text file resume in the Worldwide Resume/Talent Bank service. See Appendix C to identify other online resume database services on commercial network services, on private BBS services, and on the Internet that might be appropriate for posting your resume.

When you've completed this step, your resume will be "online" and available to millions of viewers around the globe. It will be posted on America Online, the nation's largest commercial computer network service, as well as on the Internet, the world's largest computer network system.

_____ *Step 8:* Distribute your electronic text file and/or multimedia resumes via email, email with Attached File, File Transfer Protocol (FTP), or diskette (whichever is appropriate for the receiver) whenever you identify:

❏ An employer that has posted an employment announcement that matches your career goals.

❏ An employer that you believe can benefit from the use of your expertise, even if that employer has posted no help wanted advertisement.

❏ An employment agency that can help you secure employment.

❏ An individual who you believe can assist you in finding and securing employment.

See the list of contacts that you developed in Step 6 above.

_____ *Step 9:* Upload your electronic and/or multimedia resumes to various online resume libraries that can be found on commercial computer network services, on BBS services, and on the Internet. See Step 10 for suggestions concerning how to find these locations.

_____ *Step 10:* Spend some time each week "surfing" either the commercial network services that you belong to or the Internet, to discover new locations where you can post your resume. New sites are being developed daily!

If you belong to a commercial computer network service, browse through the main menu system, check your software user's manual, use keywords to jump to locations that you think might exist, look for special announcements from the service informing members of new locations, or ask an online guide (if such a resource exists on your services) for new services and how you can navigate to the new locations.

If you have access to the Internet, use some of the Internet search programs, such as Yahoo, to find new resume posting services. Use the Uniform Resource Locator (URL) address of http://www.yahoo.com to reach Yahoo. Once there, follow the directions on screen for finding existing and new Internet resume posting resources.

7
Necessary Equipment

PCs Are Still King

When creating the enclosed software programs, the authors had to decide on which computer platform—PC or Apple Macintosh—to support. This is a most difficult decision since many computer users are extremely loyal to their machines and become upset when software is not made available for their operating systems.

Because far more PCs are in use today than Apple Macintosh computers, the authors elected to develop the programs for the PC platform. As a result, the software bundled with *Electronic Resumes* is intended to be used with an IBM or IBM-compatible personal computer (PC). Also, the terminology used in this chapter regarding equipment is in great part appropriate for PC users. The software will not operate on most Apple Macintosh computers, except Macintosh systems that have been designed or equipped to run Windows programs. *Note:* A Macintosh version of *Resumaker* is available from Techno-Marketing.

What Other Equipment Do You Need?

What equipment you should purchase or have on hand to distribute resumes electronically depends on which lane of the Information Superhighway you wish your resume to travel.

Logging on to BBS Services

If your objective is nothing more than to visit a few BBS services locally to post your resume, and if you do not plan on joining a commercial network service or traveling the Internet, then a 386-class PC equipped with a 2400-baud modem should be fine. If you plan to call up BBS services outside your local calling area, then buy the fastest modem you can afford (i.e., 28.8-baud) to reduce your long-distance bills.

Logging onto Commercial Network Services

If you wish to become a member of any of the more popular commercial computer network services, such as America Online, CompuServe, Delphi, GEnie, Prodigy, or Ziffnet, then a faster machine would be appropriate, such as a 486-class PC equipped with a 9600- or 14.4-baud modem. Most of these services will provide you with a local access number to call when logging on to avoid long-distance phone calls, but uploading and downloading files with a slow system or slow modem can be frustrating.

Logging onto the Internet

If you wish to travel the Internet, a fast machine with a very fast modem is mandatory to handle the volume of data (especially graphics) that will be transmitted to your computer when accessing various locations or sites. For Internet travelers, the top-of-the-line 486-class PCs (such as the 486 DX4 100 model) or a Pentium PC with at least a 28.8-baud modem is recommended.

Other Equipment, Features, and Peripherals

❏ *Memory.* Generally speaking, the more memory your computer has, the faster and better it will run your software programs. For most applications, 4–8 megs of memory are fine. However, with today's memory-hungry programs, and for effective multitasking, such as with Windows 95, 12–16 megs of memory are recommended.

❏ *Monitors.* Today's software programs and online services are loaded with beautiful graphics and video clips. (Everything today is going multimedia.) To fully appreciate the artwork that can be displayed, a SVGA monitor, with a .28 pitch or better resolution, and at least 1 meg of memory on the video card is recommended.

❏ *Mouse.* Today's software programs and online services have been developed for "point and click" use. Clicking the mouse button is far faster and easier than pressing keys on your keyboard. As a result, a mouse is mandatory if you intend to move quickly and easily through today's leading-edge software programs and online services.

❏ *Printer.* How your resume looks in print is an important factor if you intend to present yourself professionally to employers. Dot matrix printers—the least expensive of all printer options, equipped with "near letter quality" printing—are acceptable. Ink jet printers are the next evolution and can produce a professional output and are priced only slightly higher than dot matrix printers. However, for the very best in print quality, buy a laser printer. Some laser printers are priced the same as ink jet printers. Get the best your pocketbook can afford.

❏ *Sound card and speakers.* While not mandatory, having a sound card and speakers attached to your computer is recommended, as many multimedia resumes now include sound. Seeing is only half the fun; hearing someone's voice or appropriate sound clips adds more dimension to any program, including resumes.

❏ *Fax card.* Also not mandatory, a fax card is recommended. At times you will want to fax a copy of your printed resume to an employer, employment agency, or personal contact. If you do not already have access to a stand-alone fax machine, you should consider installing a fax card in your computer. *Note:* Most modems today come with built-in fax capability. When you purchase your modem, ask for a fax/modem.

❏ *CD-ROM drive.* This is another item that is not mandatory, but very useful. Many programs today can be obtained on CD-ROM disk. These programs are usually faster to operate and contain far more data than programs that arrive on 3.5-inch diskette. For example, several software companies offer phone books on CD-ROM. With such a program, you can obtain the phone and fax numbers for most companies in the United States—a very nice resource to have on hand when you're searching for employment!

❏ *Special software programs.* Accessing BBS services requires a communication software program. Many general-purpose communication software programs are available on the market today, such as Procom Plus for Windows. Check with your software retailer for other suggestions.

If you plan on accessing commercial computer network services, you will first need to obtain a copy of their proprietary software program. You cannot access commercial network services with a general-purpose communication program. Software for all commercial network services can be obtained at your local software retailer or by contacting the service of your choice directly. Some services offer their software at no charge, such as America Online.

If you plan to access the Internet, specialized software is required. Again, this software can be purchased at your local software store.

A word processing program is also recommended if you wish to prepare documents, such as cover letters, thank you letters, etc. If you plan to fax letters and/or copies of your resume from your computer, a fax software program is also necessary.

If you have questions regarding what equipment you should purchase, you can often find answers by contacting a computer equipment or software retailer in your area. Also, many excellent books on the market can help you build the appropriate system.

8

Precautions to Keep in Mind

Have a Safe Trip

As with any mode of travel, certain rules apply when traveling the Information Superhighway that, if adopted, can help keep you safe and away from harm's way. Foremost are some precautions concerning whether you should disclose your job search activity to your current employer.

You may wish not to have your current employer know of your job search, to avoid the risk of retaliation, which can often result in your being fired, being passed over for promotion, and other such penalties when your employer discovers you're looking for employment elsewhere. If this is the case, make sure you do not include any identifying information in the electronic resume that you post online.

For example, do not include such information as:

❑ Your name.

❑ Your address.

❑ Your phone or fax number.

❑ Your email address or screen name that has been widely publicized.

❑ Your current employer's name and address.

❑ The names of references that other people may recognize as your references.

Considering the large and growing number of employers that travel online searching through resume databases, it is possible that your employer could come across your electronic resume. If this happens, it's a dead give-away that you're planning to leave. Also, if your employer has hired the services of a placement agency to find new employees, it is possible that the recruiter could discover your resume online and inform your employer of your job search activities.

Another possibility, although rare, is that someone who has discovered your identity online may contact you by phone, mail, fax, or email with harassing or sexually implicit comments. Recently, several national news programs carried reports outlining how one Prodigy member used that network service to *stalk* another member who was actually located on the opposite coast.

Create a Blind Resume

If you are concerned about keeping your identity confidential, you can take steps to avoid these potentially hazardous situations. To limit your exposure, consider sanitizing your resume. You can actually post a resume even if no name, address, or other identifying information is included. This type of resume is often referred to as a *blind resume*, because your identity is not revealed, only your work experience and general qualifications.

In such cases, it is appropriate to include the following statement at the very beginning of your resume:

The identity of the person holding the following qualifications and experience is being withheld for security reasons until a mutually interesting situation exists. If you wish to discuss my employment history and qualifications, please contact me at the address given below.

Then provide reviewers of your electronic resume with a secure, but safe, means of contacting you. For example, you could use any of the following as a means of establishing communication with potential employers without revealing your identity:

❏ *Post office box.* Purchase a post office box from a commercial post office box service (such as Mail Boxes Etc), or from the U.S. Postal Service. Register your box under your real name (which will be known only to the post office box service) and then create a fictitious name, such as E. J. Jones, that you use when communicating with individuals interested in your background. Then include in your electronic resume the following message:

All interested parties are invited to contact me at:

E. J. Jones
PO Box 123
City, State, Zip

Please indicate the nature of your interest and provide a return address and/or phone number.

Then you can determine which parties you wish to contact.

- *Nonpublished fax number.* If you have a fax machine that is safe from prying eyes or located at home, you could obtain from your local phone company a nonpublished telephone number. Then connect your fax to the nonpublished number and list it in your resume. Invite all interested parties to contact you via fax.

- *Nonrecognizable screen name or email address.* If you have an email address or screen name that does not reveal your identity, and if that address and/or screen name is *not* known to your colleagues and employer, you could include either in your resume as the means by which people could contact you.

  Note: Many commercial computer network services allow you to create several screen names of your choice. If your original screen name is a giveaway, create a new confidential screen name.

- *Private employment placement service.* If you prefer, many private career counseling and placement services or agencies, often for a modest fee, will provide you with a "screening service." Essentially, these professionals will allow you to use their company name and address in your resume. Parties interested in talking to you should be instructed to contact you at the screening service's address. You then, in turn, contact the screening service each day to obtain information on any contacts that have arrived.

Posting on Bulletin Boards

All commercial computer network services, most private and public BBS services, and many sites on the Internet will provide a bulletin board of some sort for you to post and read messages. Bulletin boards are a convenient method of sharing information. Think of them as a bulletin board in school or at your office—a place to post messages yourself and read messages left by others.

While these are valuable ways in which to connect with other onliners, it is not wise to leave your address or phone number, unless you are interested in and prepared to receive phone calls and letters from anyone at any time. If you want people to contact you, it is recommended that you leave an email address or screen name and let people contact you electronically.

Credit Card Information

Much has been said in the national news media concerning the misuse of credit cards by certain people online. Certainly, you should never leave your credit card number on any bulletin board where all the world can see it—and use it!

However, should you include your credit card number in an email message that you want to send to someone? The answer is yes and no! There will be times when you wish to purchase a service or product online, and your credit card number will be required to process your order. The email systems offered by the major commercial computer network services, such as America Online, CompuServe, Microsoft Network, and Prodigy, are secure and confidential. Any email message you send on these network services can be read only by the person you intend.

However, this may not be the case when you're sending email to an Internet address. We say "may not" as it depends on the security of the computers that are routing your message from the computer you're using to the computer that is used by the recipient of your message. Often, your message may be passed along by dozens of computers before it arrives at its destination.

As a general rule for the safety of your credit card account, you should not include your credit card number in any email message that is being sent via the Internet—not today at least!

However, it is usually very safe to share your credit card number when you are actually visiting an Internet site, such as a Gopher or Web location, and find something there that you wish to purchase. Usually, a "fill in the blank" form is provided for you to place your order. One of the requested fields is usually your credit card number and expiration date. Entering your credit card number here is safe since this information usually travels no further than the computer where you are currently visiting. In short, it is not sent out via email on the Internet.

We say "usually" because the Internet is still in development, and not all sites subscribe to the same level of customer security. You should exercise precaution when asked for your credit card number. A wise option is to enter your phone number and allow the merchant to call you directly to obtain your credit card information.

Virus Infection

As most computer users who travel online will tell you, eventually your computer will become infected with some sort of computer virus. A virus is a special software program that ends up on your computer and that is written by someone who intentionally wishes to do harm to your computer. A virus can do all kinds of things to your computer, from something as mild and unobnoxious as displaying a warm and friendly message when you start your computer that wishes you a happy day, to something as malicious as completely erasing everything on your hard drive.

If you are in the habit of downloading files from private BBS services, the Internet, and, in some cases, commercial computer network services, or if you exchange files and programs via diskette with other computer users, then you run the risk of infecting your computer with a virus. A virus can cause damage only if it is transferred to your computer, entering either via your modem or from a diskette.

All the major commercial computer network services (i.e., America Online, etc.) clean out all virus files before you get a chance to download them, but some do slip through the cracks. However, you are much more likely to become infected when you download files from an Internet site or from a BBS service, as some of these services pay little attention to disinfecting files as compared to the commercial networks.

How can you protect your system from becoming infected? Easy; just do two things. First, buy a good antivirus program for your computer. These programs search your entire computer system looking for viruses, and destroy any that are found. Second, every time you download a file, or copy a file from a diskette, run your antivirus program *before you run the program or open the file* to make sure it is not carrying a virus.

Your local software retailer can help you select a good antivirus program.

9

How to Create an Electronic Online Resume

Caution: Due to programming design limitations, it is not recommended that you attempt to run the *Resumes Online* program at the same time that you are attempting to run the *Resumaker* program. Neither program will operate correctly if both are run simultaneously.

Using *Resumes Online*

This chapter will guide you in using the first of two software programs that have been bundled with your copy of *Electronic Resumes*. The first program, *Resumes Online*, can be used to create a text version of your existing resume. Having a text version of your resume is necessary for posting with the Worldwide Resume/Talent Bank service. *Resumes Online* has been specially created to help you do this. With *Resumes Online*, you can send your resume out onto the Information Superhighway, where it can be read by any one of the 40-million-plus people who travel through cyberspace daily. In Chapter 10, you will learn how to use the second software program that came with this book. *Resumaker* will help you create a multimedia resume for distribution electronically.

As previously mentioned, several computer online resume database services today will allow you to enter your resume for viewing online by employers, employment recruiters, and other individuals interested in finding people with certain skills, experiences, interests, and characteristics. Placing your resume into an online resume database is an excellent way of connecting with employers nationwide—and worldwide!

To actually register your resume with the Worldwide Resume/Talent Bank service, see Appendix A.

Resumes Online will help you properly convert your existing resume to an electronic resume and format it properly for use with the Worldwide Resume/Talent Bank service.

To create a text version of your existing resume, complete three easy steps:

Step 1: Install the *Resumes Online* software program. Follow the directions below for installing your copy of the *Resumes Online* program onto your computer.

Step 2: Create your electronic resume with *Resumes Online*. Use the automatic resume creation feature called Run Resume Wizard or our step-by-step directions to enter the information necessary to create your electronic resume. See below for more information about both options.

Step 3: Export your electronic resume as a text file (using *Resumes Online*). In a single click of the mouse your resume will be formatted for use in uploading to our online resume database service. See below for more information.

After creating your text resume, you will be ready to forward it to such online resume database services as the Worldwide Resume/Talent Bank service (see Appendix A).

What Is *Resumes Online*?

Resumes Online is a specialized word processing program, created for one and only one purpose: to enable you to create a *text* version of your existing resume. The program is basic in design and function, making it very easy to use; no user's manual is necessary. The resume that you create with this program will not contain any special character formatting, such as **bolding,** *italicizing,* <u>underlining</u>, centering, right margin alignment, or other text formatting options typically found in most word processing programs. Actually, the text that appears on the screen will look somewhat plain compared to many of today's sophisticated word processing, desktop publishing, and resume writing software programs. However, that's the way the program has been designed—to create a simple text version of your resume.

Why Use *Resumes Online*?

The *Resumes Online* program was not designed for creating a standard, printed resume from scratch. While it could be used for this purpose, it lacks the program functions that are built into most resume writing software programs. Its main purpose is to *convert* your existing printed resume into a text file format suitable for uploading to the Worldwide Resume/Talent Bank service. Therefore, it is recommended that you place a printed copy of your current resume next to your computer, and refer to it when the program prompts you for various information about yourself. Otherwise, you will have to recall from memory the information required to complete this program.

Technical Help

Following the directions for installing and using the *Resumes Online* software program is very easy, and it is highly unlikely that you will need any assistance. However, if you have any difficulty with the program, please contact us during normal business hours:

Gonyea and Associates, Inc.
New Port Richey, Florida
813-372-1333—voice
813-372-0394—fax
Email: Careerdoc@aol.com

System Requirements

This program should run on any IBM-compatible personal computer with a 386 or higher processor. DOS and Windows 3.1 or Windows 95 are required, with at least 4 megs of memory (8 megs for Windows 95) and 1 meg of free hard disk space. A mouse is highly recommended. A printer is optional.

Note: The screen shots found in this chapter are taken from a computer running Windows 3.1. If you're running Windows 95, your screens will appear slightly different.

This program will also operate on Apple Macintosh computers that have been equipped to run Windows programs.

Assumed Knowledge

The directions for using the *Resumes Online* software program assume that you are familiar with basic Windows operations, such as how to select menu items and dialog box items with a mouse, how to open and close applications, how to save a document, how to print a document, and other routine operations. If you are unfamiliar with these tasks, please refer to your copy of the Windows user's manual for instructions on how to operate within a Windows application (program).

Step 1: Install the *Resumes Online* Software Program

For Windows 3.1

1. Start your computer.
2. Start Windows.
3. Insert the disk found in the back of this book into your 3.5-inch disk drive.
4. In Program Manager, select Run from the File menu.
5. Type "a:setup1" (or "b:setup1") and click on the OK button.

6. When requested, you may change the directory path and file names used for installing the program files. We recommend you use the default path of c:\resumeso.

You will see a message on the screen when the installation process is completed. The install program will create a new program folder with a launch icon, both labeled Resumes Online.

For Windows 95

1. Start your computer.
2. Start Windows and select the Settings option from the Start menu.
3. Select the Control Panel option.
4. Double click on the Add/Remove Programs option.
5. Click on the Install button.
6. Insert the disk found in the back of this book into your 3.5-inch drive.
7. Change the default install path from "a:setup1" to "b:setup1" if necessary.
8. Click on the Finish button.
9. You may change the default install directory if desired. However, we recommend you keep the c:\resumeso option.
10. Click on the OK button.

The install program will notify you when it is finished, and will add the *Resumes Online* program item to the list of Programs found in your Start/Program menu area.

Starting the Program

For Windows 3.1

1. Start your computer.
2. Start Windows.
3. From Program Manager, open the *Resumes Online* folder.
4. Select the *Resumes Online* icon.

For Windows 95

1. Start your computer.
2. Start Windows.
3. Select Programs from the Start menu.
4. Select *Resumes Online* from the list of programs.
5. Select the *Resumes Online* item from within your *Resumes Online* folder.

The Main Window of the program will appear in the background, with the Run Resume Wizard dialog box appearing in the foreground.

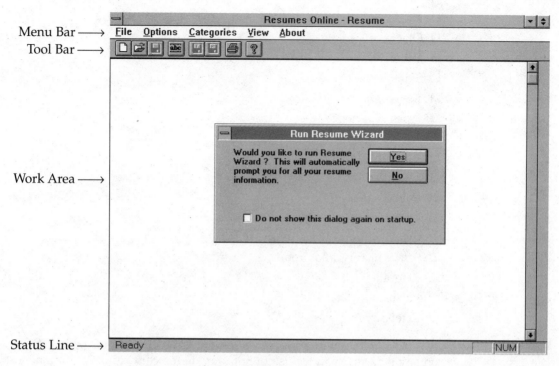

Note the following items:

❏ *Menu bar.* These menu items (when opened by clicking with your mouse) provide you with access to all the program's functions and features.

❏ *Tool bar.* These icons provide quick access to some of the most important and most often used functions. Rather than opening menus, you can click on these icons to perform a function quickly.

❏ *Work area.* This is where your resume will appear as you create it, and where it will appear when you wish to edit your resume. Now it is empty since you have not yet entered any information.

❏ *Status line.* This is where descriptive information will appear when you select a menu bar item or tool bar icon. Use this item to identify the purpose of unknown features.

❏ *Run the Resume Wizard dialog box.* This is where you can select the Run Wizard option to have the program prompt you through the creation of your electronic resume (see Step 2).

Step 2: Create Your Electronic Resume

Categories

To create your electronic resume, you will be asked to enter the following information about yourself:

❑ Name and address
❑ Objective
❑ Summary
❑ Skills/expertise
❑ Keywords
❑ Work experience
❑ Educational background
❑ Accomplishments
❑ Awards
❑ Publications
❑ Trademarks/patents
❑ Organizational affiliations
❑ Salary history/requirements
❑ Relocation
❑ Personal
❑ References

Important: You may elect to enter any or all of this information, or pass on any item that you feel is not appropriate for your resume. You may also edit or delete any information after it has been entered and saved. As you enter information, it will be displayed on the screen in the exact same layout as it will appear in the actual online resume database. It is not expected or recommended that you should use all the categories. Be discriminate, use only the categories that pertain directly to the resume you wish to create.

Automatic or Manual Options

If you prefer to have *Resumes Online* automatically prompt you for the information that it needs to create your electronic resume, please select the Yes button when the Run Resume Wizard dialog box appears. If you wish to manually navigate through the program, select the No option.

If you select the Wizard option, the program will then display the first category (Name and Address) and allow you to enter the required information. After completing the first category, the program will automatically take you to the second category, then the third, and so on until all 16 categories have been completed. You may complete or not complete any category as you wish.

Pace Yourself

Depending on the length and depth of your background, entering all the suggested information into the program could take several hours. It is not necessary that you complete this project in a single sitting or session. Feel free to stop at any time and return at a later time to complete your resume. Check off each category as it is completed.

If you elect to stop the Run Resume Wizard program before completing all categories, you may restart it where you left off by selecting the Resume Wizard option from the Categories menu. The program will determine where you last entered data and calculate where you should now continue. You may elect to start where the program suggests or at any category you wish.

If you prefer that the Run Resume Wizard dialog box not appear when the program starts up, check the "Do not show this dialog again on startup" item on the Run Resume Wizard dialog box. If you have closed the Run Resume Wizard dialog box and now wish to use this feature, select Run Wizard from the Categories menu.

Save Your Work

To avoid losing the data that you have entered into the program, *Resumes Online* will ask you if you wish to save your data when you attempt to exit the program.

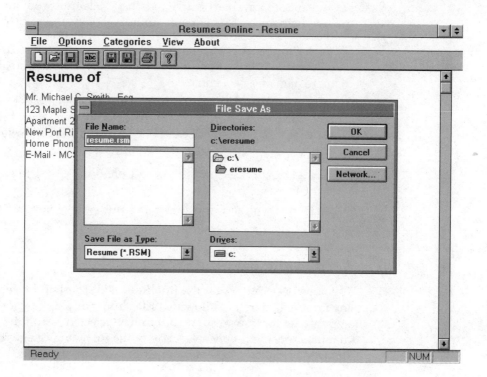

To save your data for accessing at a future time, make sure you select the Yes option when prompted by the save function. If you select the No option, your data will be discarded. When saving your resume, you should specify:

❑ *A file name.* The program will always suggest resume.rsm. You should change this to avoid overwriting existing resumes you have created.

❑ *A directory location.* The default is the directory where the program is stored.

❑ *A drive location.* The default is drive c.

To be safe, it is wise to periodically select the Save option from the File menu. This will allow you to save your data whenever you wish and continue to work without exiting the program.

Built-in Help System

If you are uncertain as to what information should or could be entered for a particular category, select the "What to enter?" button on the category dialog box for advice.

Special Keyboard Commands

Several special keyboard commands have been incorporated into the program to help you enter data more quickly. For example:

Tab key. By pressing the tab key, you may advance the cursor to the next data entry field within any of the Category dialog boxes that contain more than one data entry field.

Cut/Copy/Paste/. Use the following key combinations to cut, copy, and paste text from one data entry field to another. *Note:* When cutting or copying text, the text to be cut or copied must first be selected.

Hold down the Control key and press the X key to cut text from a field.

Hold down the Control key and press the C key to copy text from a field.

Hold down the Control key and press the V key to paste text into a field.

Let's Begin

If you have elected to use the Run Resume Wizard option, enter the following information in the following order. You may skip categories that are not appropriate for your resume. If you have elected to run the program in its manual mode, you may select any of the following categories in any order that you wish and then enter the appropriate information.

Name and Address

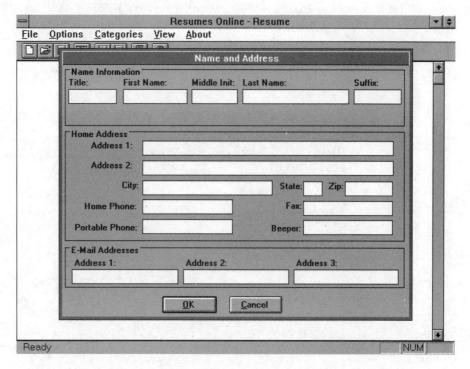

1. Select the Categories menu, and select the Name and Address menu item.
2. Enter into the Name and Address dialog box any or all of the following information (use the tab key to move from one item to the next):

    Title (example: Dr.)

    First name

    Middle name (or initial)

    Last name

    Suffix (example: Esquire)

    Home address 1

    Home address 2

    City

    State

    Zip

    Home phone [including area code]

    Fax [including area code]

    Portable phone [including area code]

    Beeper [including area code]

Email address(es) [*Examples:* 1234,567—CompuServe; HSimpson—America Online; MrQuick—Prodigy; bcotton@nsnet.com—Internet]

3. Click the OK button to display your data on the screen or select the Cancel button to discard your information.

Note that your information is aligned flush to the left margin, and displayed one line after another.

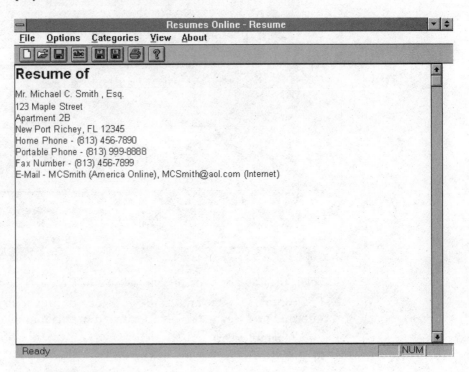

At this point you can ...

❑ *Continue* to enter information into your electronic resume.

❑ *Save your data and remain within the program.* From the File menu, select the Save option, and assign a name and directory where you wish to save your resume.

❑ *Edit your data.* By selecting the Name and Address item from the Categories Menu, you may edit any or all of the information that you just entered into this category.

❑ *Save your data and exit.* From the File menu, select Exit and select Yes when asked if you wish to save the changes to your resume. Your resume will be saved, and may be opened at a later date.

❑ *Not save your data and exit.* From the File menu, select Exit and select No when asked if you wish to save the changes to your resume. Your data will be discarded.

❏ *Print.* From the File menu, select Print to print a copy of your resume.

❏ *Change the text formatting.* By using the Format option on the Options menu, you can:

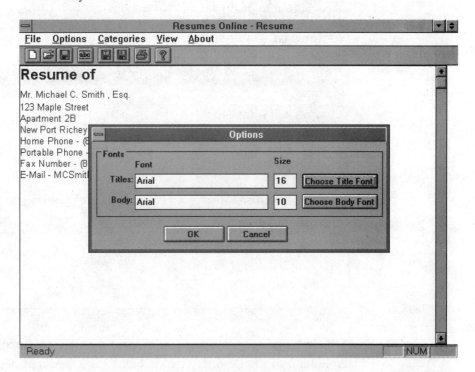

Choose Title Font. Use this option to change the font style, size, and characteristic (bold, italic, etc.) of the category titles.

Choose Body Font. Use this option to change the font style, size, and characteristic (bold, italic, etc.) of the text within each category.

Objective

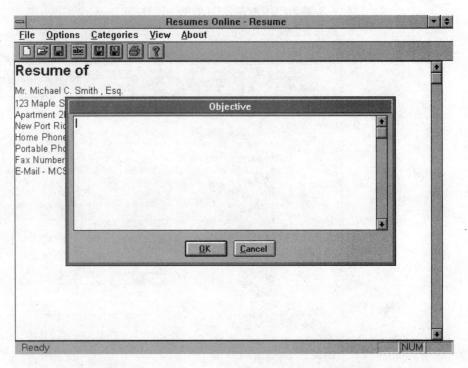

1. Select the Categories menu, and select the Objective menu item.

2. Enter into the Objective dialog box a statement that describes your job search objective.

   Example:

   Looking for an upper-management level position with a large liberal arts university where I can use my specialized knowledge in curriculum development to guide faculty in the development of liberal arts and nonliberal arts course work that is relevant to the needs of students in the 21st century.

3. Select the OK button to save your data and display it on screen.

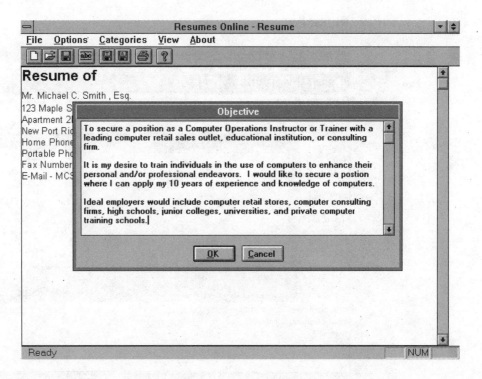

Summary

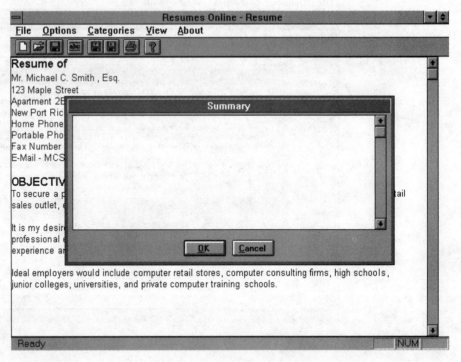

1. Select the Categories menu, and select the Summary menu item.
2. Enter into the Summary dialog box a statement that describes your over-all qualifications.

   Example:

   Nationally recognized expert in Liberal Arts Curriculum Development with 20 years of experience guiding faculty, from all disciplines, in the development of course work that is relevant to liberal arts and nonliberal arts students. Author of seven books on curriculum development and liberal arts education.
3. Select the OK button to save your data and display it on the screen.

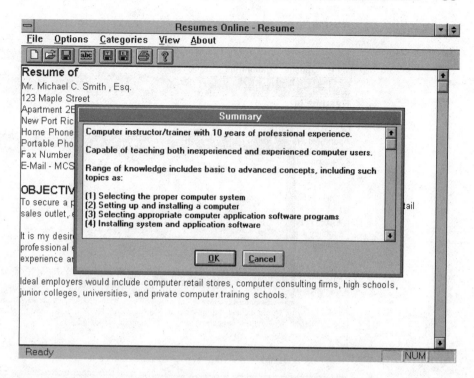

Resumes Online - Resume

File   Options   Categories   View   About

Resume of

Mr. Michael C. Smith , Esq.
123 Maple Street
Apartment 2B
New Port Ric
Home Phone
Portable Pho
Fax Number
E-Mail - MCS

OBJECTIV

To secure a p   tail
sales outlet,

It is my desir
professional
experience a

Summary

Computer instructor/trainer with 10 years of professional experience.

Capable of teaching both inexperienced and experienced computer users.

Range of knowledge includes basic to advanced concepts, including such topics as:

(1) Selecting the proper computer system
(2) Setting up and installing a computer
(3) Selecting appropriate computer application software programs
(4) Installing system and application software

OK   Cancel

Ideal employers would include computer retail stores, computer consulting firms, high schools, junior colleges, universities, and private computer training schools.

Ready   NUM

Skills/Expertise

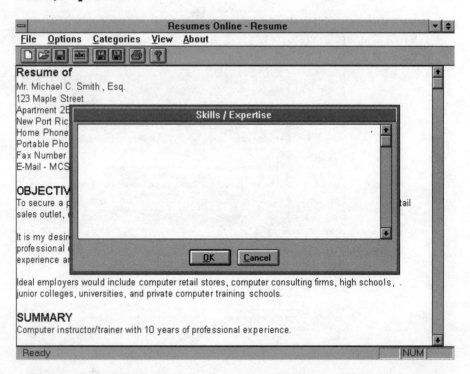

1. Select the Categories menu, and select the Skills/Expertise menu item.
2. Enter into the Skills/Expertise dialog box a statement or a list that describes your main skills and expertise.

   Example:

   Curriculum Design and Development

   Management of Diverse Faculty Groups

   Teaching of American History

   Administrative Budgeting and Finance

   Practical Employment Applications of a Liberal Arts Education

   Articulate and Dynamic Speaker

   Team Organizer and Manager
3. Select the OK button to save your data and display it on the screen.

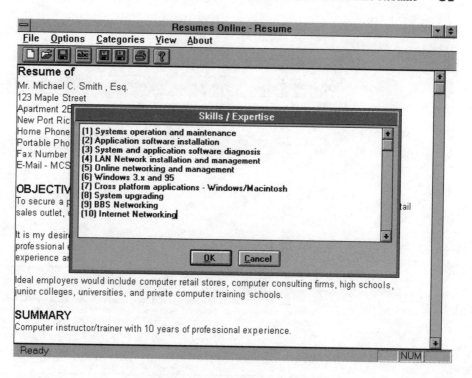

Resume of

Mr. Michael C. Smith , Esq.
123 Maple Street
Apartment 2B
New Port Ric
Home Phone
Portable Pho
Fax Number
E-Mail - MCS

OBJECTIV

To secure a p ... tail
sales outlet, ...

It is my desir ...
professional ...
experience a ...

Ideal employers would include computer retail stores, computer consulting firms, high schools, junior colleges, universities, and private computer training schools.

SUMMARY

Computer instructor/trainer with 10 years of professional experience.

Skills / Expertise dialog:

(1) Systems operation and maintenance
(2) Application software installation
(3) System and application software diagnosis
(4) LAN Network installation and management
(5) Online networking and management
(6) Windows 3.x and 95
(7) Cross platform applications - Windows/Macintosh
(8) System upgrading
(9) BBS Networking
(10) Internet Networking

OK   Cancel

Keywords

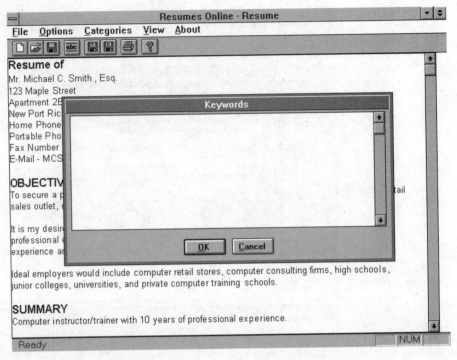

1. Select the Categories menu, and select the Keywords menu item.
2. Enter into the Keywords dialog box words that describe your overall qualifications, background, or career goals that are not found in any other section of your resume.

   Note: Most online resume databases are "full text searchable." This means that employers and recruiters who are about to conduct a search will enter into the search function a word or words that describe the person they are attempting to find. Then the computer system will check *every word in every resume* to find the requested information. If the computer finds the same word or words anywhere in your resume, it considers your resume to be a match, and will then present your resume, along with others that are also considered to be a match, to the person doing the searching.

   To ensure that your resume will be found, it is imperative that you include as many of the appropriate search words as are likely to be used by employers and recruiters who are looking for someone with your qualifications.

   For example, suppose you have experience as a "Scheduler," and you use the word "Scheduler" in your resume. Suppose also that an employer or recruiter is searching for someone with your experience, but uses the term "Expediter." If this word is not in your resume, the employer or recruiter will never see your resume. To make sure your resume is selected, a special paragraph called Keywords has been created to allow you to enter other words that are not used in your resume that describe your qualifications and career objectives.

3. Select the OK button to save your data and display it on the screen.

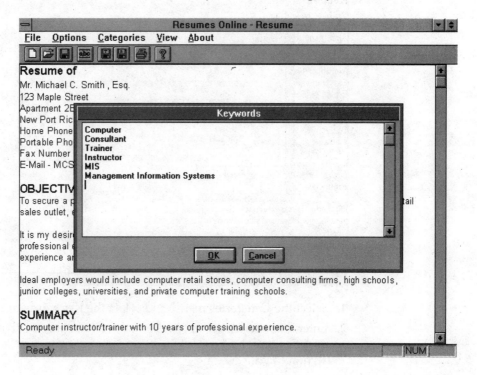

Work Experience

```
┌─────────────────────────────────────────────────────────────────────┐
│ ─              Resumes Online - Resume                      ▼ ▲     │
├─────────────────────────────────────────────────────────────────────┤
│  File   Options   Categories   View   About                          │
├─────────────────────────────────────────────────────────────────────┤
│  ▯ ▱ ▤ ▦ ▦ ▦ ▤ ▯                                                    │
├─────────────────────────────────────────────────────────────────────┤
│ R ┌──────────────────── Work Experience ─────────────────────────┐  │
│ M │  Start Date: [        ]      End Date: [        ]             │  │
│ 12│                                                    ┌───────┐   │  │
│ A │       Title: [                              ]      │  OK   │   │  │
│ N │                                                    └───────┘   │  │
│ H │ Starting Salary: [        ]  Ending Salary: [        ]  ┌──────┐│  │
│ P │                                                    │Cancel ││  │
│ F │ Employer Name: [                            ]      └──────┘│  │
│ E │     Address 1: [                            ]              │  │
│   │     Address 2: [                            ]              │  │
│ O │     Address 3: [                            ]              │  │
│ T │     Address 4: [                            ]              │  │
│ sa│          City: [            ]  State: [  ]  Zip: [      ]   │  │
│ It│         Phone: [            ]    Fax: [           ]         │  │
│ pr│   Description: [                            ] ▲             │  │
│ ex│                [                            ]               │  │
│ Id│                [                            ] ▼             │  │
│ ju└──────────────────────────────────────────────────────────┘  │  │
│ SUMMARY                                                            ▼ │
│ Computer instructor/trainer with 10 years of professional experience.│
├─────────────────────────────────────────────────────────────────────┤
│ Ready                                              NUM               │
└─────────────────────────────────────────────────────────────────────┘
```

1. Select the Categories menu, and select the Work Experience menu item.
2. Enter into the Work Experience dialogue box any or all of the following information for your *most recent* employment position:

   Starting date

   Ending date

   Job title

   Starting salary

   Ending salary

   Employer name

   Address 1

   Address 2

   Address 3

   Address 4

   City

   State

   Zip

   Phone [including area code]

Fax [including area code]

Description (position)

3. Select the OK button to save your data and display the Work Experience Listing screen.

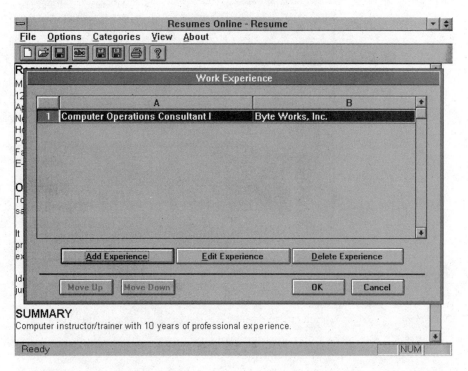

This screen will list all the work experience positions that you enter into the program. From this screen you may:

❏ Add additional work experience positions.

❏ Edit an existing work experience position.

❏ Delete an existing work experience position.

To add an additional position, just click on the Add Experience button. To edit or delete an item, first select (single click) the position you wish to edit or delete, and then click on the Edit Experience or Delete Experience button.

4. Select the OK button to save your data and display it on the screen.

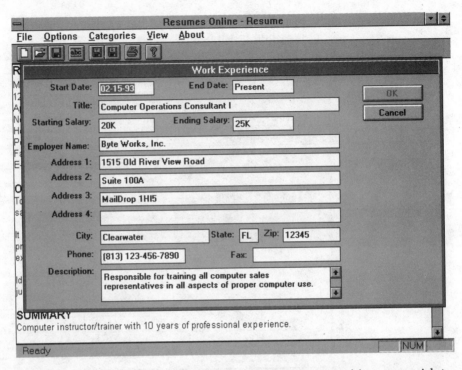

5. Continue this procedure for all the work experience positions you wish to include in your resume. Enter them in reverse chronological order, starting with the most recent and going back in time to the earliest positions.

Educational Background

```
┌─────────────────────────────────────────────────────────────────────┐
│ ⊟              Resumes Online - Resume                        ▼│ ♦   │
├─────────────────────────────────────────────────────────────────────┤
│  File  Options  Categories  View  About                              │
│ ┌──────────────────────────────────────────────────────────────┐    │
│ R│              Educational Background                           │    │
│ M│                                                               │    │
│ 12│  Starting Date: [        ]      Ending Date: [        ]      │    │
│ A│  Degree / Program: [                                    ]     │    │
│ N│    Major / Minor: [                                     ]     │    │
│ H│  Institutional Name: [                                  ]     │    │
│ P│     Address 1: [                                        ]     │    │
│ F│                                              ┌──────────┐     │    │
│ E│     Address 2: [                             │    OK    │ ]   │    │
│ O│     Address 3: [                             └──────────┘ ]   │    │
│ T│     Address 4: [                             ┌──────────┐ ]   │    │
│ sa│                                             │  Cancel  │     │    │
│ It│        City: [            ] State: [ ] Zip: [        ]       │    │
│ pr│       Phone: [            ]       Fax: [          ]          │    │
│ ex│                                                              │    │
│ Id│  Graduation Date: [      ]  Grade/Grade Point Average: [   ] │    │
│ ju│      Honors: [                                          ]    │    │
│ S│                                                               │    │
│ Computer instructor/trainer with 10 years of professional experience.│
│ Ready                                                    NUM        │
└─────────────────────────────────────────────────────────────────────┘
```

1. Select the Categories menu, and select the Educational Background menu item.
2. Enter into the Educational Background dialog box any or all of the following information for the *highest or most advanced* (i.e., Doctoral or First Professional Degree) educational program of study that you have completed (or are in the process of completing):

   Starting date

   Ending date

   Degree/program

   Major/minor

   Institutional name

   Address 1

   Address 2

   Address 3

   Address 4

   City

   State

   Zip

Phone [including area code]

Fax [including area code]

Graduation date

Grade/grade point average

Honors

3. Select the OK button to save your data and display the Educational Background Listing screen.

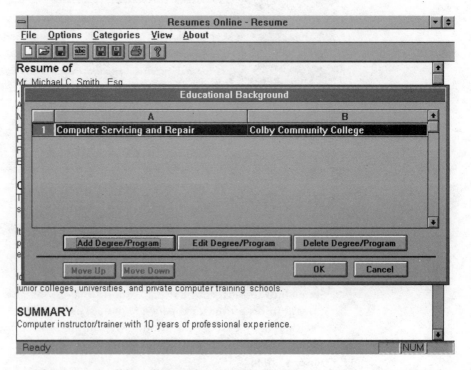

This screen will list all the educational experiences that you enter into the program. From this screen you may:

❑ Add additional educational experience.

❑ Edit an existing educational experience.

❑ Delete an existing educational experience.

To add an additional experience, just click on the Add Degree/Program button. To edit or delete an item, first select (single click) the educational experience you wish to edit or delete, and then click on the Edit Degree/Program or Delete Degree/Program button.

4. Select the OK button to save your data and display it on the screen.

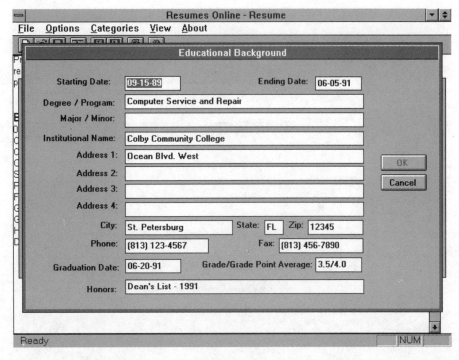

5. Continue this procedure for all the educational experiences you wish to include in your resume. Enter them in order of priority. Most people usually start with the most advanced program they have completed (or are in the process of completing) and continue back in time to their high school experience. However, you may also begin with the experience that is most applicable to the position you are attempting to secure.

Accomplishments

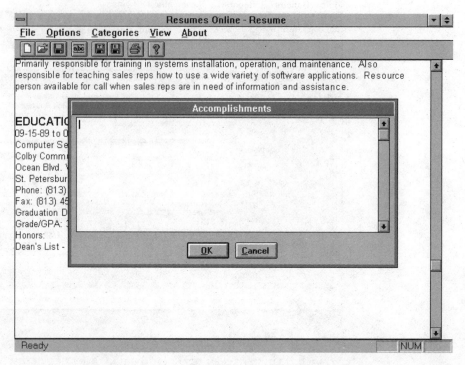

1. Select the Categories menu, and select the Accomplishments menu item.

2. Enter into the Accomplishments dialog box a statement that describes your major accomplishments in life. You could include accomplishments that are work and/or educationally related, those that you achieved in other activities in life (such as those related to certain volunteer activities) or all accomplishments.

   Example:

   Successfully designed, implemented, and managed a new university-wide faculty review program to effectively evaluate faculty performance, merit payment increase awards, and career promotions. Procedure has now been adopted by all California state universities. Procedure approved by over 90% of all tenured faculty.

3. Select the OK button to save your data and display it on the screen.

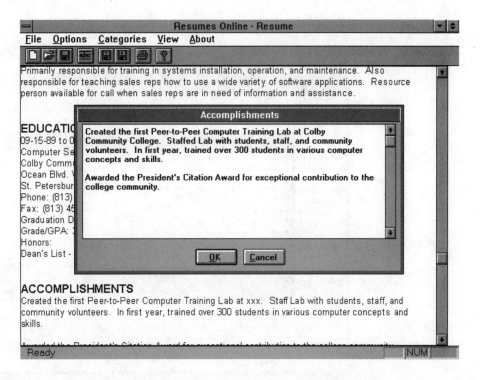

Primarily responsible for training in systems installation, operation, and maintenance. Also responsible for teaching sales reps how to use a wide variety of software applications. Resource person available for call when sales reps are in need of information and assistance.

EDUCATION
09-15-89 to
Computer Se
Colby Comm
Ocean Blvd.
St. Petersbur
Phone: (813)
Fax: (813) 45
Graduation D
Grade/GPA:
Honors:
Dean's List -

Accomplishments

Created the first Peer-to-Peer Computer Training Lab at Colby Community College. Staffed Lab with students, staff, and community volunteers. In first year, trained over 300 students in various computer concepts and skills.

Awarded the President's Citation Award for exceptional contribution to the college community.

[OK] [Cancel]

ACCOMPLISHMENTS
Created the first Peer-to-Peer Computer Training Lab at xxx. Staff Lab with students, staff, and community volunteers. In first year, trained over 300 students in various computer concepts and skills.

Ready   NUM

Awards

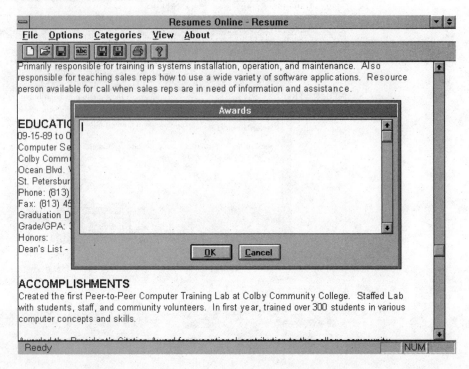

1. Select the Categories menu, and select the Awards menu item.

2. Enter into the Awards dialog box a statement that describes the awards that you have received in your lifetime. As with Accomplishments, you may include only awards that are work and/or educationally related, those that you achieved in other activities in life, or both.

    Example:

    Recipient of the Bainridge award for the "Most Outstanding Educator of 1992"

3. Select the OK button to save your data and display it on the screen.

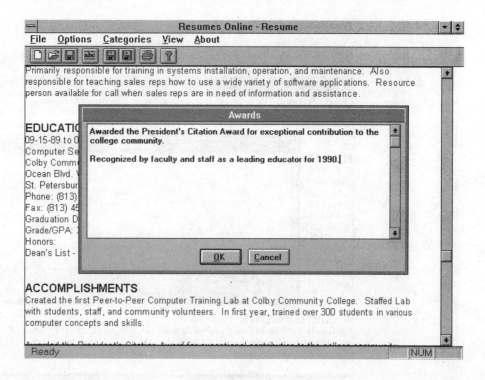

Primarily responsible for training in systems installation, operation, and maintenance. Also responsible for teaching sales reps how to use a wide variety of software applications. Resource person available for call when sales reps are in need of information and assistance.

EDUCATIO

09-15-89 to 0

Computer Se

Colby Comm

Ocean Blvd. \

St. Petersbur

Phone: (813)

Fax: (813) 45

Graduation D

Grade/GPA: 1

Honors:

Dean's List -

Awards

Awarded the President's Citation Award for exceptional contribution to the college community.

Recognized by faculty and staff as a leading educator for 1990.

[OK] [Cancel]

ACCOMPLISHMENTS

Created the first Peer-to-Peer Computer Training Lab at Colby Community College. Staffed Lab with students, staff, and community volunteers. In first year, trained over 300 students in various computer concepts and skills.

Ready   NUM

Publications

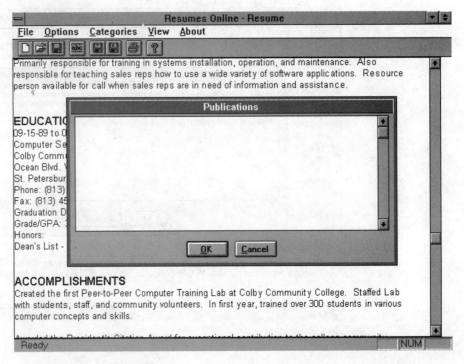

1. Select the Categories menu, and select the Publications menu item.
2. Enter into the Publications dialog box a listing of the various publications that you have authored.

   Example:

   Liberal Arts in a High-Tech World (Summer Press, 1991)

   Are Liberal Arts Too Liberal? (First Edition Books, 1990)

   Traditional Liberal Skills in a Modern Day World (Bath Publications, 1989)
3. Select the OK button to save your data and display it on the screen.

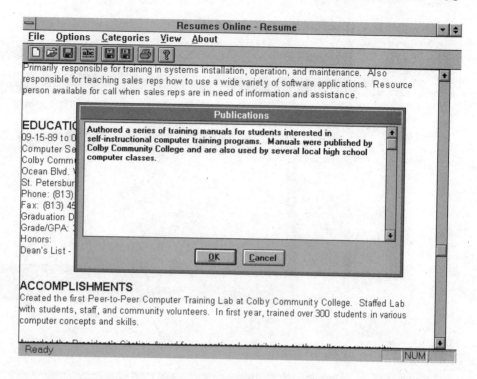

Primarily responsible for training in systems installation, operation, and maintenance. Also responsible for teaching sales reps how to use a wide variety of software applications. Resource person available for call when sales reps are in need of information and assistance.

EDUCATIO
09-15-89 to D
Computer Se
Colby Comm
Ocean Blvd.
St. Petersbur
Phone: (813)
Fax: (813) 45
Graduation D
Grade/GPA:
Honors:
Dean's List -

Publications

Authored a series of training manuals for students interested in self-instructional computer training programs. Manuals were published by Colby Community College and are also used by several local high school computer classes.

OK   Cancel

ACCOMPLISHMENTS
Created the first Peer-to-Peer Computer Training Lab at Colby Community College. Staffed Lab with students, staff, and community volunteers. In first year, trained over 300 students in various computer concepts and skills.

Ready   NUM

Trademarks and Patents

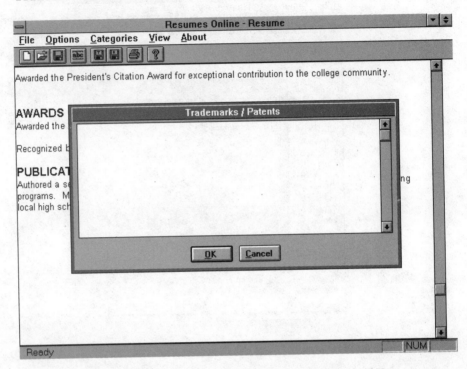

1. Select the Categories menu, and select the Trademarks and Patents menu item.
2. Enter into the Trademarks and Patents dialog box a listing of the various trademarks and patents that you have registered with the U.S. Office of Trademarks and Patents.
3. Select the OK button to save your data and display it on the screen.

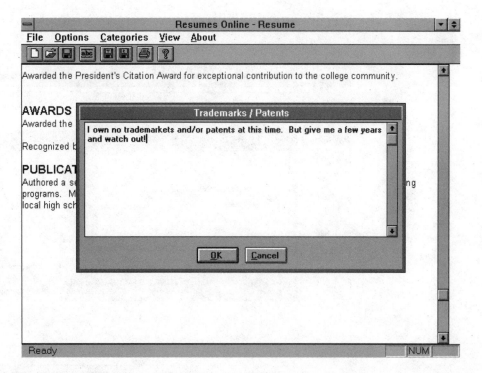

Organizational Affiliations

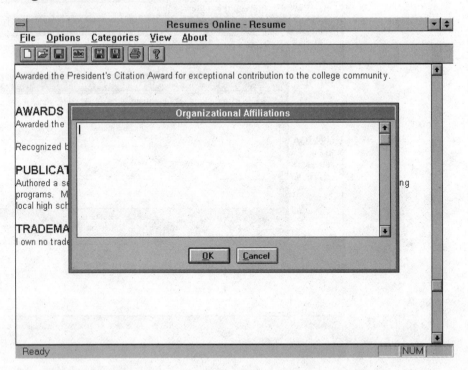

1. Select the Categories menu, and select the Organizational Affiliations menu item.
2. Enter into the Organizational Affiliations dialog box a listing of the various organizations of which you have been a member.

   Example:

   Knights of Columbus: 1982–present

   Greater Hartford Committee on the Environment: 1986–1988

   President's Committee on Education: 1989 (Chairperson)
3. Select the OK button to save your data and display it on the screen.

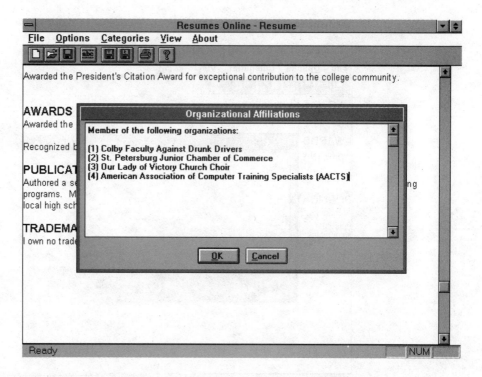

Awarded the President's Citation Award for exceptional contribution to the college community.

AWARDS

Awarded the

Recognized b

PUBLICAT

Authored a se
programs. M
local high sch

TRADEMA

I own no trade

Organizational Affiliations

Member of the following organizations:

(1) Colby Faculty Against Drunk Drivers
(2) St. Petersburg Junior Chamber of Commerce
(3) Our Lady of Victory Church Choir
(4) American Association of Computer Training Specialists (AACTS)

OK   Cancel

Salary History/Requirements

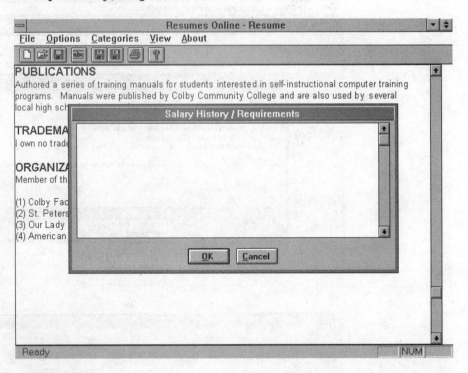

1. Select the Categories menu, and select the Salary History/Requirements menu item.
2. Enter into the Salary History/Requirements dialog box information regarding your salary history and/or the salary level you hope to achieve with your new position.

   Example:

   Salary requirements: $70,000 with full benefits package.
3. Select the OK button to save your data and display it on the screen.

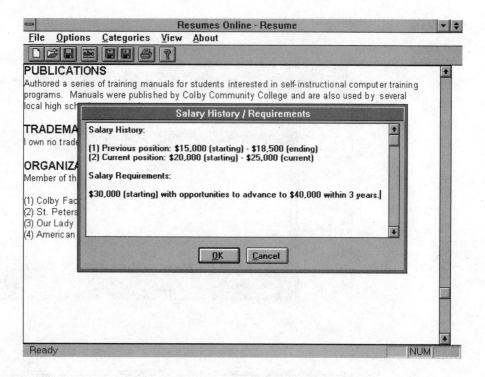

PUBLICATIONS
Authored a series of training manuals for students interested in self-instructional computer training programs. Manuals were published by Colby Community College and are also used by several local high sch

Salary History / Requirements

Salary History:

(1) Previous position: $15,000 (starting) - $18,500 (ending)
(2) Current position: $20,000 (starting) - $25,000 (current)

Salary Requirements:

$30,000 (starting) with opportunities to advance to $40,000 within 3 years.

TRADEMA
I own no trade

ORGANIZA
Member of th

(1) Colby Fac
(2) St. Peters
(3) Our Lady
(4) American

Relocation

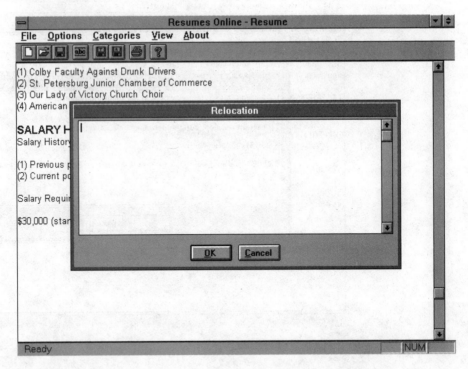

1. Select the Categories menu, and select the Relocation menu item.
2. Enter into the Relocation dialog box information regarding your relocation needs and preferences.

   Example:

   Willing to consider employment in California, Washington, Oregon, and Arizona. Willing to negotiate relocation expenses.
3. Select the OK button to save your data and display it on the screen.

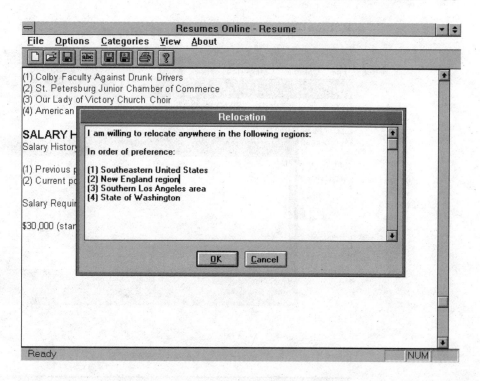

Resumes Online - Resume

File   Options   Categories   View   About

(1) Colby Faculty Against Drunk Drivers
(2) St. Petersburg Junior Chamber of Commerce
(3) Our Lady of Victory Church Choir
(4) American

SALARY H
Salary History

(1) Previous p
(2) Current po

Salary Requir

$30,000 (star

Relocation

I am willing to relocate anywhere in the following regions:

In order of preference:

(1) Southeastern United States
(2) New England region
(3) Southern Los Angeles area
(4) State of Washington

OK   Cancel

Ready   NUM

Personal

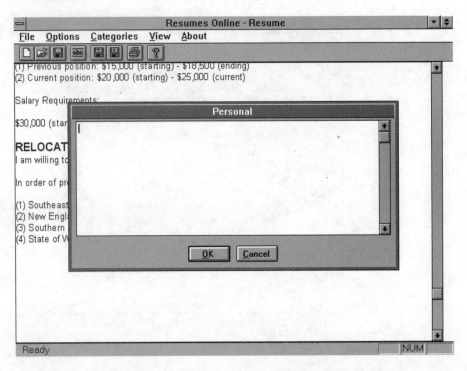

1. Select the Categories menu, and select the Personal menu item.

2. Enter into the Personal dialog box any information you wish to share with the readers of your resume that does not fit within other categories.

   Example:

   As a strong advocate of a Liberal Arts education, I am fully committed to the advancement of the liberal arts as a means of preparing college students for upper-level graduate training, as well as for a career in today's world of work.

3. Select the OK button to save your data and display it on the screen.

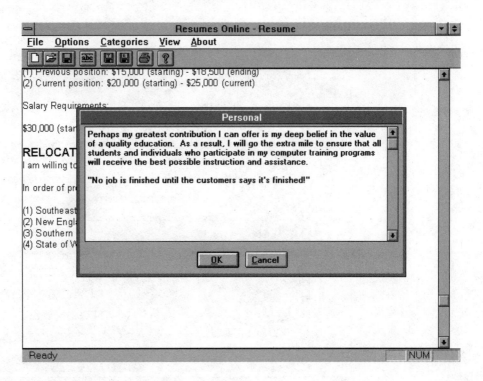

— Resumes Online - Resume

File   **Options**   **Categories**   **View**   **About**

(1) Previous position: $15,000 (starting) - $18,500 (ending)
(2) Current position: $20,000 (starting) - $25,000 (current)

Salary Requirements:

$30,000 (star

RELOCAT
I am willing to

In order of pr

(1) Southeast
(2) New Engl
(3) Southern
(4) State of V

Personal

Perhaps my greatest contribution I can offer is my deep belief in the value of a quality education. As a result, I will go the extra mile to ensure that all students and individuals who participate in my computer training programs will receive the best possible instruction and assistance.

"No job is finished until the customers says it's finished!"

OK   **Cancel**

Ready   NUM

References

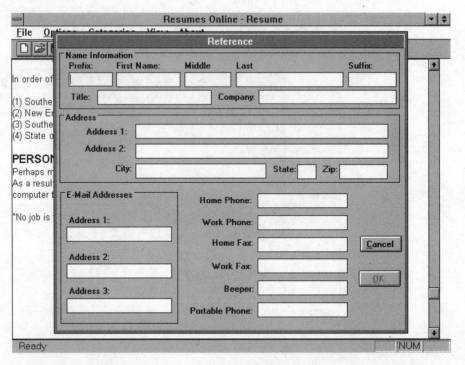

1. Select the Categories menu, and select the References menu item.
2. Enter into the References dialog box any or all of the following information:

   Prefix (example: Dr.)

   First name

   Middle name (or initial)

   Last name

   Suffix (example: Esquire)

   Title

   Company

   Home address 1

   Home address 2

   City

   State

   Zip

   Home phone [including area code]

   Work phone [including area code]

Home fax [including area code]

Work fax [including area code]

Beeper [including area code]

Portable phone [including area code]

Email address(es) [*Examples:* 1234,567—CompuServe; BW10556—America Online; MrQuick—Prodigy; bcotton@nsnet.com—Internet]

3. Select the OK button to save your data and display the References Listing screen.

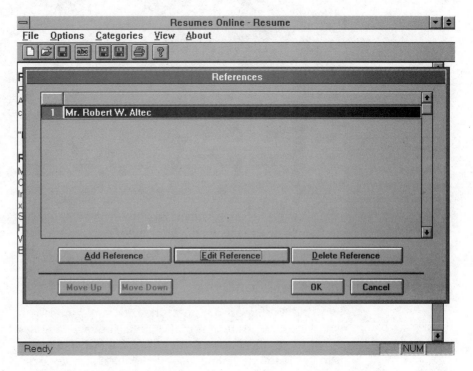

This screen will list all the references that you enter into the program. From this screen you may:

❑ Add additional references.

❑ Edit an existing reference.

❑ Delete an existing reference.

To add an additional reference, just click on the Add Reference button. To edit or delete an item, first select (single click) the item you wish to edit or delete, and then click on the Edit Reference or Delete Reference button.

4. Select the OK button to save your data and display it on the screen.

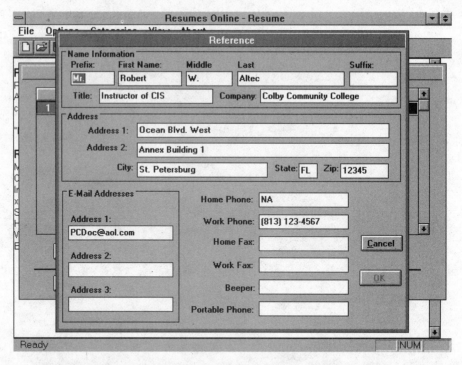

This would be an excellent time to review the wording of your electronic resume and make whatever changes you feel are necessary.

Step 3: Export Your Electronic Resume as a Text File

By using the Export option in the program, you can change the format of your electronic resume from its native language (as a *Resumes Online* file, referred to as <filename>.rsm) to a text file (<filename>.txt), thereby enabling it to be "read" by online resume database services, such as the Worldwide Resume/Talent Bank. This step is necessary if you wish to upload your resume to an online service.

Directions:

1. If necessary, start the *Resumes Online* program.
2. Using the Open option on the File menu, open the resume you wish to Export.
3. From the File menu, select the Export option to display the Export dialog box. Or click on the Export icon on the Tool bar.

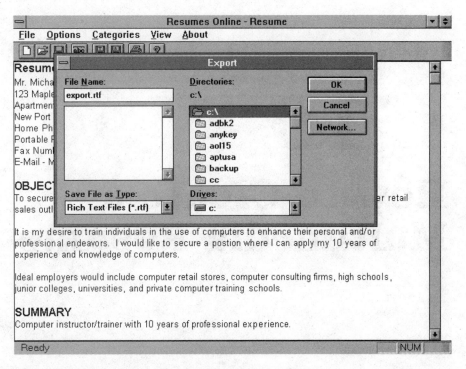

4. If you prefer, rename the resume (file).

5. Specify where you wish to save the Exported resume (drive and directory location).

6. From the "Save file as type:" area, select the "Online Format (*.txt)" option.

7. Click on the OK button to Export your resume to a text file, or the Cancel button to cancel the Export function.

Now you are ready to forward your electronic resume to the Worldwide Resume/Talent Bank service. To do so, refer to Appendix A for additional directions.

10

How to Create a Multimedia Resume

Caution: Due to programming design limitations, it is not recommended that you attempt to run the *Resumes Online* program at the same time that you are attempting to run the *Resumaker* program. Neither program will operate correctly if both are run simultaneously.

Using *Resumaker*

This chapter will guide you in using the second of the two software programs that have been bundled with your copy of *Electronic Resumes.* The second program is entitled *Resumaker,* and can be used to create a multimedia version of your existing resume, or a printed copy of your standard resume. Once you have completed this process, you can distribute your multimedia resume electronically—on diskette, as an attached email file, or via regular file transfer. In addition, you can also upload and post your multimedia resume in file libraries found on various commercial computer network services, such as America Online, as well as on any number of private BBS services.

Note: Follow the directions in Chapter 9 if you wish to create a text version of your resume for use with online searchable resume database services.

With *Resumaker,* you can send your resume out on to the Information Superhighway—where it can be read by any one of the 40 million people who travel through cyberspace.

Before you begin, it is suggested that you place a copy of your existing printed resume next to your computer as you work with the *Resumaker* program. *Resumaker* should operate on any IBM or IBM-compatible computer equipped with Windows 3.x or 95, with at least 4 megs of memory and 1 meg of free hard disk space. A mouse is highly recommended. A printer is optional. This program will also operate on Apple Macintosh computers that have been equipped to read DOS and/or Windows programs.

Remember, if you are currently employed and do not want your current employer to become aware of your job search activities, it is recommended that you *not* include your name, address, phone number, or other identifying information about yourself in your resume. Instead, it is recommended that you create a blind resume. See Chapter 8 for more information regarding this subject matter.

For Technical Support with *Resumaker,* please contact:

Techno-Marketing, Inc.
5170 West 76th Street
Edina, MN 55435
612-830-1984

The screen shots that appear in this chapter were taken of the program running under Windows 3.1. If you are using Windows 95, your screens will appear slightly different. However, all functions and features will operate the same regardless of which interface you are using.

Creating a multimedia version of your existing resume will be accomplished by completing four easy steps:

Step 1: Install the *Resumaker* software program.

Step 2: Edit the *Resumaker* multimedia display area.

Step 3: Prepare your *Resumaker* display and print files.

Step 4: Create your own stand-alone resume.

Assumed Knowledge

The directions for using the *Resumaker* software program assume that you are familiar with basic Windows operations, such as how to select menu items and dialog box items with a mouse, how to open and close applications, how to save a document, how to create a basic document and then save it, how to print a document, and other similar concepts. If you are unfamiliar with these concepts, please refer to your copy of the user's manual for Windows for instructions on how to operate within a Windows application (program).

Step 1: Install the *Resumaker* Software Program

1. Start your personal computer.
2. Start Windows.
3. Insert the disk found in the back of this book into your 3.5-inch disk drive.
4. For Windows 3.1, in the Program Manager, select Run from the File menu. For Windows 95, select Run from the Start menu.
5. Type in "a:setup2" (or "b:setup2") depending upon your system, and click on the OK button.
6. (Optional) When requested, specify a path location if the default is not acceptable. We recommend you use the default location.

You will be notified on the screen when the installation process is completed.

Starting the Program

1. If necessary, start your computer.
2. If necessary, start Windows.
3. For Windows 3.1, from the *Resumake* folder, select (double click) the *Resumake* launch icon. For Windows 95, select *Resumaker* from the Start/ Programs menu.

The program will first display a photograph of Jenny Johnson, a sample job seeker, and then the screen will automatically dissolve to an Introduction screen. Soon you will learn how you too can display your picture. The Introduction screen is actually a place where you can display the contents of a cover letter that you wish to send to potential employers or employment recruiters. Click on the Continue button to display the main menu of the *Resumaker* program.

Step 2: Edit the *Resumaker* Multimedia Display Area

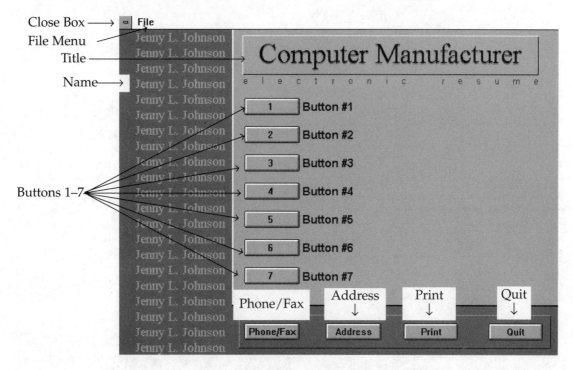

This is the main display area of the *Resumaker* program. The information that you will soon enter into the program will appear on this screen. Employers who wish to view your multimedia resume will use this same screen to access the contents of your resume.

1. Note the use of the following features:

   Close Box. By double clicking on this item, or by opening this box and selecting Close, you can exit the *Resumaker* program. This box can also be used to move or minimize the program, or to gain access to the About information (i.e., information about the developers of the *Resumaker* program).

   File Menu. By opening this menu, you can gain access to the Edit function, or you can view the About, or exit the program. Select the Upgrade item on the File menu to learn how you can obtain a copy of *Resumaker Pro* ($14.95) from Techno-Marketing, Inc., which will allow you to add sound and video to your multimedia resume.

   Title (Computer Manufacturer). This is where the title of your resume will appear.

   Name (Jenny L. Johnson). This is where your name will appear.

   Menu Buttons 1-7. These buttons, when edited by you and then selected, will provide access to the following sections of your resume:

- Career Objective

  Employment History

  Educational Background

  Skills and Expertise

  Accomplishments

  Awards and Honors

  References

Click on any of these buttons and a screen will appear informing you that you have accessed the location where certain information will be displayed (which you will soon enter). Click on the Continue button to return to the main display area.

Phone/Fax. This is where your phone and/or fax number will appear.

Address. This is where your address will appear.

Print. For use when you wish to print a copy of your resume.

Quit. To exit the program.

2. From the File menu, select the Edit menu item to display the Edit screen and Edit functions.

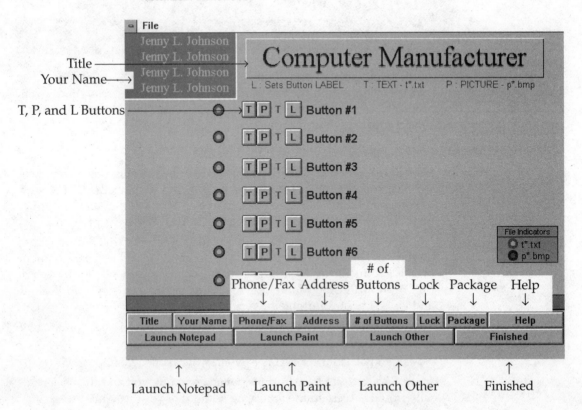

3. Note the use of the following edit functions:

Title. This is where you will enter the title of your resume.

Your Name. This is where you will enter your name.

T, P, and L Buttons. With these buttons you can set the format characteristic of each of the 7 main menu buttons: Career Objective, Employment History, Educational Background, Skills and Expertise, Accomplishments, Awards and Honors, and References.

Each button may be set to display either text information (T) or graphic or pictorial information (P). In addition, you may also edit the label or title of each button (L). All buttons are currently set to display text, and are labeled as Button #1 through Button #7.

Phone/Fax. This is where you will enter your phone and/or fax numbers.

Address. This is where you will enter your address.

# of Buttons. This function will allow you to set the number of buttons that will actually appear on the main display area. You can set the number from 1 to 7.

Lock. Use this function if you wish to distribute a copy of your resume without first packaging (explained below) your program files into a stand-alone Windows application. When you lock the program, the end user cannot edit the program settings that you have established.

Package. This function, when selected, will lock your program, compress your program files, and package all files with a Windows installer program into a stand-alone package. You may then distribute your resume freely. Users will simply install your resume as they do any Windows application by clicking on a file named Install.exe.

Help. Use this option to obtain a quick description of the various Edit functions.

Launch Notepad. Use this option to launch the Windows 3.1 Notepad (or Windows 95 Wordpad) program. Because Notepad comes bundled with Windows 3.1, it is a convenient program to use in creating text files for use with buttons 1-7. However, any word processing or text editing program that can create a text file may be used. You can easily access Notepad from within the Edit area of the *Resumaker* program. *Caution:* If you launch Notepad and while it remains open, click on Launch Notepad again, two copies of Notepad will be operational at the same time. Always close one copy before launching the program again.

Launch Paint. Use this option to launch the Windows 3.1 or 95 Paint program. Like Notepad, Paint comes bundled with Windows 3.1 and 95, and is therefore a convenient program to use in creating graphic files for use with any of the 1-7 buttons. However, any graphic or paint program that can create a .bmp file may be used. You can easily access Paint from within the Edit area of the *Resumaker* program. *Caution:* If you launch Paint and while it remains open, click on Launch Paint again, two copies of Paint will be operational at the same time. Always close one copy before launching the program again.

Launch Other. Use this option if you wish to launch some other Windows program, other than the Notepad or Paint programs. If you wish to use a program other than Notepad or Paint to create any files for buttons 1-7, this is where you would launch that program.

Finished. When you have completed any editing and wish to view the results, or to exit the Edit area, select the Finished button. By selecting Finished you can save the changes you have made to your resume.

4. Edit the Title of your resume:

   a. Click on the Title button.

   b. In the Title dialog box,

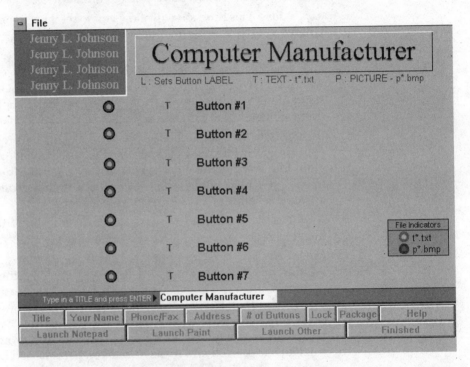

type in a title for your resume (up to 21 characters) and press the Enter key. Note that the Title of your resume has now changed. You may type in your name, or a phrase that describes your overall qualifications or career objective. For example, Dynamic Speaker or Quality Control Chief. It is suggested that you not use your name as this information will be entered in the Name area.

If you make a mistake, or wish to change your entry, simply repeat the process.

5. Edit your Name:

   a. Click on the Your Name button.

   b. In the Your Name dialog box,

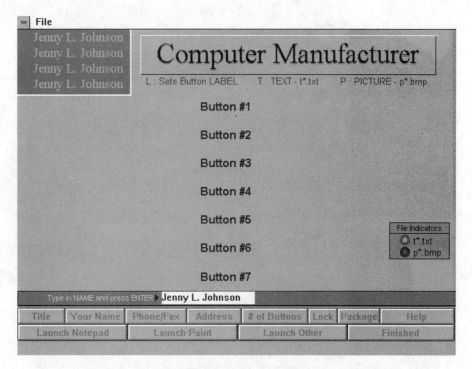

   type in your name (up to 16 characters) and press the Enter key. Note that the Your Name area has changed.

6. Edit your Phone/Fax numbers:

   a. Click on the Phone/Fax edit button.

   b. In the Phone/Fax dialog box,

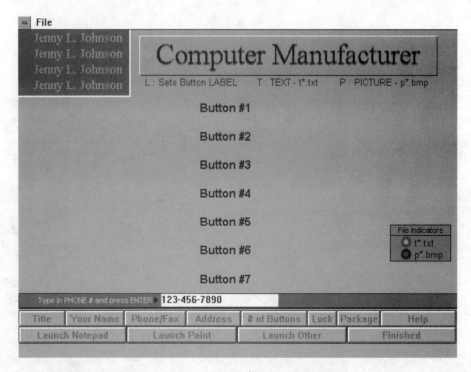

type in your phone number (with area code) and press the Enter key. Example: 123/456-7890

c. Then enter your fax number in the same manner.

If you do not wish to enter a phone and/or fax number, then enter any of the following: Not Available, Contact via Mail, Contact via Email, etc.

7. Edit your Address:

a. Click on the Address button.

b. In the Address dialog box,

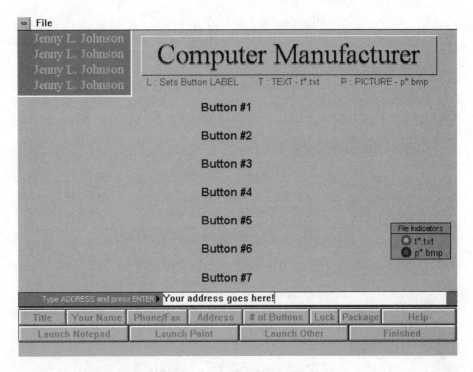

type in your address.

If you do not wish to enter your residential mailing address, then you might consider advising readers to contact you via a post office box, via email, by phone, or by fax. Whatever is your preference, enter in the appropriate information.

8. Edit the 7 button labels:

Click on the "L" button located to the left of the words Button #1 on the Edit screen. Enter the phrase Career Objective in the data entry field that will appear, and then press the Enter key. Note the button is now labeled Career Objective.

Follow the same procedure to label the remaining buttons. We recommend you use the following categories, but you are free to label the buttons whatever you wish. If you make a mistake, just repeat the process to label the buttons correctly.

Label Button #2 as Employment History

Label Button #3 as Educational Background

Label Button #4 as Skills and Expertise

Label Button #5 as Accomplishments

Label Button #6 as Awards and Honors

Label Button #7 as References

9. Click on the Finished button to view the changes you have made to your resume. If you wish to make further changes to these areas, simply return to the Edit screen and repeat the above steps.

Step 3: Prepare Your *Resumaker* Display and Print Files

You are now ready to prepare the files that will appear when buttons 1 to 7 are selected, plus a special file that will print when the Print button is used. Before you actually prepare the display and print files, you need to make three decisions.

Decision #1: Number of Buttons

Resumaker will allow you to display anywhere from 1 to 7 buttons. Your copy of *Resumaker* has been preset for 7 buttons. Therefore, you first need to determine how many sections you wish to use to display your resume, and then set the program to display the same number of buttons. You must use at least one button.

Decision #2: Button Labels

Resumaker will allow you to name (label) the buttons whatever you wish. While we have suggested labels that reflect typical resume categories, you are free to use your own labeling system.

Decision #3: Text or Graphics

Resumaker will allow you to display for each of the seven buttons either text information *or* a graphic image, but not both. Depending upon what information you wish to display within your resume, and your ability to produce or obtain such information, you should determine for each button whether you wish to display text information or a graphic image. As found within the program's install directory (c:\resumake), all button text files must be labeled t1.txt, t2.txt, t3.txt and so on where t*x* (e.g., t1) defines the button number. All graphic image files must be labeled similarly, p1.bmp, p2.bmp, p3.bmp, etc.

Actually, *Resumaker* will allow you to display up to eleven text and/or graphic image files as listed below:

File #	Description/Location	Format	File Name*
1	First Screen w/dissolve	Graphic	intro.bmp
2	Introduction Screen	Text	cover.txt
3	Button 1	Text (or Graphic)	t1.txt (or p1.bmp)
4	Button 2	Text (or Graphic)	t2.txt (or p2.bmp)
5	Button 3	Text (or Graphic)	t3.txt (or p3.bmp)
6	Button 4	Text (or Graphic)	t4.txt (or p4.bmp)
7	Button 5	Text (or Graphic)	t5.txt (or p5.bmp)
8	Button 6	Text (or Graphic)	t6.txt (or p6.bmp)
9	Button 7	Text (or Graphic)	t7.txt (or p7.bmp)
10	Printed Resume	Write file	resume.wri
11	Exit Screen w/dissolve	Graphic	exit.bmp

*As found in the program's install directory (c:\resumake).

All files *must* be labeled as indicated above in the File Name column, as the program will look for these file names when a particular function (e.g., Button 1) is selected by the user.

File #10 must be created with the use of the Windows 3.1 Write (or Windows 95 WordPad) word processing program, and the file must be labeled as resume.wri.

Text files should pose little problem for you to create, as you are more than likely familiar with how to use a word processing program (or in this case the Notepad program) to create a text (*.txt) file. Creating a text file is a very easy task. However, if you are not familiar with how to use a paint or illustration program to create a graphic (*.bmp) file, or how to convert a photograph into a .bmp file, then you should seek professional assistance with the creation of your graphic files.

Since the purpose of the resume is to display information about yourself, many of the graphic image files used by job seekers are actual pictures of themselves. However, other kinds of graphic image files are appropriate. For example, if you are a water color artist, you may wish to include a sample of your art work as one of the 7 buttons, or perhaps as the First or Last screen displays. Use your imagination to determine how best to combine text and graphic image files—*Resumaker* will display whatever you wish!

Refer to Appendix C to learn about a graphic scanning service that will convert your 35 mm photos into graphic (*.bmp) files for use in your *Resumaker* program.

Setting the Number of Buttons

1. From the File menu, select the Edit item to display the Edit screen.
2. Select the # of Buttons button to display the # of Buttons dialog box.

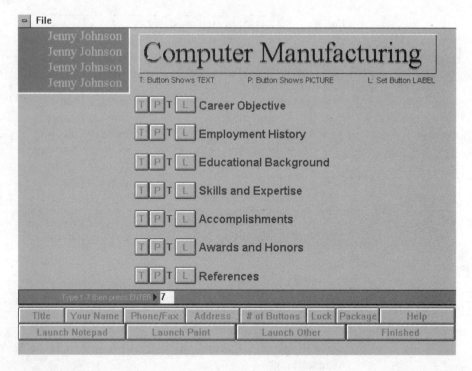

3. Enter in the number of buttons you wish to display (1, 2, 3, 4, 5, 6 or 7), and press the Enter key.

4. Select Finished to view the change to your resume.

Setting the Format Characteristic of Each Button

1. From the File menu, select the Edit item to display the Edit screen.

2. Starting with the first button and depending upon the plans you have for button 1, click on the T button to set the button for text, or P to set the button for a graphic image. Note that a red T or P will appear to indicate which option has been selected.

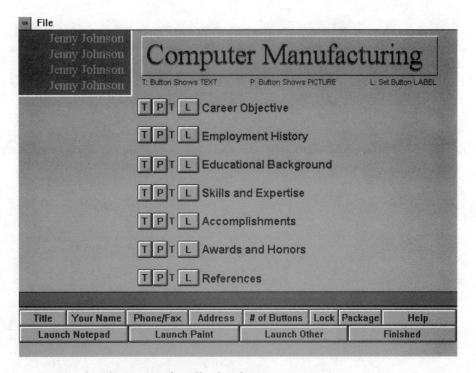

3. Repeat the above step for all other buttons.

4. Select the Finished button when you have set all buttons.

Editing the Button Labels

1. From the File menu, select the Edit item to display the Edit screen.

   Starting with the First button, click on the L button to display the button label dialog box.

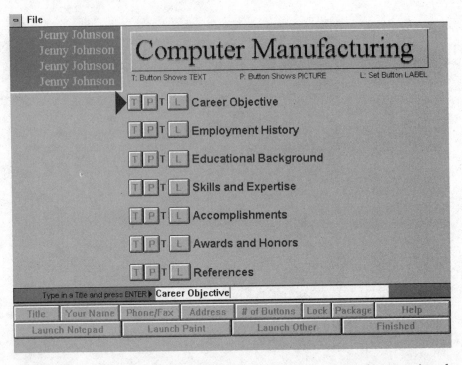

2. Enter in the label you now prefer for button #1 (up to 40 characters) and then press the Enter key.

3. Repeat the above steps for any other button labels you wish to edit.

4. Select Finished to view the changes to your resume.

Preparing or Editing Text Files

Follow this procedure when you wish to display text information for any of the 1-7 buttons. If you wish to display graphic images, proceed to the "Preparing graphic file images" section below.

1. From the File menu, select the Edit item to display the Edit screen.

2. Select the Launch Notepad button to display the Windows 3.1 Notepad program (or the Windows 95 WordPad program).

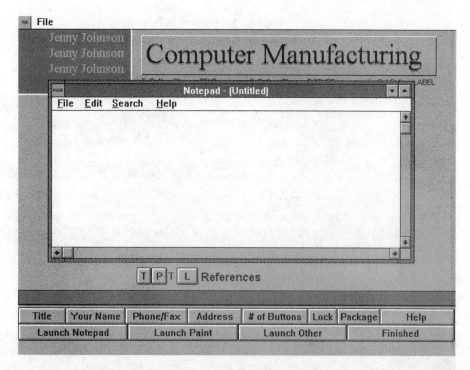

3. From the File menu in the Notepad (or Wordpad) program, select the Open option.

4. Determine what information you wish to edit. Depending upon which file you wish to edit, select the following:

   To edit data associated with Button #1—select file: t1.txt

   To edit data associated with Button #2—select file: t2.txt

   To edit data associated with Button #3—select file: t3.txt

   To edit data associated with Button #4—select file: t4.txt

   To edit data associated with Button #5—select file: t5.txt

   To edit data associated with Button #6—select file: t6.txt

   To edit data associated with Button #7—select file: t7.txt

   To edit data associated with the Introduction screen—select file: cover.txt

5. Remove our sample text and then type in the information that you prefer. Remember, your information will be saved as text, therefore, no special character formatting is possible, such as **Bold,** *Italic,* <u>Underlining</u>, etc.

   Caution: Considering that your resume is the tool that will help you make your first impression with potential employers, check your spelling and grammar carefully! Each line should not be longer than 80 characters wide. Tabs will not be supported; use spaces to indent text if desired.

6. After entering in the desired information, select the Save option from the File menu to save your new text.

7. Repeat the steps above to edit any of the remaining buttons (text files).

   This step may take up to a few hours to complete depending upon how much information you wish to enter, and how long it takes you to draft the information. Feel free to complete this step over several sessions, taking breaks in between each session.

   Do not specify a different location where the file should be saved. *Resumaker* will save the *.txt files to the same directory as the *Resumaker* program (making it easy for it to find the file when needed).

8. Click the Finished button to return to the main display screen, and then select the appropriate button to view your new information. To view the Introduction screen, you must first exit the program and then restart *Resumaker*.

Preparing or Editing Graphic Image Files

Follow this procedure whenever you wish to create or edit graphic images for any of the 1-7 buttons, or for the First and Last screens.

1. From the File menu, select the Edit item to display the Edit screen.
2. Select the Launch Paint button to display the Windows Paint program.

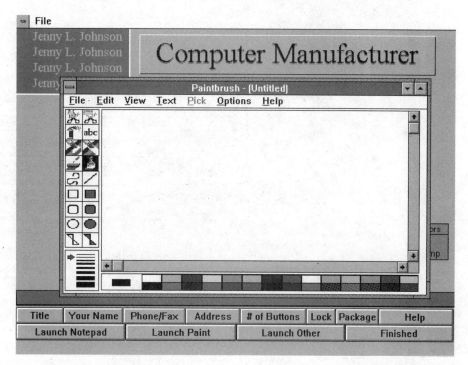

3. Create or edit the graphic image that you wish to display when a particular button is selected.

   Note: If you plan to use existing clip art images or photos, open the appropriate file using the Open command on the Paint File menu. Then perform the desired changes (if any) and continue with the directions below to import that file into your resume.

4. From the Paint File menu, select the Save option to save your image. Note: For VGA display, select the 16-color bitmap option. For SVGA display, select the 256-color bitmap option.

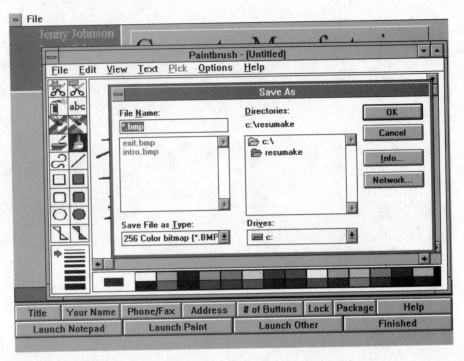

5. Label your files according to the following directions:

For Button 1—label the file as p1.bmp

For Button 2—label the file as p2.bmp

For Button 3—label the file as p3.bmp

For Button 4—label the file as p4.bmp

For Button 5—label the file as p5.bmp

For Button 6—label the file as p6.bmp

For Button 7—label the file as p7.bmp

For the First Screen—label the file as intro.bmp

For the Last Screen—label the file as exit.bmp

6. Do not specify a different location where the file should be saved. *Resumaker* will save the *.bmp files to the same directory as the *Resumaker* program (making it easy for it to find the files when needed).

7. Click the Finished button to return to the main display screen, and then select the appropriate button to view your new display.

8. Repeat the above procedure for all buttons for which you wish to display graphic images. This step may take up to a few hours to complete depending upon how long it takes you to create or edit your graphic image files. Feel free to complete this step over several sessions, taking breaks in between each session.

Preparing a Printed Copy of Your Resume

Located on the main display screen of the *Resumaker* program is a button labeled "Print." If it is configured properly, and if a printer is attached to your computer, you can print out a copy of your standard resume. The Print option is also convenient for those readers of your multimedia resume who wish to have a printed copy.

To configure the *Resumaker* program to allow for printed copies, follow the directions below. Please note that the print option does *not* generate a printed copy of any of the text that you have entered into Buttons 1 to 7 or into the Introduction (cover letter) area. Rather, the text to be printed is generated from a separate file labeled "resume.wri" that must be stored within the same directory as the *Resumaker* program. Also note that to prepare the resume.wri file, you must use the Write word processing program that is bundled with your Windows 3.1 program (or the Windows 95 WordPad program). When the Print option is selected, *Resumaker* will search its directory for the resume.wri file. If it cannot find this file in this directory, the Print function will not work.

Because the print option is created with the use of the Write word processing program, the output file is not a text file. Rather, it is a "Write" file, hence the file extension name "resume.wri" (wri = Write). As such, you may incorporate into this version of your resume any or all of the special character formatting:

bold

italic

<u>underlining</u>

centering

superscript

subscript

In addition, you may use any of the font styles and sizes that are supported by the Write program. In short, you can make the print version of your resume as eye appealing and as professional looking as you wish. The printed version will look the same as it does on screen.

Directions

1. If necessary, start your personal computer.
2. If necessary, start Windows.
3. For Windows 3.1, display the Program Manager and open the Windows Accessory group and double click on the Write icon.

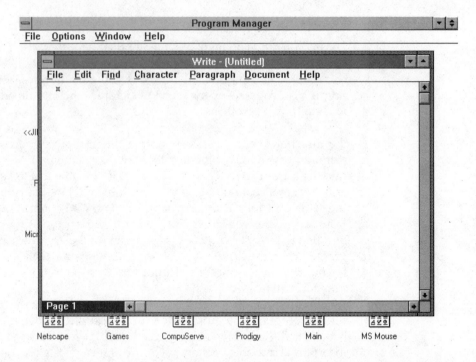

4. For Windows 95, click on Start, select Programs/Accessories/WordPad.

5. Using your existing printed resume as a guide, type in your resume (see Special Note below).

6. When you have finished creating your resume, select the Save item from the File menu. Label the file as resume.wri and save it to the same directory as the location of your copy of the *Resumaker* program.

7. Exit the Write program.

8. If necessary, turn on your printer.

9. Start the *Resumaker* program, and from the main display screen, select the Print option. If the Print function fails to operate, double check all of the above steps.

Special Note: If you have prepared your existing printed resume using a word processing program other than Write, your program may be able to save a copy of your resume as a "Write" file. By doing so, you can save the time required to enter your resume into the Write program. Check with the user's manual for your word processing program to determine if it can save a file as a "Write" file. If so, launch the word processing program that you used to create your resume, from the File menu, select the Open option to display your resume, and then select Save As from the File menu. Select Write for the save style, and label the output file as resume.wri. Save the file to the same directory as the one where your copy of the *Resumaker* program is stored.

Step 4: Create Your Own Stand-Alone Resume

Now that you have configured your multimedia resume, you are ready to convert it into a stand-alone Windows application. By doing so, you will then be able to freely distribute copies of your multimedia resume to potential employers and employment recruiters. Your stand-alone copy has a built-in installer program. When a user attempts to install your resume onto his computer, the installer program will copy all necessary files to the user's preferred drive and directory location, and create a Program group folder and launch icon in Windows. Then, all the user has to do to view your multimedia resume is double click on the *Resumaker* icon.

Please note that distribution of copies of your multimedia resume is royalty free—you may distribute as many copies as you wish without need for compensation to Techno-Marketing.

Directions

1. If necessary, start your personal computer.
2. Launch Windows.
3. Launch the *Resumaker* program.
4. From the File menu, select the Edit option.
5. Select the Package button.

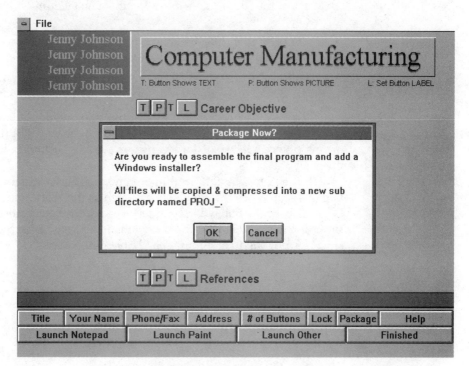

6. You will be prompted on the screen when the Packaging process is complete. The Packaging process will create the following files and save them to a subdirectory called PROJ1 within your *Resumaker* directory:

❏ compresd.exe

❏ install.dta

❏ install.exe

❏ resume.ico

Note: The number that follows the subdirectory PROJ will increase by a factor of one each time the Packaging option is run. For example, if you run the Packaging function for a third time, the subdirectory will be labeled PROJ3.

7. These are the files that you may distribute. Copy them to a 3.5" diskette for distribution. Label your diskette: Resume of <your name>. Instruct the viewers of your resume to follow the directions below for installing a copy of your multimedia resume on their computer system:

❏ Start your personal computer.

❏ Start Windows.

❏ Insert your diskette into the 3.5-inch drive.

❏ For Windows 3.1: Display the Program Manager. From the File menu, select the Run option, and type in "a:install" (or "b:install") and press OK.

❏ For Windows 95: Select Start and then the Run option. Type in "a:install" (or "b:install") and press OK.

❏ Follow the directions on the screen to select a program directory. After the install program has finished, launch the *Resumaker* program.

Important! If you wish to distribute your resume via email, as an attached file to an email message, or via file transfer (FTP) (in short, via any means other than on diskette), please see the section below called Compressing Files.

Please note that your multimedia resume is not suitable for posting online in a searchable resume database, such as the Worldwide Resume/Talent Bank. These searchable database services require that your resume be in the form of a text file. Follow the directions in Chapter 9 for preparing your resume for posting in an online searchable database.

Compressing Files

This information applies only if you plan to distribute your *Resumaker* program via any means other than on diskette.

If you wish to transfer your multimedia resume via email, as an attached file to an email message, or by File Transfer Protocol (FTP), you must first compress the four files that comprise your multimedia resume into one single file.

This is necessary for two reasons. First, you can attach only one file at a time to an email message. Without compressing your four files into one file, you'd have to send four separate email messages to transfer your entire resume. Compression programs can "zip up" any number of individual files into one single file. Second, compression programs actually squeeze your program down in size. Therefore, it will take less time (and cost less) to upload it to other individuals, and less time (and cost) for end users to download your resume to their computers.

Compression, or zipping a file as it is most often referred to, can be done easily using a program called PKZIP. To enable end users to easily open your compressed file without having to have a copy of PKZIP's decompression program (PKUNZIP), it is suggested that you convert your PKZIP file into a *self-extracting* file.

Free (shareware) copies of PKZIP may be downloaded from services such as America Online and CompuServe. Check the computer forum areas of these services for directions regarding how to download PKZIP, and how to use it to compress files. Commercial copies of PKZIP are also available from most computer software stores and mail-order services, or directly from PKWARE, Inc. by calling 414-354-8699.

11

Sample Resumes

In preparing your own resume, it is often helpful to view the resumes of others, especially resumes developed by experts in the field of resume preparation and employment placement. The sample resumes found in this chapter and the sample cover letters found in Chapter 12 were developed by our team of resume writing experts.

It is intended that the sample resumes found here will help you more easily determine what information you should include in your resume, as well as how the information should be laid out on paper or on screen.

As you prepare your electronic resume (see Chapter 9) for posting in an online searchable database, refer to these sample resumes to determine what content should be included in your own resume. Remember, since your online resume must be in a text format, you need not concern yourself with page layout—how each piece of information should be laid out on each page for an electronic resume.

As you prepare your multimedia resume (Chapter 10), you will be asked to prepare a version for use when a printed copy is desired. Since the Print option will be created with the use of the Windows Write word processing program, and since Write supports various character and page formatting options, the following sample resumes can help you decide on both content and page layout design for your multimedia resume.

For information regarding resume writing resources, see Appendix B.

Type of Resumes in This Chapter

You will find four different styles of resumes here:

1. *Chronological.* This resume format is the most commonly used style, and one that traditionally employers are most familiar with. As its name suggests, this type of resume presents information about your work experience in a (reverse) chronological order, starting with your current or most recent work experience and moving back in time to your past work experiences. Your work experience or history is the focus of this style of resume. Other information, such as Career Objective, Summary, Educational Background, and References, is also usually included.

   Some of the sample chronological resumes featured here include a keyword summary. In printed resumes these keywords are included to catch employers' attention as they quickly glance over the resume. Some of the keywords featured in a printed resume may be identical to those appearing as keywords in an electronic resume. The keywords included in an electronic resume are used to ensure that your resume is found when an employer's computer is scanning a database. Often an electronic resume may contain more keywords than a printed resume because additional alternate words are included. For example, if a job candidate were seeking a position as a secretary, keywords would include "secretary," "administrative assistant," "executive assistant," and so on. (An example of an electronic resume can be found in Chapter 9, "How to Create an Electronic Online Resume.")

   The chronological resume style is appropriate for most job seekers who have a work history with appropriate experiences and skills for the position they now seek to secure, or for young persons starting their first job search.

2. *Functional.* This style of resume centers around a listing of your most advanced skills, that is, the "functions" or "tasks" that you are best able to complete. This listing of skills is the centerpiece of the resume. Job seekers usually list only the skills related to the career or position they wish to secure. Less space is devoted to other topics, such as Work History, Educational Background, Career Objective, Summary, and References.

   This style of resume is used less often than the traditional chronological style, and has become popular only within the last few decades. Some employers may not be familiar with the content of a Functional resume, and some may even question the motives of job seekers who use such a format (i.e., what is the job seeker trying to hide?). However, for certain individuals who have a gap in their work history, or a history of work experiences unrelated to their career objective, or a heavy concentration of talent and expertise in a particular skill area, the use of a Functional resume may be most appropriate.

3. *Combination.* As its name implies, a combination resume combines the main features of a chronological and a functional resume into one format. A combination resume includes both a listing of your functional skills and a listing of your work history. Such a resume format is appropriate when you wish to emphasize both your skill set and your work history. The combination resume, while not as common as the chronological or functional style, is quickly becoming the preferred style as it offers readers information about the job seeker's most important qualifications.

4. *Targeted.* While used less frequently than any of the other resume styles, the targeted resume is crafted in such a way as to focus the resume in the direction of one single career or occupational objective. In a targeted resume, you include information from your past history that is appropriate only to the career or job objective that you wish to achieve.

This style of resume is most appropriate for individuals who have a clear and focused job objective, who have a strong background related to the same job objective, and who wish to be considered for no other positions other than the job objective mentioned in their resume.

Following is a list of sample resumes included in this chapter with information indicating the format style of each resume. (For information regarding resume writing resources, see Appendix B.)

Title	Format Style
Accounting/Financial Analyst	Combination
Administrative/Clerical Position	Chronological
Administration/Management	Combination
Advertising Manager	Targeted
Air Conditioning and Refrigeration Technician	Combination
Association Management	Combination
Athletic Director/Coach	Combination
Banking and Financial Development Specialist	Combination
Business Manager	Chronological
Career Guidance/Counseling Specialist	Chronological
Chef	Combination
Clothing Manufacturing Administrator	Chronological
Computer Aided Design/Manufacturing Programmer	Combination
Credit/Collections Management	Combination
Customer Service	Combination
Educational Psychology/Human Development	Chronological
Electronics Technician	Combination
Elementary Teacher	Combination
Engineering/Facility Management	Functional
Environmental Manager	Chronological
Finance/Investments Management	Combination

Financial Operations Management	Chronological
General Management	Chronological
Geologist	Targeted
Health Care Operations Management	Chronological
Health Care Sales and Marketing	Combination
Human Resource Management	Chronological
Information Technology Manager	Combination
Insurance Professional	Chronological
Laboratory Technician	Chronological
Legal Secretary	Combination
Logistics Management	Combination
Management	Combination
Marketing Professional	Combination
MIS Management/Networking Professional	Combination
Occupational Health Specialist	Chronological
Pilot/Aircraft Mechanic	Functional
Product Design/Development	Combination
Production/Distribution Management	Combination
Public Relations Specialist	Chronological
Quality Management Specialist	Combination
Real Estate Appraiser	Combination
Retail Sales	Chronological
Risk Management	Combination
Sales/Customer Service	Combination
Sales Director	Chronological
Sales Management	Functional
Sales Operations Management	Combination
Sales Representative	Targeted
Software Programming	Targeted
Technical Writing/Editing	Targeted
Truck Mechanic	Combination
Warehouse Management	Combination
Writing and Communications Specialist	Combination

Accounting/Financial Analyst

Name • Street Address • City, State, Zip • Phone Number

PROFESSIONAL PROFILE

Possess over sixteen (16+) years of combined corporate accounting, financial analysis, and internal auditing experience with a major multinational. Experience includes:

❏ Financial analysis responsibilities and supervision for support staff and accounting activities of a large, multi-user master planned community developer in Houston.

❏ Accounting functions associated with a separate $300+ million construction project lasting three years.

❏ Financial matters related to property acquisition and the leasing of temporary facilities for the relocation of corporate headquarters from Thistown to Thattown.

❏ Exhaustive research for and analysis of tens of thousands of oil & gas properties from a four state region for divestiture valuation and marketing candidacy.

FINANCIAL EXPERTISE

Aside from demonstrating a comprehensive understanding of Generally Accepted Accounting Principles (GAAP), also command a hands-on knowledge of financial concerns related to real estate, land development, commercial construction, homebuilding, property leasing, and property management. These include:

Cost Accounting	Revenue Accounting	Tenant Build-Out Accounting
Payroll Accounting	Book Basis Accounting	Real Estate Accounting
Tax Basis Accounting	Utility District Accounting	Federal, State, and Local Tax Accounting
Financial Reporting	Economic Modeling	Accounting System Automation
Land Sales Costing	Financial Forecasting	Property Divestiture & Acquisition
Cost Basis Research	General Ledger Accounting	Payables/Receivables Processing
Cash Flow Projections	Oil & Gas Property Analysis	State Franchise Tax Reporting
Market Price Valuation	Bank Account Reconciliations	Long/Short Term Debt Financing & Tax Benefits

Repeatedly recognized for ability to constructively fuse creative and analytical skills with this body of knowledge to reduce costs, gain tax advantages, and recoup potentially lost revenues through identification of strategic opportunities, operational streamlining, the development of enhanced tracking and forecasting tools, and compliance with regulations which impact properties.

PROJECT & MANAGEMENT EXPERTISE

While capable of handling numerous and sizable responsibilities independently, provide direction and focus to projects as both a leader and contributor.

Staff Supervision	Contractor Auditing	Contract Billing Negotiations
Property Research	Management Reporting	Financial Exhibit Preparation
Organizational Planning	Capital Budget Revisions	Year End Financial Statement Presentation

Execution increases group productivity and likelihood of goal attainment within resource constraints. Communicate equally well with superiors, peers, and subordinates, as well as with Engineers, Geologists, Auditors, Executives, and Clerical Staff. Effectively translate financial and accounting issues into comprehensible terms.

EDUCATION

UNIVERSITY OF THE SOUTHWEST, Somewhere, Southern State
Bachelor of Business Administration in Accounting (1976)

Continued

Accounting/Financial Analyst

Name • Street Address • City, State, Zip • Phone Number

PROFESSIONAL HIGHLIGHTS

BIG COMPANY   1991–1994
Lead Financial Analyst
   Identified non-performing oil & gas properties for divestiture. Developed current valuation
   of properties for determination of minimum pricing. Marketed properties for sale through
   competitive bid process.
   *Analyzed tens of thousands of properties for divestiture, successfully identifying 250+ high value
   properties which did not meet divestment criteria. Efforts also yielded the identification of $500,000
   in unrecorded revenue/receivables due from gas sales.*

PAL DEVELOPMENT (An affiliate of BIG)   1985–1991
Pal is a fully integrated commercial and residential real estate company.

Project Financial Analyst (1990–1991): *On loan to BIG*
   Handled financial matters related to corporate relocation from Heretown to Theretown, concentrating on the acquisition of temporary leased corporate HQ facility and future owned HQ
   building representing $100+ million capital project. Project Manager reported directly to Pres-
   ident of BIG.
   *Set up proper procedures and documentation to support a separate corporate structure to own the
   HQ facility and lease to the Corporation to capitalize on specific debt finance tax benefits. Developed
   economic model of long-term lease options to maximize cash flow and tax benefits.*

Project Financial Analyst (1989–1990): *On loan to Something Else, Inc.*
   Accountable for all financial matters related to the sale and divestment of this BIG real estate
   affiliate. Supervised general ledger and financial reporting activities during marketing and
   divestment phase.
   *Devloped detailed inventory of project assets, researching original cost basis to ascertain write-offs
   for book and tax purposes. Revised and streamlined revenue accounting for multi-family residential
   units to more accurately reflect income from these properties.*

Accounting Services Supervisor (1987–1989)
   Supervised general accounting activities, directing a staff of 5 professional, 3 clerical, and 2
   contract personnel for this BIG affiliate and the Land Management Department of BIG. Aside
   from revenue accounting, cost accounting, receivables, payables processing, and bank account reconciliations, activities included short- and long-term debt obligation, utility district
   advances, payroll, and sales commission accounting.
   *Streamlined and consolidated activities to reduce staffing demands, thereby reducing overhead by
   $70,000. Recouped $453,000 in tax savings by changing reporting utilized State Franchise Tax returns and initiating amended returns for periods prior to 1989. Automated costing of land sales and
   revised procedures to more accurately reflect land development project models.*

Financial Analyst (1985–1987)
   Prepared intermediate and long-term financial forecasts. Compared current operating and financial data to plans. Presented monthly financial and operating highlights to management
   and BIG's domestic Division HQ.

Continued

119

Accounting/Financial Analyst

Name • Street Address • City, State, Zip • Phone Number

BIG SHIPPING COMPANY   1980–1985
Financial Analyst (1985)/**Tax Accountant** (1982–1985)
  Prepared financial information required for federal, state, and local tax return filing, coordinating activities with BIG's Tax Department.

Construction Accountant (1982–1985)
  Served as on-site accountant for a $200 million ocean tanker construction project contracted on a cost-plus basis. Activities included auditing contractor charges, negotiating revisions to contractor billings, arranging payment of contractor invoices, supporting capital budget revisions, and management reporting functions.

BIG COMPANY, CONTROLLER'S DEPARTMENT   1978–1980
Internal Auditor

Additional information furnished upon request.

Continued

Accounting/Financial Analyst

Name • Street Address • City, State, Zip • Phone Number

POSITION STATEMENT

Accounting & Other Disciplines

Accounting performs a vital function for every business. The ability to accurately apply a comprehensive knowledge of Generally Accepted Accounting Principles means everything to managing cash flow, reducing tax liability, and helping maintain a strong bottom line. However, as accounting does not exist in a vacuum, it is imperative that the practitioner have a reasonable grasp of complementary disciplines. The varieties of accounting vary greatly, and the areas to which its principles apply are even more numerous.

It is my sound understanding of accounting and financial analysis principles applied to real estate and land development, especially in this state, which distinguishes my level of competence from that of my peers.

Texas Real Estate & Accounting

My experience with Pal, a large master planned community developer in Thattown, necessitated that I acquire a firm grasp of this state's real estate standards for both residential and commercial development. My scope of activities encompassed the management of accounting related to the development of the community's:

Infrastructure: Water Systems, Sewer Systems, Drainage Systems, Thoroughfares

Amenities: Golf Courses, Tennis Centers, Swimming Facilities, Country Clubs

To fulfill my obligations to the best of my ability, I actively blended my knowledge of accounting standards and practices with an awareness of key issues which impacted ongoing financial viability. These included accounting for:

Land Sales Costing & Modeling

Municipal Utility Districts (MUDs)

Bond Anticipation Notes (BANs)

Long- & Short-Term Debt Obligations

Tenant Build-Out & Lease Concessions

Texas State Franchise & Sales Tax Reporting

My understanding of these and other key issues, coupled with the identification of applicable circumstances, directly contributed to the success of master planned community development by Pal, with total assets in excess of $700 million, in the Thattown area.

Continued

Accounting/Financial Analyst

Name • Street Address • City, State, Zip • Phone Number

Diversified Excellence

Over the course of my career, BIG and Pal repeatedly entrusted me with key projects. Whether working independently, as part of a team, or in a leadership role, I have earned the right to accept greater challenges.

Construction Accounting: My experience in successfully handling financial responsibilities and controlling costs on a $200+ million construction project demanded that I actively get involved in negotiations with contractors and be able to distinguish legitimate cost claims from inflated ones.

Land Development Accounting & Supervision: Pal, with its spectrum of accounting issues, provided the opportunity to successfully demonstrate supervisory abilities on an ongoing basis.

Pinch Hit Accounting: From 1989 to 1994, whenever Pal and BIG needed help, I would plug and play. The diversity of my assignments—the sale and divestment of an affiliate, financial matters pivotal to the relocation of corporate headquarters, and oil & gas property divestiture consulting—only broadened my inventory of technical knowledge and better prepared me to surmount the most overwhelming tasks.

Market seasoned with a proven track record, I look forward to contributing my expertise in the assessment and management of diversified accounting and financial issues to facilitate your organization's unencumbered growth.

Administrative/Clerical Position

Name
Street Address
City, State, Zip Code
Telephone Number

KEYWORD SUMMARY: Budget Accounts. Tracking of Grants and Contracts. Payroll. Supervised Work Study. Macintosh. IBM. Microsoft Word. Excel. WordPerfect. Quattro Pro. Internet. Dictaphone.

OBJECTIVE: An administrative/clerical position that includes opportunity to utilize previous office management skills.

EXPERIENCE: **Virginia Tech, Center for Public Administration and Policy. 1991 to Present.**

Office Services Specialist.
Interact with Director, faculty, and students to provide administrative, clerical, and fiscal support in an efficient and orderly manner. Work independent of the Director.

- ❏ Advise Director, 24 faculty, 339 students and numerous alumni of daily, ongoing activities and deadlines.
- ❏ Responsible for all budgeting activity for operating budget, overhead accounts, grants, contracts and computer accounts.
- ❏ Handle payroll for all department employees.
- ❏ Interact successfully with variety of individuals and departments on and off campus.
- ❏ Coordinate travel arrangements and schedule meetings.
- ❏ Coordinate catered meals, welcome guests.
- ❏ Hire work study students and train new employees in Blacksburg and Northern Virginia.
- ❏ Order supplies for department.

Virginia Tech, Extension Animal Science Department. 1987 to 1991.

Senior Secretary.
Interact directly with the Program Chairman and Extension Animal Scientist for the Virginia Beef Cattle Improvement Association, with approximately 370 members, to operate three test stations in Virginia, serving Virginia and bordering states.

Continued

Administrative/Clerical Position

Name
Street Address
City, State, Zip Code
Telephone Number

❑ Confidential secretary, typing correspondence, speeches, reports, news articles, visual aids, publications, and newsletters.
❑ Maintain an accurate set of books.
❑ Prepare financial statement, tax report.
❑ Process information from three test stations on approximately 600 animals annually.
❑ Independently gather and disseminate relevant information to Extension Agents and BCIA members.
❑ Interact with prestigious corporation owners and executives.

Virginia Tech, Registrar's Office and Office of Housing and Residence Life. 1986 to 1987.

Office Services Assistant.
Process transcript requests for the University with working knowledge of the record management system.

Personal secretary to the Assistant Director and Manager for Furnishing and Facilities. Assisted students with their individual needs, and directed them to appropriate office.

EDUCATION: **Attended: Virginia Tech, Blacksburg, Virginia. 1987, 1960, 1959.**

Courses Included: Business Administration and Psychology.

Attended: New River Community College, Dublin, Virginia. 1983–1984.

Courses Included: Data Entry, Shorthand, Psychology, English, History, Math, Biology, Music and Art.

OTHER: **Virginia Notary Public.**

Administration/Management

Name
Street Address
City, State, Zip
Telephone Number

ADMINISTRATION/MANAGEMENT

PROFILE:
- ❏ Proven abilities in human relations, staff training and motivation; well-versed in group dynamics and processes.
- ❏ Plan & conduct written and oral presentations in a professional manner; organize meetings, programs and events.
- ❏ Hands-on experience in vendor relations, customer service and sales; write & distribute correspondence; coordinate budgets and business operations.

EDUCATION:
University of Illinois, Urbana-Champaign, IL
Bachelor's Degree, Major: Psychology   Graduated 5/93
- ❏ Pledge class Social Chairman: Delta Upsilon Fraternity.

Elgin Community College, Elgin, IL
Activities required extensive human relations, motivational, and organizational skills:
- ❏ Elected to ECC's College Community Council, representing the student body among various community groups and the general public.
- ❏ Represented ECC at various conferences: NACA, ACUI & ICCSAA.
- ❏ Served as coordinating Vice President for the Student Senate.
- ❏ Co-founder of first Phi Alpha Delta pre-law fraternity at any Junior College.
- ❏ Awarded Leadership Scholarship for two consecutive years.
- ❏ Served as Chairman of the Clubs and Organizations Committee.
- ❏ Attended numerous Leadership seminars.

EMPLOYMENT:
Land's End, Bloomingdale, IL   11/92–1/93
Sales Associate
Handled direct customer service, sales and inventory control.
- ❏ Ranked #2 in sales of 16 Associates in first month.

Super Sealers, Bartlett, IL   Summer, 1991
Co-Owner
Hired, trained, motivated, and supervised four employees.
Responsible for marketing, sales promotions and professional customer relations.

Rosati's Pizza, Bartlett, IL   Summer, 1991
Shift Leader
Trained and supervised several employees in sales and all store operations.

C.B.G.B., Inc., Chicago, IL   Summers & Breaks, 6/85–8/89
Inventory Control Clerk
Placed incoming equipment & supplies; assisted in shipping & receiving.
Tracked sales and configured a computerized vendor system.

Advertising Manager

Name
Street Address
City, State, Zip
Phone Number

JOB TARGET: Manager of Advertising Department

CAPABILITIES

- ❏ Consult with clients, initiate sales and services, and negotiate contracts.
- ❏ Initiate, design and orchestrate all creative points in the development of advertising campaigns utilizing a diversity of media: video, animation of all print, and computer generated art and graphics.
- ❏ Organize and manage all aspects and details in the execution of the projects from start through completion.
- ❏ Manage and supervise advertising and design units.
- ❏ Speak and write Spanish fluently.

ACCOMPLISHMENTS

- ❏ Organized, planned, and executed the design, schedule, and direction for over 42 catalogs, direct mail pieces, brochures, and other print materials.
- ❏ Planned and art-directed commercial photography and video sessions for major commercial clients, television and video producers, retail catalogers, and retail industry utilizing multi-formats.
- ❏ Art-directed and coordinated a multi-media campaign for an international television film series in the United States and Spain; designed the promotional package and secured $2 million in funding for this project.
- ❏ Automated the Design Department for Arizona Public Television with new hardware/ software purchases which generated a 150% increase in production rates for an extensive client base.
- ❏ Conducted negotiations with printers and other vendors which resulted in a 15% cost savings over previous years.

WORK HISTORY

1991–present ARIZONA PUBLIC TELEVISION   Phoenix, AZ
Associate Manager of Advertising Services

1986–1991   Desert Graphics, Inc.   Phoenix, AZ
Advertising Production Assistant

EDUCATION

1986   EASTERN MICHIGAN UNIVERSITY   Ypsilanti, MI
Bachelor of Arts—Business Administration, Marketing

Air Conditioning and Refrigeration Technician

Name

Street Address • City, State, Zip • Phone Number

PROFILE

❑ Competent air conditioning and refrigeration technician with over four years experience. Skilled at troubleshooting; a thorough knowledge of optimum working conditions for components of a system.

❑ Excellent interpersonal skills developed through good customer relations. Able to explain to a customer the problem with a system, and the possible remedies required.

❑ Positive approach to problem solving. Encourage proactive goal setting to solve a problem.

❑ Organized and able to delegate tasks. Follow up to monitor the progress, coaching if required, and inspection to see that completion is timely and done with utmost quality.

SKILLS

❑ Skilled in: ❑ *Problem Determination* ❑ *Troubleshooting* ❑ *Customer Relations* ❑ *Administration*

❑ Extensive knowledge in: ❑ *air-conditioning* ❑ *refrigeration compressors*
❑ *associated salt/fresh water pumps*
❑ *IBM O/S 2 and Windows applications* ❑ *Micrographix 5 Auto CAD*

❑ Rebuilt a 150-ton centrifugal air conditioning compressor and supervised the rebuilding of two 50-ton refrigeration compressors. Received commendations for outstanding performance.

EDUCATION

Course work toward a Bachelor's Degree, Austin Community College, Austin, Texas 1994–1995

PROFESSIONAL EXPERIENCE

MARVINS MECHANICAL, Austin, Texas   **Sept/1994–present**
Automation Systems Operator—responsible for writing programs to initiate systems and shut down systems based on the operating needs of the system.

❑ Repaired heating and air conditioning equipment for facilities and inspected and replaced electrical components.

❑ Scanned floor plans into computer and modified structural changes as required using Auto-CAD.

❑ Maintained roof-top split systems.

UNITED STATES NAVY, Yokosuka, Japan   **Sept/1990–Aug/1994**
Supervising Technician, Training Supervisor, General Technician

❑ Operated and maintained eight air conditioning plants and five refrigeration plants aboard the aircraft carrier Independence.

❑ Provided cooling air for ship's electronics/computer spaces and ship's crew.

❑ Maintained twelve walk-in freezer boxes.

❑ Supervised five men and was responsible for preventive and corrective maintenance.

WALKER CREEK PLAZA HOTEL   **Feb/1990–Sept/1990**
Front Desk Clerk

SPEAKERS BURGER HOUSE   **Oct/1987–May/1988**
Shift Manager

Association Management

Name
Street Address
Telephone Number/Day   **City, State, Zip Code**   Telephone Number/Evening

PROFESSIONAL OBJECTIVE   Association Management

PROFILE

Seasoned management professional and proven leader with over 12 years of diverse experience including election to successful terms as President of the Pennsylvania Cowpokes and the United States Excelsior Club. Prior background in operations and credit management positions with Sushi and Mid-Belly. Demonstrated abilities include public speaking, media relations, and building coalitions among association, community, corporate and government leaders. Strongest skills in fundraising, written and verbal communications, problem solving, internal and external marketing efforts, strategically positioning an association for growth and empowering teams to achieve more.

AREAS OF EXPERTISE AND EXPERIENCE

- Operations
- Strategic Planning
- Building Coalitions
- Team Development/Training
- Client Relations
- Communications
- Public Speaking
- Community Relations
- Business Development

SELECTED ACCOMPLISHMENTS IN ASSOCIATION MANAGEMENT, 1993–1994

Operations

Decreased operating costs and increased the efficiency of staff operations through a restructuring based on delivering service to members. Reduced senior management layer by over 50%, while increasing accountability and timeliness of service.

Business Development

Implemented an inside telemarketing department. Successfully increased non-dues revenues over 50% by increasing emphasis on major corporate sponsorship solicitation, most of which will recur annually.

Strategic Planning

Researched and developed a groundbreaking five-year strategic plan for the USEC. Won an overwhelming mandate to position the organization for growth into the 21st century.

Communications/Client Relations

Developed a member services publication, created a toll-free member hot line and increased member support services. Increased member satisfaction and improved incoming communications from members by over 300%.

Building Coalitions

Launched the USEC into the advocacy and governmental arenas by personally building upon key relationships with dignitaries such as Past President Ronald Reagan, Vice President Al Gore, and Senator Wendell Ford (KY) and through involvement in constituent-based issues-oriented programming that match community and corporate interests.

Continued

Association Management

Name
Street Address
Telephone Number/Day   **City, State, Zip Code**   Telephone Number/Evening

UNITED STATES EXCELSIOR CLUB, WACO, TX   JUNE 1991 TO JUNE 1994

National President (7/93–6/94)—Elected to provide overall direction to the U.S. Excelsior Club (the Cowpokes), one of the nation's largest civic and business membership associations serving 175,000 members in 4,000 chapters.

National Vice President (7/92–6/93)—Elected to provide management oversight and consulting to five diverse state Excelsior Clubs (PA, TN, MO, ND, AZ).

State President (6/91–7/92)—Elected to provide organizational leadership for the 7,500 members of the Pennsylvania Excelsior Club.

MID-BELLY SEE KING, KING OF PRUSSIA, PA   DECEMBER 1989 TO AUGUST 1991

Operations Manager—Initiated and implemented the Operations Department for this inventory finance division of Bell Atlantic, a new venture for the company.

AMERICAN ALRIGHT ALREADY CORP, CHUCKSVILLE, PA   JANUARY 1987 TO DECEMBER 1989
                                                          DECEMBER 1981 TO JUNE 1985

Unit Operations Manager (1/87–12/89)—Responsible for all operational functions and supervision of personnel within a unit handling a portfolio of accounts in various captive inventory finance programs.

Account Executive (12/81–6/85)—Managed a portfolio of specialized accounts.

SUISHI ELECTRIC SALES AMERICA, INC.   JULY 1985 TO JANUARY 1987
SUISHI ELECTRONICS, INC., MOUNT PROSPECT, IL

Assistant Regional Credit Manager (8/86–1/87)—Managed a portfolio of computer-related accounts.

Credit Manager, Mobile Electronics Division (7/85–8/86)—Managed all accounts nationwide for this division.

EDUCATION

Grads 'R Us University, Philadelphia, PA. Majored in Business Administration, emphasis on finance and accounting. Completed over 90% of undergraduate study.

Additional course work taken at the Chicago Institute of Credit and JCI Training Institute (Accredited Certified Member Trainer) including management and communications dynamics, leadership training, time management, stress management, public speaking, media training, coaching/counseling, and critical behavior interviewing.

PERSONAL

Raised in da Bronx. Married in 1982. Enjoy community service work, travel, guitar and sports. Conversational in French. Skilled in WordPerfect 5.1 and Lotus 1-2-3.

Athletic Director/Coach

Name • Street Address • City, State, Zip • Phone Number

PROFESSIONAL OVERVIEW

More than 20 years experience as an educator, head coach, and athletic director, as well as collegiate-level coaching and recruiting experience. Specialize in rebuilding losing and piloting successful men's and women's programs, emphasizing commitment, discipline, and the learning experience. Career reflects dedication to both scholastic and athletic excellence.

SUMMARY OF QUALIFICATIONS

Instruction and Curriculum: State Evaluation System (SES) certified. Hold Permanent Lifetime Secondary Teaching Certificates in:

Biology	*Drivers' Education*	*Physical Education*	*Social Studies*

Experienced in development and coordination of K–12 physical education curriculum guides and the supervision of faculty teaching 4,200 students.

Athletic Programs: Head coaching and athletic director experience with high schools includes, but is not limited to:

Sport	Record	District Championships
Football	*224-102-6*	*15 (Coach)*
Basketball	*74-49*	*2 (Coach)*
Track	*N/A*	*12 (Coach)*
Golf	*N/A*	*7 (AD)*
Tennis	*N/A*	*10 (AD)*

Coordinate activities among up to 34 coaches and 12 sports programs at schools with 1,400+ student athletes. Consistently demonstrate willingness to pursue programs which engender excellence and a determination to build excellence in programs with marked deficiencies.

Collegiate Athletics & Recruiting: Experienced as a running back and junior varsity head coach for a 1-AA college program. Certified by the NCAA as a recruiter, concentrating on recruiting student athletes from across the state at all positions.

Administration: Skillfully manage annual budgets of as little as $900 in excess of $274K. Administer comprehensive athletic insurance programs. Spearheaded facility expansion for all sport programs, directly engaging in the design of facilities to offer student athletes the best available tools and venues for:

Football	*Baseball*	*Basketball*	*Tennis*	*Track*

FOOTBALL HEAD COACHING SUMMARY

SCHOOL	RECORD	PRIOR	SCHOOL	RECORD	PRIOR
Bush	*61-33-3*	*2-7-1*	**Lee**	*31-12-1*	*0-10*
Reagan	*15-15*	*1-9*	**Grant**	*42-8*	*0-10*
Carter	*40-13*	*2-7-1*	**Sherman**	*28-5*	*0-20*
Nixon	*47-15-2*	*3-6-1*	**Beauregard**	*28-5*	*0-22*

EDUCATION

THE UNIVERSITY
Graduate Studies in Education

BIGONE UNIVERSITY
Bachelor of Science in Biology with studies in Physical, Drivers', and Social Studies Education

WHOSAYS INSTITUTE
Associate of Arts in Education

Continued

Athletic Director/Coach

Name • Street Address • City, State, Zip • Phone Number

PROFESSIONAL HIGHLIGHTS

ANOTHER UNIVERSITY, Somewhere, His State   1993–Present
Running Back Coach • JV Head Coach • NCAA Certified Recruiter
Coach the Conference's top running back for the top rated offense. Successfully recruit top high school and junior college prospects, conducting interviews with student athletes, coaches, and parents.

BUSH ISD   1986–1993
Athletic Director • Head Football Coach • Physical Education Coordinator
Supervised 31 coaches and 6 support staff in 12 sports programs for grades 7–12 with an annual budget of $274K. Expansion included a new track, press box, and 2,800 seats. Supervised construction of a $295K baseball field. 61-33-3 football coaching record earned 3 District Championships and playoff berths in 5 years. Supervised 14 P.E. faculty with 3,000+ students.

REAGAN—LONGVIEW ISD   1984–1986
Assistant Football Coach • Head Track Coach • Instructor

CARTER ISD   1981–1984
Athletic Director • Head Football Coach • Physical Education Coordinator
Supervised 34 coaches and 5 support staff in 12 sports programs with 1,100+ students and an annual budget of $195K. Designed and supervised construction of a 15,870 square foot field house complex, a high school and junior high gymnasium, and 6 football practice fields. Initiated construction of a new football stadium and track. Designed and constructed a new baseball field. Compiled a record of 40-13 for a school which had never had a winning football season.

NIXON ISD   1976–1980
Athletic Director • Head Football Coach • Physical Education & Drivers' Ed Coordinator
Supervised 29 coaches in 9 sports programs with 1,100+ students and a $153K annual budget. Facility improvements included 12 tennis courts, a new track, new press box, and 2,500 new seats. Compiled a 47-15-2 record in football for a school which had 6 prior consecutive losing seasons.

LEE ISD   1973–1976
Assistant Coach, Football & Track • Off-Season Coordinator • Instructor

GRANT ISD   1967–1973
Athletic Director • Head Football & Track Coach • Drivers' Ed Coordinator • Instructor
Supervised 5 coaches in 6 sports programs with 145 students and an annual budget of $8,500. Compiled a football record of 42-8 to help school reach playoffs in 5 of 6 years. Track program recorded 6 district championships and one regional championship.

Continued

Athletic Director/Coach

SHERMAN ISD   1963–1967

Athletic Director • Head Football, Track, and Basketball Coach • Drivers' Ed Coordinator

Supervised 3 coaches in 6 sports programs with 130 students and an annual budget of $900. Took over a football program with a 0-20 record; compiled a record of 28-5 to help school reach playoffs in 3 of 4 years and a season-end state ranking of #1 in 1964. Basketball team assembled two district championships, including a single season 22-1 mark in 1964–65. Track program recorded 3 district championships and 2 second place finishes in regional competition. Directed district, regional, and state championships in boys' and girls' tennis.

BEAUREGARD ISD   1959–1963

Athletic Director • Head Football, Track, and Basketball Coach • Instructor

Supervised 3 coaches in 5 sports programs with 107 students and an annual budget based solely upon gate receipts at Hermleigh (1962–1963). Supervised 1 coach in high school and junior high sports programs with 72 students at Divide. Took over a football program which had not won a game in 2 years; compiled a record of 28-5 to help school earn 3 district championships in 3 years.

Additional information furnished upon request.

Banking and Financial Development Specialist

Name • Street Address • City, State, Zip • Telephone Number

❏ *Dedicated professional offering more than 15 years* in a corporate banking environment, with expertise in middle market and asset based lending. Experience in analysis, leveraged transactions, new account generation, cross selling and loan administration.

❏ *Spearheaded and secured* BANK OF MONEY'S *$50,000,000 gain* through the successful sale of the factoring division. Performed extensive research, analysis and evaluation of sales strategy.

❏ *Drove efforts to revitalize* BANK'S *Special Business;* accumulated more than $50,000,000 in new loan business with a modified franchise concept. Increased volume of loans by $100,000,000.

❏ *Initiated restructuring of* BANK OF MONEY'S *Asset Based Lending.* Motivated and bolstered efficiency of marketing team; generated over $1,000,000,000 in transaction reviews and yielded in excess of $5,000,000,000 in revenues within 1 year.

❏ *Innovated the turn-around of the Special Division.* Initiated detailed strategic planning after loss of top employees; hired new management team. Implemented intensive marketing campaign to regain client confidence and rebuild strong bonds of loyalty.

❏ *Employed risk management expertise to determine* potential areas of control weakness. Achieved passing grades in all internal risk reviews and targeted OCC review.

❏ *Highly skilled manager; provide leadership by example to 20 personnel;* proffer technical support in sales, marketing, portfolio administration, strategic planning and credit relationships. Set effective and realistic goals and motivate staff to accomplish objectives.

EXPERIENCE

BANK OF MONEY • New York • Tokyo • London • Brussels

Division Executive: Asset Based Lending & Franchise Finance	1993–Present
Division Executive: Special Projects	1991–1993
First Vice President: United States Lending	1990–1991
Vice President: Middle Market Lending	1989–1990
Vice President: Middle Market Lending	1987–1989
Assistant Vice President	1984–1987
Loan Officer	1982–1984
Lending Officer Trainee	1980–1982

EDUCATION & TRAINING

MASTER OF BUSINESS ADMINISTRATION
University of Somewhere, Graduate School of Business—Boston, Massachusetts

BACHELOR OF SCIENCE IN HUMAN ENVIRONMENT & DESIGN
Wonderful University—Boston, Massachusetts
Dean's List • Cum Laude

Additional courses, workshops and seminars include:
Numerous Bank of Boston Credit, Sales Management, Finance and Management courses

REFERENCES & FURTHER DATA AVAILABLE UPON REQUEST

Business Manager

Name
Street Address
City, State, Zip Code
Telephone Number

KEYWORD SUMMARY: Business Manager for 5 years. College Degree. Detail Oriented. Bookkeeper. Independent Worker. Payroll. General Financial Summaries. Cost Proposals. Invoicing. Tax Records. Prepared Contracts. Peachtree Accounting Software. WordPerfect.

OBJECTIVE: A position as business/financial manager with a small to medium size research and consulting organization in the New River Valley area.

EXPERIENCE: **Business Manager,** Paradigm, Inc.
Blacksburg, Virginia. 1991–Present.

Helped to organize and subsequently managed an engineering research firm that included a staff of 6 and contracts of up to 1/2 million dollars.

❑ Managed gross annual receipts of $250,000.
❑ Handled government defense research contracts.
❑ Acted as liaison to legal and accounting services.
❑ Responsible for all business operations.

Manager, So Fro Fabrics.
Monmouth, New Jersey. 1980–1981.

Promoted after 3 months to manager. Responsible for retail operation of a fabric store for a national chain.

❑ Supervised a staff of 6 to 8 individuals.
❑ Worked effectively with the public.

EDUCATION: **Bachelor of Science,** University of Vermont, 1982.
Graduated: Cum Laude
Major: Home Economics
Additional Courses: Accounting, Virginia Tech.

Career Guidance/Counseling Specialist

Name
Street Address
City, State, Zip Code
Telephone Number

KEYWORD: Computer Proficient. IBM Compatibles. WP. Statistical Packages. On-line Services. Organizational. Oral and Written Communication. Supervised Student Staff. Group and Individual Counseling Techniques.

PROFESSIONAL HIGHLIGHTS:
❑ Experienced Career Counselor.
❑ Leader in Business Sector.
❑ Excellent Interpersonal Skills.
❑ Strong Academic Background.

EXPERIENCE:

Virginia Tech, Blacksburg, Virginia. 1992–1994.
Special Assistant to Vice President Student Affairs and Assistant to Associate Provost.

Developed and conducted a campus climate assessment for the Division of Student Affairs. Presented results to 525 employees. Organized a statewide conference for female administrators working in higher education.

❑ Excellent organizational and communication skills.
❑ Able to supervise details of programming in higher education.
❑ Effective interpersonal abilities.

Virginia Tech, Blacksburg, Virginia. 1992–1993.
University Placement Counselor.

Responsible for all placement activities in College of Agriculture and Life Sciences. Supervised a career fair, acted as liaison to student organizations, and wrote career newsletter for the faculty and students of the College.

❑ Developed solutions to inform college population about current job opportunities.

Radford University, Radford, Virginia. 1988–1991.
Assistant Director, Career Planning and Placement.

Presented career information to student body of 9,000. Worked in individual and small group counseling settings. Presented seminars at request of faculty. Wrote department newsletter and served as senior class advisor.

Continued

Career Guidance/Counseling Specialist

Name
Street Address
City, State, Zip Code
Telephone Number

❏ Excellent counseling skills.
❏ Demonstrated effective writing and marketing strategies.

EDUCATION: **Doctor of Philosophy,** Student Personnel/Affairs. Virginia Tech, Blacksburg, Virginia. 1994.

Received Academic Scholarship four semesters.
Served as special assistant to Vice President of Student Affairs.

Master of Science, Counseling. Radford University, Radford, Virginia. 1982.

Elected to Academic Honorary Society. Phi Kappa Pi. Internships Financial Aid. Career/Placement Services, Secondary School. Nominated for First Year Teaching Award by the City of Radford.

Bachelor of Arts, Sociology. College of William and Mary, Williamsburg, Virginia. 1971.

AFFILIATIONS: Member, NASPA, 1991–Present.
Member, ACPA, 1991–Present.
Member, VCPA, 1988–1991.

OTHER: **Community/Civic/Volunteer Experience.**

Radford Main Street, Radford, Virginia. 1984–1995.
President, 2 terms.
Board Member, 3 terms.

Developed concepts of economic redevelopment in City of Radford. Guided competition for selection into National Main Street Program.

❏ Leadership of 250-member volunteer organization.
❏ Facilitated long-term funding of program.
❏ Completed fund-raising drive of $150,000.

Chef

Name
Street Address
City, State, Zip
Telephone Number

OBJECTIVE: SOUS CHEF / HEAD CHEF

Profile of Experience:

❑ More than 12 years of professional experience in cooking and the restaurant industry with a thorough working knowledge of regional American cuisine.
❑ Effectively train, supervise and motivate staff in kitchen operations.
❑ Creative strengths in Southwest, Caribbean and French cuisine.

Career Background:

HEAD CHEF   1987–Present
Prospector's Kitchen (American/Regional), Prospect Heights, LA
Responsible for all kitchen operations including menu planning, daily specials, ordering and food costing.
Created a seasonal menu to incorporate local ingredients in imaginative preparations.
❑ Prospector's Kitchen is a consistent leader in its regional market and has received critical acclaim from electronic and print media in Prospect Heights.

EXECUTIVE CHEF   1986–1987
Columbus' Hideaway (Caribbean, American/Regional), Virgin Gorda, British Virgin Islands
Supervised menu planning, daily specials, ordering and food costing.
Positioned restaurant as a successful culinary leader in the Virgin Islands.
❑ Created restaurant-brewed beers that sold successfully and increased bar revenue 25 percent.
❑ Gained experience in handling a seasonal, tourist-impacted industry.

SOUS CHEF   1984–1986
Foodtypes, (Eclectic, American/Regional), Glencoe, LA
Planned menus and created daily specials.
Responsible for sautés, grilling, soups and sauces.
Handled cost-effective purchasing of all foods and equipment.
❑ Gained an extensive education in the use of ethnic and regional American foodstuffs.

INDEPENDENT CONTRACTOR   1978–Present
Developed "Oasis," an independently owned and operated catering service featuring a wide variety of home-brewed beers.

ADVERTISING AND PUBLIC RELATIONS MANAGER   1978–1984
Employed as Copywriter in the advertising industry.
Subsequently became Advertising Manager for Champion Auto Parts, Inc.
Developed communication, PR and business skills that have proven invaluable in the restaurant industry.

Education:

B.S. Degree, Advertising/Journalism, Arizona State University, Tempe, AZ
American Restaurant Association, Certified for completing the Restaurant Management Program.

Clothing Manufacturing Administrator

Name
Street Address
City, State, Zip Code
Telephone Number

KEYWORD SUMMARY:
Extensive Experience in Apparel Industry. Master of Science in Apparel Design. Virginia Tech. Instructor. Teaching Assistant. Research Interest in Design Needs of the Non-Average Body. Sizing and Fit. Physical Aspects of Aging. Certificate in Gerontology. Business/Banking Experience. Excellent Communicator. Good Listener. Interpersonal Skills. Customer Service. Sales. Computer Familiarity. Autocad. Lectra System. IBM. Macintosh. WordPerfect. Lotus 123. WordStar.

PROFESSIONAL EXPERIENCE:
❏ Experienced in both the business and academic side of the apparel industry.
❏ Worked in production.
❏ Emphasis on design and sizing issues.
❏ Significant business background.
❏ Classroom teaching experience.

OBJECTIVE:
An administrative position in the clothing manufacturing industry with particular emphasis on those involved as pattern maker, marker maker, and design issues.

EMPLOYMENT:
Teaching Assistant, College of Human Resources.
Virginia Tech. Blacksburg, Virginia. 1990–Present.

Taught clothing construction class including apparel draping, structure, and fit.
❏ Assisted with design using Autocad and Lectra System.

Graduate Assistant, College of Human Resources.
Virginia Tech. Blacksburg, Virginia. 1990–Present.

Worked with the State Extension Service Activities.
❏ Assisted with the Virginia Home Economist Newsletter.
❏ Helped with 1991 4-H Congress Fashion Review.
❏ Revised 4-H Clothing Judging Forms.

Continued

Clothing Manufacturing Administrator

Name
Street Address
City, State, Zip Code
Telephone Number

Bookkeeper, The Peoples Bank. Ripley, Mississippi. 1976–1988.

Responded to customer service account issues.
❏ Entered transactions into computer system.
❏ Balanced daily documents.
❏ Developed excellent interpersonal skills.

OTHER EMPLOYMENT:

Sales Associate, Joann Fabrics. Christiansburg, Virginia. 1992–1993.

Office Assistant, University of Mississippi. Oxford, Mississippi. 1988–1990.

Teachers Aid, Tippah County School System. Ripley, Mississippi. 1967–1968.

EDUCATION:

Master of Science, Virginia Tech. Blacksburg, Virginia. 1995.

Major: Clothing and Textiles.

Bachelor of Science, University of Mississippi. Oxford, Mississippi. 1990.

Major: Home Economics. Minor: Business.

VOLUNTEER:

4-H Leader. Mississippi and Virginia. 1978–1995.
❏ President, State Leaders Association.
❏ State Coordinator, Southern Regional Leaders Forum.

Student Government. Virginia Tech. Blacksburg, Virginia. 1990–1995.

❏ Student Assembly Representative.
❏ Graduate Student Assembly Representative to Commission of Public Services and Extension.
❏ College of Human Resources Representative to Graduate Re-granting Budget Board.

Computer Aided Design/Manufacturing Programmer

Name
Street Address
City, State, Zip
Telephone Number

OBJECTIVE: *DESIGN ENGINEERING*
A position where proven skills in CAD/CAM systems will be utilized, preferably related to new products and business environments.

PROFILE:
- More than seven years in virtually all aspects of product design, development, production and inspection on CAD/CAM systems.

- Assist in staff training and supervision in 2-D & 3-D design and drafting; assign/organize work and interface with technical staff and engineers in a professional manner.

- Utilize 3-D finite element analysis and solids modeling; skilled in IBM CAD-PAK, SuperLaunch and CADAM systems.

EMPLOYMENT: Sparrow-Hoffman Corp., Cylinder Division, Norridge, UT   1987–Present
Design Engineer, CAD/CAM Systems
Perform product design and development for this major manufacturer of cylinders, pistons, rods and all types of hydraulic and pneumatic equipment. Train and supervise up to five employees.
Responsible for work scheduling, assignments and special projects.
Assist in all development functions for parts and finished products.
- Work extensively with R&D personnel for new CAD/CAM designs.

Robert Morris College, Salt Lake City, UT   1985–1987
Teacher's Assistant
Instructed students in drafting and design techniques.
Performed CAD-PAK 2-D drafting, BRAVO 2-D & 3-D design, drafting, solids modeling and finite element analysis.
Tracked individual student performance; administered tests and answered technical questions.

EDUCATION: Utah University, Calumet, UT   Expected Graduation: 1993
B.S. Degree: Mechanical Engineering

Salt Shaker College, Salt Lake City, UT
A.S. Degree: Pre-Engineering   Graduated 1987
- Completed extensive training in CADAM, BRAVO and CAD-PAK systems.

Credit/Collections Management

Name
Street Address
City, State, Zip
Telephone Number

EXPERIENCE:
- ❏ More than ten years in the management of sales, customer service and production operations, including full profit/loss responsibility.
- ❏ Staff hiring, training and supervision in tangible and intangible product sales and service.
- ❏ Skilled in strategic planning, marketing and sales staff motivation; experience in sales forecasting, budget management and cost containment.

Credit Collections:
Manage credit and collection activities. Analyze financial statements and evaluate new accounts; organize database systems for specific business needs.

Customer Service:
Manage telephone and mail order customer service operations; train staff in customer problem resolution, professional communications and full client servicing.

Management:
Plan and implement sales, service and cost reduction procedures; work directly with senior-level personnel in budget administration, distribution and materials management.

Sales:
Effectively hire, train and supervise sales and marketing teams in technical product lines, sales presentations and market penetration.

EMPLOYMENT: Walter Sales Company, Berwyn, IL   9/83–Present
Credit/Collections Manager
Supervise all credit, collections, and customer service operations, involving the supervision of more than 28 employees for this major manufacturer and wholesaler of automotive after-market products.
Manage all aspects of order processing/expediting, billing, and account updating on a WANG system.
Coordinate technical problem solving and customer correspondence via "ACD" telephone, FAX, and mail.
- ❏ Responsible for all operations and facilities in absence of company owners.
- ❏ Developed and implemented the key account sales and service program.

Continued

141

Credit/Collections Management

Name
Street Address
City, State, Zip
Telephone Number

Singer Safety Company, Chicago, IL   10/80–9/83
Customer Service and Credit/Collections Manager
Effectively managed 22 employees in order processing, client relations and account servicing.
Directed credit research on new accounts and established new accounts within credit limitations.
Supervised follow-up on accounts receivable collection activities.

Wilson Sporting Goods Company, Elk Grove Village, IL   8/78–9/80
Assistant Regional Merchandise Manager
In charge of an entire distribution center and all office staff for the midwestern region.
Managed order processing on a corporate-wide computer system, including data entry, account management and customer service.
Updated and maintained accurate inventories on a regular basis.

Performance Dynamics International, Chicago, IL   1/75–8/78
Customer Service and Inside Sales Manager
Trained and motivated sales staff in new account acquisition and management.
Supervised customer relations and special assignments for the CEO.

Sears Roebuck and Company, Chicago, IL   3/66–12/74
Customer Service and Credit Manager
Managed a complete telephone and mail order operation.
Analyzed and improved customer service procedures and sales promotions.
❑ Developed cost reduction techniques for product deliveries and installations.

EDUCATION: Loyola University, Chicago, IL
Successful completion of courses in Business Administration.

Dale Carnegie Institute
Completed training in Public Speaking, Dynamics of Human Relations, Sales Administration, Credit and Collection Management.
❑ Conducted courses as Graduate Student Instructor.

Dun and Bradstreet
Completed courses in credit and collection management, including financial statement analysis and customer service management.

Customer Service

Name

Street Address • City, State, Zip • Phone Number

OBJECTIVE

An administrative/customer service position in communications where continued success and development can be achieved.

PROFILE

❏ Conscientious, self-directed professional with experience working with multi-cultural individuals in an international setting.

❏ Team player able to work with a group of employees who are customer-driven. Excellent interpersonal skills working with customers by telephone or in person.

❏ Able to resolve conflicts in a diplomatic manner. Highly skilled at developing rapport with all types of people. Able to develop natural and spontaneous scripts for telemarketing sales; evaluate effectiveness; and rewrite as appropriate.

❏ Bilingual—English/Spanish. Recently relocated from England.

PROFESSIONAL EXPERIENCE

Account Executive   1988–1994

TTel Communications, London, England—a marketing company with clients that include computer companies, publishing companies and the Department of Trade and Industry. Sales exceeded $750,000 annually. Ranked in the top 20 for marketing companies in London.

❏ Developed a marketing plan which increased the seminar participation for one client by 300-500%.

❏ Reorganized systems and procedures in order to have day to day operations run more smoothly.

❏ Recognized for the outstanding leadership of a team which negotiated a five-year contract extension.

Real Estate Agent   1985–1988

MS Ltd., London, England—a residential properties privately owned firm.

❏ Developed a sales strategy to assist customers by doing an exceptional job in learning the properties and knowing the status at any given time.

❏ Coordinated successfully with contractors during new construction to make sure that finish dates coincided with the needs of the client.

Sales Representative   1984–1985

Bass Ltd., London, England—a direct sales company.

❏ Established a client base through aggressive research, developing leads to become a top producer.

Receptionist/Customer Liaison   1974–1984

ABC Ltd., London, England—an import/export company. Clients—American Express, Chase Manhattan Bank and other major retailers and distributors in the United States, Spain and Japan.

Educational Psychology/Human Development

Name • Street Address • City, State, Zip • Telephone Number

EDUCATIONAL PSYCHOLOGY • HUMAN DEVELOPMENT

ASSOCIATE PROFESSOR: Social Science Department   1994–Present
EDUCATIONAL INSTITUTE   Boston, Massachusetts

Engaged for this full-time, temporary position with responsibility for teaching four psychology and sociology courses. Develop course syllabi, compile and creatively utilize adjunct teaching materials. Present subject matter to provoke immediate interest while encouraging commitment to develop a thorough understanding of key concepts.

❑ *Foster student growth and development by assisting individuals with difficulties and challenging advanced learners.*
❑ *Devise and implement methods of evaluating student understanding and performance with high degree of accuracy.*
❑ *Serve as student counselor and advisor on academic performance, career planning, and related college life issues.*
❑ *Interact positively with faculty and administrative staff.*

ADJUNCT PROFESSOR: Human Services Department   1988–1991
ANOTHER INSTITUTE   Boston, Massachusetts

Taught Early Childhood Education developing course content, related materials and student activities. Sparked lively class discussions interjecting dramatic elements to gauge students' grasp of developmental concepts in practical application.

❑ *Assigned research projects to satisfy individual interests, use strengths and develop areas of weakness.*
❑ *Designed, administered and graded exams.*

EXECUTIVE DIRECTOR   1980–1988
CHILD CARE FACILITY   Boston, Massachusetts

Spearheaded organizational structure and program development and quality management for this child care center serving 98 children from infancy to school age. Recruited, selected, trained and evaluated the performance of a staff of 14 childhood professionals.

❑ *Designed and administered programs appropriate for the varied developmental levels.*
❑ *Conducted professional development sessions geared to individual staff member needs.*
❑ *Arranged parent presentations featuring variety of childhood related topics.*
❑ *Positively resolved problems involving children, staff, parents and center operations.*

PROFESSIONAL ACTIVITIES

American Psychological Association • Association for Supervision and Curriculum Development
National Association for the Education of Young Children

EDUCATION

DOCTOR OF PHILOSOPHY IN EDUCATION   1994
BOSTON COLLEGE   Boston, Massachusetts
  Dissertation: *On an incredible exciting topic*

MASTER OF SCIENCE IN EARLY CHILDHOOD ADMINISTRATION   1986
A UNIVERSITY   Boston, Massachusetts
  Thesis: *An outstanding one, you can be sure*

BACHELOR OF ARTS IN ELEMENTARY & EARLY CHILDHOOD EDUCATION   1982
A COLLEGE   Boston, Massachusetts
  Honors: *Class Valedictorian*

Electronics Technician

Name

Street Address • City, State, Zip • Phone Number

OBJECTIVE

A position as **Electronics Technician**

QUALIFICATIONS

❑ Electronics technician with five years of experience in component level troubleshooting and miniature component repair.

❑ Knowledge of computer networking and setting up systems configurations for different needs and preferences.

❑ Computer literate. Proficiency with Windows, DOS, Lotus 123, WordPerfect, Harvard Graphics, Ami Pro, and other word processing and graphics software.

❑ Proficient with oscilloscope, spectrum analyzers, frequency meters, multimeters, and many other types of test equipment.

❑ Excellent with installing, making, and repairing cable.

❑ Ability to adapt to new work environments. Can work as an individual, but prefer to be part of a team. Excellent communicator.

WORK EXPERIENCE

1988 to present: **United States Air Force**

❑ Served as an electronics technician for five years on communications equipment, microwave systems, computer systems, printers, and copiers.

❑ Responsible for maintaining and repairing all equipment. Performance evaluation never below outstanding.

❑ Monitored and recommended standard of quality control to ensure accurate reporting.

❑ Attended different quarterly training seminars on equipment and preventive maintenance techniques.

EDUCATION

Southern Illinois University, College of Technical Careers 1994
❑ Bachelor of Science Degree in Electronics Management
United States Air Force, Non Commissioned Officers School 1992
❑ Graduated in the top 5 percent

HIGHLIGHTS

Bilingual, fluent in French: reading, writing, and speech
Dean's List at Southern Illinois University
NCO of the Quarter, fourth 92, first 93
Special Olympics volunteer, 1989

Elementary Teacher

Name
Street Address
City, State, Zip
Telephone Number

OBJECTIVE: *ELEMENTARY TEACHER*
A position utilizing leadership skills and a strong desire to work with and nurture students to achieve their greatest potential.

PROFILE:
- ❑ More than 14 years in teaching as an instructional aide and full-time substitute, including full responsibility for lesson planning, material selection and performance review.
- ❑ Utilize Macintosh systems for teaching Mathematics, Social Studies and Computer Science to normal and learning disabled students.

EMPLOYMENT: **Substitute, Full-Time Basis**   1987–Present
St. Patrick Language Academy, Boston, MA
Responsible for teaching intermediate grades in all general subjects.
Acted as Cadre Substitute for six months.

Instructional Aide—High School Section   1980–1987
Northwest Suburban Special Education Organization, Boston, MA
Developed lesson plans and evaluated students.
Worked directly with the teacher in sourcing appropriate classroom materials and creating new student challenges.
- ❑ Utilized Apple PCs in a classroom environment for the instruction of Composition, Typing, Social Studies and Mathematics.

Teacher   One Year
Bryant School and Lloyd School, Massachusetts Board of Education, Boston, MA

EDUCATION: Champaign University, Normal, IL
B.S. Degree, Elementary Education

Chicago Teaching University, Chicago, IL
Diagnosis and Remediation of Reading Problems, 1988;
Personal computer use in the Classroom, 1987; The Exceptional Child, 1986

W.R. Harper College, Palatine, IL
Completed courses in WordPerfect and WordStar, 1987.

PERSONAL: Trained extensively in Spanish; traveled in Spain, France and Italy.
Actively support the PTA. Secretary for the PPAC at Bryant School.
Seeking to volunteer for the St. Patrick's proposed after-school program.

146

Engineering/Facility Management

Name
Street Address
City, State, Zip
Telephone Number

PROFESSIONAL HIGHLIGHTS:

EFFICIENCY:
- ❑ Design and install conveyor systems that ease work flow and increase production.
- ❑ Installed computer systems that have been proven to cut production time of weekly invoices in half. Redesigned an invoice to accommodate office, production and delivery procedures more efficiently.
- ❑ Invented a pry-bar that cut a company's manual demolition time by one-third.
- ❑ Extensive experience with high pressure boilers, three-phase electricity, pipe fitting, pneumatic and electric controls, pump/motor repair and welding.
- ❑ Work with job shops to fabricate or repair obsolete and expensive parts to keep 30-year-old equipment operating.
- ❑ Skilled in the use of WordStar and Quattro for word processing and the compilation of financial data.

MANAGEMENT:
- ❑ Supervise all phases of operations including production, inventory control and maintenance.
- ❑ Work directly with inspectors, union officials, OSHA personnel, auditors and attorneys. Administer EEOC regulations and right-to-know legislation.
- ❑ Experience supervising union and non-English-speaking employees.
- ❑ Act as insurance risk manager: obtain quotes, maintain policies, verify audits and file worker's compensation reports.
- ❑ Work with general contractors, architects and engineers; develop plans for building construction and remodeling projects valued up to $500,000.
- ❑ Serve as on-site coordinator for all trades while supervising plant operations.
- ❑ Skilled in the selection, design, installation and operation of waste water pretreatment systems. Represent companies at Sanitary District hearings. Apply for local, state and federal regulatory permits and file subsequent reports.

Continued

Engineering/Facility Management

Name
Street Address
City, State, Zip
Telephone Number

EMPLOYMENT HISTORY:

1989–1990   **Project Manager,** Bison Cleaners
      Large retail facility with annual sales of $1.5 million.

1963–1989   **Plant Manager,** The Uniform Rental Service
      Industrial laundry with annual sales of $3 million.

1970–1972   **SP-5,** U.S. Army (Vietnam)
      Honorably Discharged.

LICENSES

City of Chicago **Stationary Engineer's License**

EDUCATION

Bachelor of Science, Southern Illinois University, Carbondale, IL, 1968

CONTINUING EDUCATION

Completed Studies in:
     Robotics
     Stationary Engineering
     Computers
     Welding
     Machine Shop Math

Environmental Manager

Name
Street Address
City, State, Zip Code
Telephone Number

KEYWORD SUMMARY: Experienced Manager. Supervised Staff of 60–70 Individuals. Handled All Scheduling and Training Responsibilities. Restaurant Management. Healthcare/Insurance Industry. Excellent Written and Oral Communication. Public Relations Responsibilities. Strong Work Ethic. Reliable. Problem Solver. Computer and Accounting Experience. WordPerfect. AmiPro. Lotus 123. Windows. Developed an Accounting and Inventory System. CPR. Red Cross. Certified Rescue and Scuba Diver. Bachelor of Arts.

OBJECTIVE: A management position in an environmental organization with particular interest in the aquatic/dive industries of Florida.

EXPERIENCE: **Manager,** The Allegheny Cafe. Radford, Virginia. 1994–Present.

General Manager for staff of 50 employees. Handled daily operations of a restaurant with $1 million in annual sales.
❑ Developed inventory and accounting program for restaurant operation.
❑ Strong interest in efficient management of restaurant cost and waste control.

Assistant Manager, Macado's, Inc. Radford, Virginia. 1992–1994.

Developed effective employee relationships and communication channels. Created positive working environment. Learned all phases of restaurant management.
❑ 60–70 staff supervised.
❑ $1.5 Million annual restaurant sales.
❑ Developed as training site for 7–8 restaurant facilities.

Customer Service Representative. Capital Care, Inc. Subsidiary of Blue Cross and Blue Shield. Vienna, Virginia. 1991–1992.

Handled customer relations including policy information and claims problems.
❑ Recognized as hard worker able to complete assignments.
❑ Developed interpersonal skills while on telephone.

EDUCATION: **Bachelor of Arts,** University of Pittsburgh. Pittsburgh, Pennsylvania. 1990. Major: History. Minor: English Literature and Religious Studies.

OTHER: Active Member, Theta Chi Social Fraternity.
Awarded, Outstanding Theta Chi Undergraduate, 1990.
Employed through college to defray costs.

Finance/Investments Management

Name • Street Address • City, State, Zip • Telephone Number

EXECUTIVE MANAGEMENT • FINANCE • INVESTMENT

MULTIDISCIPLINED ACHIEVER OFFERING CPA DESIGNATION WITH PROGRESSIVE CONTRIBUTIONS IN STRATEGIC BUSINESS PLANNING, FINANCIAL CONTROLS, PORTFOLIO MANAGEMENT, RISK ANALYSIS, POLICY DEVELOPMENT, COMPLIANCE, MIS OPERATIONS AND STAFF DEVELOPMENT

PROFILE WITH SELECTED ACHIEVEMENTS

❑ *Dynamic & Motivated Performer: Self-starter with strong planning, controlling, organizing and leadership skills. Initiated start-up operations and built ACCOUNTING ASSOCIATES' annual billings from $50,000 to $500,000 within two years.*

❑ *Results Oriented: Trimmed operating expenses by introducing efficient procedures and upgrading the automated systems. Improved cash flow, cut costs and boosted profit performance for BIG INDUSTRIES.*

❑ *Finance & Accounting Expertise: Includes internal audit, budget preparation and control, tax planning, investment planning, banking relations, cash management, financing debt, collections, and insurance issues.*

❑ *Systems Proficiencies: Utilize advanced technology to improve reporting performance and operating efficiencies. Successfully programmed BIG INDUSTRIES' IBM AS400.*

PROFESSIONAL EXPERIENCE

VICE PRESIDENT • CHIEF FINANCIAL OFFICER   1987–Present
BIG INDUSTRIES, INC.   Strong Assets, New York

Spearhead business development and provide critical financial leadership for this enterprise generating $100,000,000 in annual revenues. Direct operations governing financial accounting and cash management with ongoing contributions to future planning, policy development, review, risk management, compliance and MIS.

❑ *Execute forecasting and prepare capital and operating budgets; analyze multimillion dollar financial statements and related data.*

❑ *Select, develop, motivate and evaluate the performance of support staff inspiring a team commitment to goals, management objectives and high quality standards.*

❑ *Ensure that all processing and reporting conform to established procedures and meet all legal and regulatory criteria.*

❑ *Cultivate excellent relations with bank officers and regulatory agency personnel.*

❑ *Identify complex problems; employ resourcefulness and creativity in implementing solutions resulting in increased profitability.*

INVESTMENT CONSULTANT   1993–1995
BIG SECURITIES   Strong Assets, New York

Designed and implemented client marketing programs and investment strategies ensuring they met and exceeded their target investment returns. Conducted detailed company research and made consistently sound recommendations while delivering outstanding client service.

Continued

Finance/Investments Management

Name • Street Address • City, State, Zip • Telephone Number

❏ *Created results-getting sales strategies and monitored account performance.*
❏ *Assisted qualified investors with financial planning, effectively presented investment product options.*
❏ *Maintained current knowledge of economic indicators, exchange and interest rates, inflation rates, political and competitive considerations.*

OWNER 1990–1992
ACCOUNTING ASSOCIATES   Strong Assets, New York

Marketed and managed the delivery of small business and tax accounting services combined with software consulting. Established excellent client relations; scheduled and performed reviews, compilations and audits. Prepared financial statements; made critical recommendations and trained clients in accounting software applications.

❏ *Initiated start-up operations and built annual billings from $50,000 to $500,000.*
❏ *Recruited and oversaw the performance of all firm associates.*
❏ *Filed personal and corporate tax returns; reconciled general ledger, created and reviewed financial statements.*

ACCOUNT REPRESENTATIVE 1988–1990
FINANCIAL MANAGEMENT FIRM   Strong Assets, New York

Marketed the company product line to individuals and businesses. Provided consultations with recommendations employing a command of product knowledge, sales technique, client service and operating protocols to negotiate sales.

❏ *Evaluated weekly performance to determine best sales strategies.*
❏ *Processed policy applications in compliance with policy and procedure developing a track record for client satisfaction and loyalty.*

EDUCATION

BACHELOR OF SCIENCE IN ACCOUNTING   1990
University of Massachusetts   Boston, Massachusetts

LICENSES & CERTIFICATIONS

NASD SERIES 7 BROKER'S LICENSE • HEALTH AND LIFE INSURANCE LICENSE
CERTIFIED PUBLIC ACCOUNTANT

REFERENCES & FURTHER DATA AVAILABLE UPON REQUEST

Financial Operations Management

Name • Street Address • City, State, Zip • Telephone Number

GREATBIG COMPANY—Chicago, Illinois 1986–Present

DIRECTOR OF REGIONAL OPERATIONS   1994–Present

Drive the division's strategic business planning, marketing / sales development and coordinate manufacturing and warehousing operations to maximize revenues and profits. Develop and implement policy collaborating with the President on major finance and operations issues.
❑ *Identify sales trends; develop products and services; plan effective promotional programs.*
❑ *Train, motivate and supervise the efforts of a national sales team.*

RESIDENT MANAGER   1988–1994

Spearheaded P&L performance of a newly purchased manufacturing facility employing 68 employees in marketing, sales and operations. Managed cash flow including implementing highly effective tax planning initiatives.
❑ *Boosted sales and dramatically increased profits.*
❑ *Reduced inventory by 50% and effected 5.5 total turnover.*
❑ *Structured operations to minimize federal sales and excise tax obligations.*

CONTROLLER: Operations Accounting / Financial Analysis   1987–1988

Provided leadership in development of improved reporting systems with key responsibility for generating quality financial information, making incisive analyses with recommendations.
❑ *Trained and developed talented accounting and management support personnel.*

MANAGER: Financial Analysis & Budgets   1986–1987

Developed and implemented a formal budgeting system and financial analysis department for regional operations. Directed a staff of 4 in analysis and accounting support work.
❑ *Designed a highly effective reporting protocol.*

EVENANOTHER COMPANY—Chicago, Illinois • 1977–1986

SPECIAL PROJECTS ACCOUNTANT   1985–1986

Selected to work directly with the corporate treasurer on financial matters critical to the future of profitable operations.
❑ *Designed formal budgeting procedure, profit planning and analysis functions for a restructure of the operation into the corporate group of companies.*
❑ *Researched and analyzed audit allowance disputes and briefed IRS representatives on accounting procedures.*

INVESTOR RECEIVABLES ACCOUNTING MANAGER   1984–1985
BRANCH CONTROLLER   1981–1984
MANAGER OF FINANCIAL ACCOUNTING SYSTEMS   1980–1981
ACCOUNTING MANAGER   1979–1980
SINGLE FAMILY & LAND ACCOUNTANT   1978–1979
COST ACCOUNTANT   1977–1978

EDUCATION

MASTER OF BUSINESS ADMINISTRATION UNIVERSITY OF TEXAS   San Antonio
BACHELOR OF SCIENCE: Business & Economics TRINITY UNIVERSITY   San Antonio

REFERENCES & FURTHER DATA AVAILABLE UPON REQUEST

General Management

Name • Street Address • City, State, Zip • Telephone Number

PROFESSIONAL EXPERIENCE

MY COMPANY—Somecity, Massachusetts

GENERAL MANAGER   1994–Present

Plan and coordinate all sales and marketing activities and operations. Formulate results-getting sales programs and marketing campaigns for over 500 accounts including convenience stores, chain stores, chain supermarkets, package facilities and national accounts.

❑ *Increased sales above state average in the midst of an industry downturn.*
❑ *Conduct training and development for 50 personnel encompassing changes in contract options, sales techniques, operations, staff training and administrative procedures.*
❑ *Utilize knowledge of prevailing market and consumer trends to devise long-range business strategies and forecast sales projections.*
❑ *Provide leadership in supplier training; bolster sales by implementing supplier and in-house incentive programs.*

ANOTHER SALES COMPANY, INCORPORATED • Somecity, Massachusetts

PRESIDENT & CEO   1992–1994

Directed, managed and orchestrated business and financial operations encompassing fiscal planning, forecasting, strategic plan development and implementation, sourcing of funds and grant writing, contract negotiation and administration, and personnel functions.

❑ *Increased company profits by successfully introducing new products and maintaining sales above state averages.*
❑ *Accountable for annual budget preparation, administration and oversight, overall financial responsibilities and operational forecasting / business planning.*
❑ *Developed a resource network and cultivated excellent relations with industry agencies.*
❑ *Consistently reviewed and analyzed existing policy and procedures with a view toward enhancing sales productivity, efficiency and quality performance.*

GENERAL MANAGER   1980–1992

Provided effective leadership and supervision to all areas of distributorship. Managed time, resources and multiple projects to consistently meet deadlines and management objectives.

❑ *Utilized market expertise to analyze current factors and forecast trends; implemented successful promotions to maximize market penetration and share.*
❑ *Negotiated freight rates with trucking companies which led to $50,000+ savings.*
❑ *Evaluated and installed management information systems linking distributor to suppliers.*

EDUCATION & TRAINING

MASTER OF BUSINESS ADMINISTRATION PROGRAM
University of Arkansas Graduate Center   Little Rock, Arkansas

BACHELOR OF SCIENCE IN EDUCATION University of Arkansas   Monticello, Arkansas

Additional courses, seminars and professional enrichment:

Effective Selling Through Psychology • Managing Marketing Effectiveness • Advanced Selling Skills • Sales Forecasting • Spaceman II • Display Building • Effective Management • Strategic Planning • Business Planning • Effective Meetings • Merchandising

Geologist

Name
Street Address
City, State, Zip
Phone Number

GEOLOGY:

- ❑ Supervised and directed drilling, logging, and coring activities during well site operations.
- ❑ Evaluated, examined, and prepared drill cuttings and core samples during well site geological investigations.
- ❑ Conducted surface mapping investigations by taking field measurements of dip and strike.
- ❑ Testified numerous times before the State Oil and Gas Commissions of Texas and Louisiana.

TECHNICAL/HAZARDOUS WASTE:

- ❑ Certified in OSHA Safety and Health Training for hazardous waste site investigations.
- ❑ Monitored CERCLA, RCRA, SARA Title III, TSCA and other environmental requirements and regulations.
- ❑ Proficient in the theory and application of gamma, geophysical, and resistivity logs.
- ❑ Designed and created computer programs used in the development of drilling programs.
- ❑ Utilized technical writing skills and constructed graphs and charts for government publications.

WORK HISTORY:

1990–Present EXXON, USA, INC. Tumwater, WA
Geotechnical Consultant

1989–1990 BURGER CHEF, INC. Tumwater, WA
Manager and Area Marketing Director

1986–1989 MHQ Corporation Tumwater, WA
Geological Consultant

1983–1986 KUFACKER EXPLORATION CO. Walla Walla, WA
Area Geologist

1977–1983 ENERGY DEVELOPMENT CORP. Walla Walla, WA
Geologist, Drafter

EDUCATION:

Present Tumwater Community College
Major: Hazardous Materials Management

1976 Missouri School of Mines—B.S. Geology

Health Care Operations Management

Name
Street Address
City, State, Zip
Phone Number

WORK EXPERIENCE:

1991–present   ROSS HEALTHCARE CENTERS   Minneapolis, MN
                Operations Supervisor

- ❑ Supervised all functions of the Operations Department consisting of three route drivers, one repair technician, and two shipping/receiving clerks.
- ❑ Purchased all inventory and established stock levels.
- ❑ Negotiated purchase agreements with vendors to establish best pricing and to return obsolete inventory for full credit.
- ❑ Developed purchasing system to reduce inventory on hand and fill back orders more efficiently.
- ❑ Implemented procedures for transporting hazardous wastes.

1988–1991   ST. CYRUS HOSPITAL   Minneapolis, MN
                Supply, Procurement and Distribution Technician

- ❑ Established and maintained stocking levels of medical and surgical supplies for all hospital wards, emergency room, and surgery.
- ❑ Checked, cleaned, and sterilized instruments used for surgery and the emergency room.
- ❑ Purchased and maintained inventory stocking levels for the central supply department.

1980–1985   KSZZ RADIO STATION   Minneapolis, MN
                Radio Announcer

- ❑ Prepared and broadcasted an eight-hour radio music program including hourly news, weather, and sports.
- ❑ Wrote and produced commercial copy for local sponsors.
- ❑ Designed and maintained top-40 play list with Billboard of top 100.

EDUCATION:

1988   MANKATO TECHNICAL COLLEGE
              Associate's Degree in Business Administration

Health Care Sales and Marketing

Name

Street Address • City, State, Zip • Phone Number

OBJECTIVE

A position in sales or marketing in the health care services industry.

PROFILE

❑ Highly motivated recent college graduate with experience gained while attending college and preparing for career. Self-starter with excellent investigative skills.

❑ Can work cooperatively with a wide range of personalities; diplomatic and tactful with both professionals and nonprofessionals.

❑ Able to learn difficult terminology related to a specific industry, as witnessed by intensive training in medical terminology, prescription medicines, medicinal procedures and understanding diagnoses. Familiar with Medicare regulations as related to private insurance.

❑ Licenses 02 and 03, issued by the Texas Department of Insurance, State of Texas, 1993.

EDUCATION

B.A., Sociology, minor in women's studies,
The University of Texas at Austin, Austin, Texas, 1994
Business courses, Washington University, St. Louis, Missouri, 1988–1989

PROFESSIONAL EXPERIENCE

Benefits Administrator   1993
Texas Association of Insurance Funds, Houston and Austin, Texas

❑ Investigate claims by reviewing witnesses' statements, doctor's diagnosis versus the injury report completed by the client and provide compensation according to the state law.

❑ Counseled with injured workers through interviews and written statements. Explained what benefits were available and what the Texas laws were governing injury compensation.

❑ Liaison between employer and medical provider. Reviewed the prognosis of a client presented by the medical provider and compared the work status allowed to the work provided by the employer. Encouraged employer to provide duty status as soon as possible to reduce the time a client was on workers' compensation.

Claims Examiner   1992–1993
Any Life Insurance Company, Houston, Texas

❑ Elected by peers to Team Improvement Committee, a self-directed committee working for the good of the client base by discussing ways to improve customer service.

Human Resource Management

Name
Street Address
City, State, Zip Code
Telephone Number

KEYWORD PREFACE:

15 Years of Human Resource Experience. OSHA Compliance. MSDS. Safety. Affirmative action. EEOC. ADA. Performance Reviews. Job Evaluations. Employee Assessment. Procedure Development. Policy Manuals. TQM. Group and Organizational Behavior. Trainer. Interviewer. Labor Relations. Emergency Medical Technician. CPR. Audiometric Technician. Hearing Conservationist. IBM Computers. WordPerfect 5.1. WordStar. Lotus 123. D-Base.

EMPLOYMENT HIGHLIGHTS:

❑ Experienced in benefits administration and employee relations.
❑ Developed procedures to satisfy safety and OSHA regulations for a large manufacturing facility.
❑ Excellent public relations and communication skills.

EMPLOYMENT EXPERIENCE:

Kollmorgen Corporation, Industrial Drives Division.
Radford, Virginia, 1980–1992.
Employee Benefits and Safety Coordinator.

Administered OSHA, Worker's Compensation, Right to Know, and Hearing Conservation programs for over 380 employees. Developed hazardous communication and safety programs for entire facility.

Carilion Health System, St. Alban's Hospital.
Radford, Virginia, 1978–1980.
Assistant, Personnel Department.

Facilitated the development of a human resources department at a 90-bed, private psychiatric hospital. Attended seminars on safety and workers' compensation. Learned the field as a human resources generalist.

Continued

Human Resource Management

Name
Street Address
City, State, Zip Code
Telephone Number

EDUCATION:

Bachelor of Science, Bluefield College.
Bluefield, Virginia, 1994.
    Major: Management, Human Resources.
    Graduated: Magna Cum Laude.

PROFESSIONAL MEMBERSHIPS:

- ❏ Society of Human Resource Management.
- ❏ International Personnel Management Association.
- ❏ Industrial Hygiene Association.
- ❏ Virginia Safety Association.
- ❏ Phi Beta Lambda Business Society.

Information Technology Manager

Name
Street Address
Telephone Number/Day   **City, State, Zip Code**   Telephone Number/Evening

OBJECTIVE   Senior Information Technology Manager

SUMMARY OF QUALIFICATIONS

Information System Professional with demonstrated management, leadership and communication skills, seeks position which will utilize my background in management, engineering, systems integration, system design, development, and implementation.

AREAS OF EXPERTISE AND EXPERIENCE

- ❏ Information Systems
- ❏ System Requirements

- ❏ System Integration
- ❏ Life Cycle Management

- ❏ Cost Reduction
- ❏ Marketing

SELECTED ACCOMPLISHMENTS AND EXPERTISE

Information Systems Management

❏ As Program Manager of the Airborne Warning and Control System, I increased the productivity of software development and maintenance activities. The process entailed the establishment of a well-defined requirements baseline for software development and maintenance. The new baseline set realistic schedules and budgets for the development efforts, and the open communication of the goals and objectives for the development of the next software baseline. The productivity for software development and upgrades of software and software maintenance improved by 300% over a 12-month period.

❏ As Manager of System Software Development, I designed and managed the development of a real-time system to ascertain the safety of missile flight over the US and Europe. The system established a probability model for the safety of European over-flight. Through this modeling effort parameters that contributed to missile safe flight and probabilities of impact were ascertained. The system processed both radar and telemetry signals and used them to track missile flight and thereby provided near-real-time information to end user's decision. This software was a determining factor for allowing the advancement of the US space program and has allowed the Apollo space vehicles to be safely flown over Europe and other populated areas.

System Requirements

❏ As a senior consultant for Martin Marietta, I developed the telecommunication and computer requirements for a large facility's complex. I successfully negotiated, documented and communicated the customers' telecommunications requirements. This resulted in wholehearted acceptance and approval of proposed requirements. This single factor allowed the customer to start project development, by supporting contractors, three months early.

❏ As Manager of Data Base Administration, I developed the requirements and procurement specifications for a computer systems upgrade at the White House Communications Agency in The Old Executive Office Building. Expedited the procurement and installation of systems at the White House Communications Agency in The Old Executive Office Building. Initial operational capability was realized six months ahead of schedule.

Continued

Information Technology Manager

Name
Street Address
Telephone Number/Day   **City, State, Zip Code**   Telephone Number/Evening

System Integration
❑ As an independent consultant, I developed a software system for Wal-Mart that integrated layered geographic maps with overlaid ICONS. This system provided information to facilitate decisions, support inventory control, distribution, and transportation. This allowed global data access interfaces to information contained in many data bases located in heterogeneous hardware and software network environments.

❑ As Manager of Data Base Administration, I supervised the conversion of and redesigned the existing data files to "Total Data Base Managed System" files for the Defense Communication Agency. Enhanced the data integrity, continuity, and consistency of the Defense Communication Agency's six world-wide distributed information systems.

Life Cycle Management
❑ As Manager of Integrated Logistic Support for General Electric, I designed and managed the developed software systems that predicted maintenance actions needed for operational equipment. The system processed the signals from these sensors to determine the anticipated failure of the parts under measurement. Failure thresholds were established for all components under measurement. Before these thresholds were exceeded the parts critical to operation were replaced during preventive maintenance. This resulted in: a reduction of redundant equipment of 30%; a 25% reduction of the spare part inventory; and a 60% reduction in warehousing cost for spare parts inventory.

Cost Reduction
❑ As a senior consultant for Martin Marietta, I directed the transition hardware and software systems to the United Kingdom. I successfully transitioned hardware and software valued at $8M. Achieved a 10% reduction in cost associated with the packaging and shipment of the products. Systems were operational in the United Kingdom 4 months ahead of schedule.

Marketing
❑ As Senior Information Systems Engineer for GE, I led the efforts to develop technical volumes for 15 proposals for new business acquisition. Over a two-year period, I developed 10 winning proposals out of the 15 proposals submitted. These winning proposals generated in excess of $759M in new business.

CAREER HISTORY

VORSHT INFORMATION, Radnor, PA   1993–Present
  Senior Consultant

BILL O. FARE, ASSOCIATES, King of Prussia, PA   1992–1993
  Independent Consultant

GENERAL ELECTRIC AEROSPACE GROUP, Philadelphia, PA   1984–1992
  Senior Information Systems Engineer
    Proposal Development, Systems Analysis & Design

  Manager, Test and Verification Engineering
    Initial Systems, Checkout, Test and Verification

  Manager, Integrated Logistic Support Engineering
    Systems integration, training, system reliability and maintainability, operational readiness

Continued

Information Technology Manager

Name
Street Address
Telephone Number/Day   **City, State, Zip Code**   Telephone Number/Evening

US AIR FORCE	1964–1984
Program Manager, Airborne Warning and Control System, Tinker AFB, OK	1981–1984
Manager, Data Base Administration, Defence Communication Agency, Arlington, VA	1978–1981
Plans & Programs Officer, Allied Air Force Europe, Wiesbaden, Germany	1972–1978
Manager, Information Systems Development, Foreign Technology Division, Dayton, OH	1969–1972

Other US Air Force assignments can be discussed during the interview.

EDUCATION

MS (97% complete) Operations Research, North Carolina State University, Raleigh, NC.

BS Mathematics, Minor in Physics, Arizona State University, Tempe, AZ (1968)

Specialty Courses

GE Experienced Managers Course, GE Management Development Institute, Crotonville, NY (1985)

Program Manager Certification, Department of Defense Computer Institute, Washington DC (1980)

COMPUTER EXPERIENCE

Design Technologies:
❏ CASE Tools, Object-Oriented Design & Programming, Rapid Prototyping

LAN/WAN Technologies:
❏ Novel, Pathworks, TCP/IP, Token Rings, FDDI, Routers

Computer Platforms:
❏ IBM, Digital, Hewlett Packard, Sun Micro Systems, Apple

Operating Systems:
❏ MVS/TSO, VM/CICS, VAX/VMS, UNIX, MS-DOS, Windows, OS2, Mac OS

Programming Languages:
❏ COBOL, FORTRAN, JOVIAL, BASIC, "C," "C++," Pascal, PL1, IBM APL, X-Windows

Data Base Management Systems:
❏ IDMS, M204, DB2, Oracle, Ingres, Sybase, Rbae, Foxpro, Alpha4, dBase

Insurance Professional

Name • Street Address • City, State, Zip • Telephone Number

MARKETING • OPERATIONS • MANAGEMENT

Offer Masters training, ChFC and CLU designations combined with 10+ years of progressive accomplishment in the Life Insurance field. Expertise encompasses Sales, Market Development, Finance, Staffing, MIS and Customer Relations

SUMMARY

SEASONED PROFESSIONAL WITH STRONG PLANNING, CONTROLLING, ORGANIZING, COMMUNICATIONS AND LEADERSHIP SKILLS. SELECTED BY NEW YORK LIFE TO STRUCTURE AND IMPLEMENT NEW SALES UNITS AND DEPARTMENTS WITH COMPREHENSIVE SUPPORT ORGANIZATIONS INVOLVING STAFFING, TRAINING, RESOURCE DEVELOPMENT AND SOFTWARE APPLICATIONS. SUCCESSFULLY MANAGED AGENT DEVELOPMENT FOR THE COMPANY'S 44-OFFICE NORTHEAST REGION. WROTE AND DESIGNED AGENT AND CLIENT MATERIALS; CREATED STATE OF THE ART SALES TRAINING TOOLS. WINNER OF NATIONAL ASSOCIATION OF LIFE UNDERWRITERS SALES ACHIEVEMENT AWARD, COMPANY LIFE'S EXECUTIVE COUNCIL AND HEALTH LEADER SALES AWARDS.

PROFESSIONAL EXPERIENCE

A LIFE INSURANCE COMPANY—Hartford, Connecticut • 1986–Present

ASSISTANT VICE PRESIDENT 1994–Present

Spearhead development and operations management of a new Individual Life Department providing nationwide agent support for policies sold. Designed systems, personnel and administrative procedures and developed materials to meet assigned sales goals, management objectives and quality service standards.

❏ *Generated $14.5 million in net surrender value and $4 million in annualized premium conserved.*
❏ *Identify market opportunities and recommend new product features to boost sales.*
❏ *Developed major training programs for field agents and for Regional Service Center staff.*
❏ *Maintain communication via field training workshops, monthly magazine, field memos and audio cassettes.*
❏ *Designed and implemented effective reporting and tracking mechanisms.*
❏ *Produced consumer-focused materials including a client explanation of dividends and dividend reductions.*
❏ *Developed pre-approach letters, phone scripts, a "how-to" manual, a "Solutions Guide" and brochures.*

MARKETING DIRECTOR 1992–1994

Provided strategic leadership critical to achieving maximum penetration of the pre-retired market. Evaluated the potential and effectiveness of current products and services; established sales goals; developed distribution systems, advertising, support and software tools.

❏ *Trained personnel in all aspects of sales and conducted regular performance evaluations.*
❏ *Developed prospects by conducting consumer-oriented retirement planning seminars.*
❏ *Published articles on pre-retired market Retirement Planning.*
❏ *Troubleshot complex pre-retired matters and implemented prompt and effective solutions.*

Continued

Insurance Professional

Name • Street Address • City, State, Zip • Telephone Number

LIFE PRODUCTS FIELD CONSULTANT 1990–1991

Identified product solutions for the aggressive promotion of Individual Life Products for agents of the 44 offices of the competitive Northeast Region. Conducted meetings communicating product changes, legislative variances, underwriting principles and marketing strategies.
- ❑ *Communicated product changes, industry developments and sales innovations and provided individual consultation to agents and prospective clients.*
- ❑ *Worked with headquarters in developing and introducing quality training and sales management tools.*

SALES MANAGER 1988–1990

Selected to initiate, develop and motivate agents selected for this new sales production unit. Recruited top performing and high potential agents; designed and conducted training in product knowledge, sales technique, client service and operating protocols. Assessed sales performance to determine best sales strategies.
- ❑ *Developed and implemented training and continuing education resulting in increased sales.*
- ❑ *Contributed to the overall planning of office operations.*

SALES ASSOCIATE 1986–1988

Focused sales efforts on business owners developing employee benefit plans. Provided consultation and recommended group health and individual products with a track record for maximizing client investment return.
- ❑ *Top producer in employee benefit plans to small businesses.*
- ❑ *Employed detailed knowledge of asset allocation and diversification in taxable and tax-favored products.*

ANOTHER LIFE AND CASUALTY COMPANY—Hartford, Connecticut • 1976–1986

ASSISTANT ADMINISTRATOR: Employee Benefits 1984–1986

Provided technical support to staff analysts and consultation to field personnel, brokers and policyholders on legislation, coverage, procedures and underwriting.

CONTRACT SPECIALIST: Employee Benefits 1976–1984

Developed and presented contract seminars and trained new personnel.

PROFESSIONAL ASSOCIATIONS

American Society of Chartered Life Underwriters and Chartered Financial Consultants
National Association of Life Underwriters

EDUCATION

MASTER OF SCIENCE IN MANAGEMENT PROGRAM 1994–Present
AMERICAN COLLEGE Hartford, Connecticut

MASTER OF SCIENCE • *Kappa Delta Phi Honor Society*

BACHELOR OF SCIENCE • *Cum Laude*
CENTRAL CONNECTICUT STATE UNIVERSITY Hartford, Connecticut

Additional courses, seminars and professional development include:
AETNA LIFE AND CASUALTY CEBS • HIAA
LICENSES & CERTIFICATIONS: CHARTERED FINANCIAL CONSULTANT • CHARTERED LIFE UNDERWRITER

REFERENCES & FURTHER DATA AVAILABLE UPON REQUEST

Laboratory Technician

Name
Street Address
City, State, Zip Code
Telephone Number

KEYWORDS: Laboratory Technician. Analytical Testing. Endocrine Hormones. Esoteric Testing. Viral Hepatitis. Estrogen. Progesterone Receptors in Breast Tumor Tissues. Environmental. Supervised 9 Technical Representatives. Completed Management Training Program. Prepared and Presented Training Seminars. Bachelor of Arts and Sciences. Rutgers. Associate of Applied Science in Laboratory Technology. Certificate of Achievement for Quality Improvement. Computer Knowledge. Problem Solver. Excellent Interpersonal Skills.

EMPLOYMENT HIGHLIGHTS:
- ❏ 12 Years of laboratory experience.
- ❏ Significant management responsibilities.
- ❏ Proficient in a variety of testing areas.

EXPERIENCE: **Dental Assistant.** Dublin, Virginia. 1994–Present
Dental assisting for a general practice including chair side responsibilities, x-ray certificate, and office functions.

Senior Technical Representative. Metpath. Teterboro, New Jersey. 1981–1993
Promoted two times into progressively more responsible positions from Medical Technologist to Technical Representative to Senior Technical Representative. These promotions involved increasing administrative, management, and staff responsibilities.

- ❏ Supervised 9 technical staff members.
- ❏ Performed analytical testing procedures.
- ❏ Provided technical support to field staff and sales personnel.
- ❏ Handled all reporting from the laboratory and training of staff.
- ❏ Evaluated new assays and wrote protocols.

EDUCATION: **Bachelor of Arts and Sciences.** Rutgers. Newark, New Jersey. 1981.
Major: Zoology.
Honors Program.

Associate Applied Science. County College of Morris. Randolph Township, New Jersey. 1979.
Major: Biological Laboratory Technology.
Honor Graduate.

AFFILIATIONS: American Association for Clinical Chemistry.
Clinical Ligand Assay Society.

Legal Secretary

Name
Street Address
City, State, Zip
Telephone Number

LEGAL SECRETARY

A position where professional skills and a knowledge of legal terms would be utilized.

PROFILE:
- Secretary and Receptionist experience includes research, correspondence writing, client relations and payroll processing.
- Skilled in MS Word, WordPerfect, and WordStar as well as Lotus 1-2-3; familiar with WestLaw and Lexus; operate various switchboard systems and compile/produce detailed reports via dictaphone.
- Interface with legal staff and handle general accounting, bookkeeping and special projects in a professional manner.

CAREER BACKGROUND:

Holtz and Reinhart, Tacoma, WA   7/90–Present
Legal Secretary
Currently providing assistance in case studies and the research, preparation and updating of a wide variety of legal documents.
Operate a 12-line switchboard; write/expedite messages and handle greeting and reception of clients.
Write/type correspondence related to legal matters using WordPerfect.

Seattle, WA   4/83–7/90
Homemaker

Omaha Bank, Omaha, NE   11/79–4/83
Payroll Clerk   4/80–4/83
Maintained accuracy of over 400 time cards and processed computer input forms and reports.
Utilized MSA and ADP computer systems, as well as Addressograph equipment.
- Scheduled data processing projects and checked/distributed pay stubs; processed salary changes and updated life insurance cards.
- Developed microfilm and typed/produced monthly life insurance reports; processed employee's Savings Bonds.

Receptionist/Secretary   11/79–4/80
Primarily responsible for letter and memo typing from Dictaphone and rough drafts.
Worked directly with senior-level personnel on special projects.

EDUCATION: Alberts College, Seattle, WA
Completed the Legal Secretary Program   Diploma, 1985

Logistics Management

Name
Street Address
Telephone Number/Day   **City, State, Zip Code**   Telephone Number/Evening

OBJECTIVE   Logistics Manager

KEYWORDS

- ❏ Freight Rates Negotiations
- ❏ Pro-Active Customer Service
- ❏ Strategic Planning
- ❏ Administration

- ❏ Logistics Analysis
- ❏ US Customs Regulations
- ❏ Dept. of Transp. Compliance (CFR 49)
- ❏ Spanish / Portuguese language

PROFESSIONAL DEVELOPMENT

BLK, Inc.   1994–Present
Export Administrator / Regulatory Affairs

- ❏ Spearheaded implementation of import and export procedures for new customer base in Mexico City.
- ❏ Analyze freight rate contracts with trucking companies. Auditing freight bill plan against external auditor. Found three-year-old $43,000 overcharge by a trucking firm. Recovered entire amount.
- ❏ Designed and implemented new effective ways of transporting hazardous material to end consumers. Facilitator for Hazardous Materials Awareness Program targeting 4 different audiences.
- ❏ Negotiate rate contracts with local and foreign carriers to handle "valuable cargo."

Yawntime Electronics & Barber Corp.   1985–1993
Account Manager

- ❏ Analyzed product "bottle-neck" in a foreign country—had to develop new creative ways in which to keep goods flowing smoothly through foreign customs.
- ❏ Developed tracking report to keep all levels of management informed of possible delays in order to better track product and anticipate possible delays.
- ❏ Extensive direct interaction with product suppliers as well as service providers to ensure a uniform level of production was maintained.
- ❏ Designed and developed procedure manuals for exporting freight to Europe and South America.

Continued

Logistics Management

Name
Street Address
Telephone Number/Day   **City, State, Zip Code**   Telephone Number/Evening

Cross Ship Freight International Corp.   1983–1985
International Coordinator

❑ Identified different modes of transportation services available to potential customers.
❑ Supported Export Sales Team

The Hen's Nest   1982–1983
Traffic Assistant

❑ Implemented coordinating shipping procedures with local trucking companies and freight forwarders. Worked closely with tax / investment department to quickly clear letter of credit payment.

American Acne Society   1981
Public Relations / Intern

❑ Wrote public press releases and public service announcements for radio.
❑ Prepared layout for annual newsletter.
❑ Chaired annual "Daffodil Day" campaign. Raised $1,000 in initial attempt at raising funds.

Gas Machinery Service, Inc.   1973–1978
Purchasing Agent

❑ Supervised general office personnel.
❑ Purchased heavy machinery for parent company in Santiago, Chile.
❑ Translated office communication from Spanish to English.

EDUCATION
Bachelor of Science, Communications, 1982, Montana State University.

Associates of Arts, Liberal Arts, 1980, Pittsburgh College.

PROFESSIONAL EDUCATION
Certificate, Business Logistics Management, May 1995, Pennsylvania State University.
Transportation of Dangerous Goods, Lion Technology, 1995
ICAO/IATA Hazardous Material, Flying Tigers, 1992
Export Controls and Licenses, US Dept. of Commerce, 1990
Let's Learn Portuguese, Berlitz, 1987

Management

Name

Street Address • City, State, Zip • Phone Number

PROFILE

❑ Innovative and highly competent professional manager with 25+ years of sales, operations and administrative experience through increasingly responsible positions. Market and oversee the day-to-day operations of small to mid-sized companies, grossing $2–$35 million. Thirteen years in municipal government with the City of Houston at the division/department head level.

❑ Create a vision of the whole profit picture for a company or organization. Established systems and procedures that consistently resulted in significantly increased control and profitability.

❑ Recognized for exceptional managerial skills and effective communications at all organizational levels. Team player who develops customer-driven teams providing quality response and follow-up.

❑ Well-developed organizational, project management, troubleshooting and problem solving skills.

❑ Computer literate. Proficient in WordPerfect 5.1, 6.0, Word for Windows, and Lotus 1-2-3. Working knowledge of Microsoft Works, Excel, Quattro Pro, MAC programs and DOS.

HIGHLIGHTS OF ACHIEVEMENTS

❑ Turned around the branch of a computer company preventing closure and employee layoffs. Assumed management position with the sole intent to evaluate the daily operations of the branch, and implement radical changes in procedure. The branch went from 7th place to 2nd place in 4 months, maintained 2nd place in 1992 and moved to 1st place in customer service, profitability, overall performance, and realized a 44% growth in 1993. The branch is still #1.

❑ Developed the marketing and consultants' training program, as the COO of a start-up national career consulting firm in Santa Clara, California. Shortened the learning curve for new consultants and had the entire company operational in six weeks.

❑ As Center Manager, reorganized an environmental company in San Mateo, California. Restaffed without loss of daily client support or continuity of service. Restructured customer service procedures, decreased expenses, increased the client base and increased revenues by 45% in the first 5 months of 1990.

❑ Expanded a major party supplier in Anaheim, as General Manager. Established the northern California distribution facility. Hired and trained all personnel, developed the budget and all accounting systems, set up all office and delivery procedures. Penetrated a niche market and established all new clients. The center opened in 20 days, and attained revenues within 2% of goal even after the earthquake of 1989.

❑ Pioneered specialty retail stores in Austin, Texas. Successfully increased the presence of the goods in the market with the addition of four stores. Negotiated favorable lease arrangements, created major news coverage as a business incubator, and promoted a unique business approach.

EDUCATION AND PROFESSIONAL TRAINING

Advanced business courses, The University of Houston, Texas, 1973 and 1978
Management courses, Criminal Justice System and Civil Service, 1977–1983

Continued

Management

Name

Street Address • City, State, Zip • Phone Number

PROFESSIONAL EXPERIENCE

Vice President, Sales and Marketing   1994–present
Professional Associates, Houston, Texas—a 21-year-old full-service consulting firm that assists job seekers create successful job search skills, provides success training, and conducts job search support groups. Responsible for developing the marketing plan and advertising strategy to increase sales. Coordinates sales, community outreach, public relations, new training programs, and partnering programs with other agencies.
- ❑ Close ratio is 85%–95% with qualified leads.
- ❑ Published articles or featured in articles as a change expert.

Management Consultant   1988–present
Assumed management and consulting positions within companies during projects in progress, in the Bay area of Northern California and in Houston, Texas. Companies were involved in start-ups, reorganization, computer conversions, and new business development.
- ❑ Clients have included executive suites during major expansion; a party goods manufacturer opening a satellite distribution center; a group of psychologists who needed a client database developed for mandated State regulations; an elementary school district that needed to be computerized; a design firm that was a start-up in California; a retailer that needed marketing assistance; a start-up career consulting firm who needed a COO; a major electronics manufacturer in California who needed organization of a database.
- ❑ Consultant to clients in Houston, Texas, the Bay area of Northern California, and nationally through Internet and America Online. Clients have successfully transitioned their businesses, increased public relations, and increased revenues.
- ❑ Computerized all accounting systems, developed procedures to make a school district in Santa Rosa, California, more fiscally responsible, resulting in better record keeping and reducing personnel costs.

Branch Administrator   1991–1994
Santa Clara branch of the largest independently owned computer company in the country, based in Walnut Creek, California, with revenues of more than $32 million, over 350 employees and seven branches in California. Recently purchased controlling interest in a telecommunications company.

Supervised quality control; sales support; personnel; accounts receivable and billing; employee development; customer service; and administration.
- ❑ Authorized a Sales Coordinator's Training Manual. Adopted companywide, this document outlines the procedures required to process business from sales to installation and reduced the learning curve for new employees.
- ❑ Implemented a customer service program. Resolving installation and service problems within 48 hours of notice reduced collection problems to less than 1%, once accounting for more than 20%.

Continued

Management

Name

Street Address • City, State, Zip • Phone Number

Owner, General Manager   **1983–1987**

A Zoo, The Christmas Store, The Mercantile, and Christmas For You, Houston, Texas—Specialty retail toy stores and department stores specializing in Christmas items.

❑ Directed advertising; public relations; accounting and tax compliance; merchandising; inventory control; sales supervision; budgeting and forecasting.

Director, Police Administrative Services Bureau   **1977–1983**

Any Police Department, City of Anywhere, Texas.

❑ Directed the day-to-day operations; Fiscal Affairs Division; Property and Evidence Management; Building Services Division; $30 million budget; Personnel Division. Supervised 46 employees including 4 managers.

Accountant, Records Analysis Supervisor   **1970–1977**

City of Anywhere, Texas. Finance Department and Vehicle and Equipment Services.

Marketing Professional

Name

Street Address • City, State, Zip • Phone Number

PROFILE

❏ Innovative and creative marketing professional with over 10 years administrative and marketing experience developing marketing plans for nonprofit agencies, school districts and the business community.

❏ Proven track record of designing and implementing successful projects. Have successfully promoted new ideas to organizations and the community. Particularly skilled at directing large meetings.

❏ Outstanding communication and presentation skills, effective public speaking and the ability to command attention when necessary. Able to work with public officials, executives and other community leaders.

❏ Computer literate. Proficiency with Lotus 1-2-3, Microsoft Word, WordPerfect, DOS and Windows. Working knowledge of Filemaker, Pagemaker and Excel.

❏ Reading and writing proficiency in French.

ACHIEVEMENTS

❏ Developed a rapport with area merchants and set up a base for financing a nonprofit retail center which increased revenues and exposure to the center.

❏ Produced market analysis for a task force on special projects. Identified strategic issues such as the recommendation for future outreach programs resulting in increased community awareness of services available.

❏ Increased attendance at a Seymour College event by developing hands-on participation and setting up a speakers' bureau with celebrities.

❏ Produced a highly effective slide presentation explaining financial allocations of an agency's revenues so the membership understood where their donations were being spent. The presentation increased membership awareness of the importance of donations and involvement.

❏ Coordinated press releases and scheduled placement for the optimum exposure for several events.

❏ Developed a marketing plan for the Manheim Health Committee which increased communication. New services included an information hotline, increased public relations and a mobile unit.

❏ Raised $165,000 for a San Francisco foundation by organizing a major foundation fund-raising event. Awarded recognition for being among the top 10 best promoters.

EDUCATION

B.S. Psychology, Santa Clara University, Santa Clara, California, 1994

Continued

Marketing Professional

Name

Street Address • City, State, Zip • Phone Number

PROFESSIONAL EXPERIENCE

Marketing Consultant   1986–present
Coordinated marketing, advertising and public relations for various agencies, organizations and companies in the Bay area.

- ❏ **Project:** Financial Development Committee, Action League of Milltown, California, 1993–1994
  Duties: Planned pertinent training session for members to familiarize them with the operations. Organized orientations, sales and marketing shift for personnel. Managed contacts with area merchants, supervised volunteers and attended City Council meetings as representative for organization.

- ❏ **Project:** Planned Parenthood of Reas City, California, 1993–1994
  Duties: Counseled members of the community in various aspects of family planning.

- ❏ **Project:** Holiday Faire at Oaktown School, Parkside, California, 1992–1993
  Duties: Co-chaired and organized the Sweet Shoppe fund-raiser for the PTA. Generated $28,000 (a 20% increase over previous fairs), developing procedures and methods for achieving cost-effective results for future fairs. Planned, scheduled and recruited volunteers. Stimulated parent participation and coordinated vendors.

- ❏ **Project:** Action Environmental Foundation, San Francisco, California, 1992
  Duties: Organized and coordinated major foundation fund-raising events. Created a network of corporate donors and successfully recruited participants to an event which resulted in raising $165,000. Awarded recognition for being among the top 10 best promoters for the Selection Committee.

- ❏ **Project:** The Technology Center Committee, Action League of Milltown, California, 1991–1992
  Duties: Organized publications, developed questionnaires to promote improvement in operations, and evaluated manuals. Directed distribution of the publications. Coordinated advertising with local businesses.

- ❏ **Project:** The Manheim Health Committee, Action League of Milltown, California, 1990–1991
  Duties: Coordinated promotion, marketing, and public relations of the facility. Created an information hotline to outline services available and recommended future outreach programs such as a mobile unit.

- ❏ **Project:** Speakers Bureau for Child Abuse Project, Action League of Milltown, California, 1990
  Duties: Produced and coordinated the speakers' bureau in San Ramon. Created media announcements and recruited local organization to help sponsor the project. Enlisted qualified speakers and appeared as guest speaker at civic and Chamber of Commerce activities.

- ❏ **Project:** Drug Faire Project Committee, Action League of Milltown, California, 1988–1989
  Duties: Planned and coordinated the Drug Faire at Seymour College. Recruited high schools in the area to attend and participate. Chaired the publicity and promotional program which included flyers and brochures. Coordinated media participation.

Administrative Assistant   1983–1986
Coping, Inc., in San Jose, California, and Mercy, Inc., in Sunnyvale, California.

MIS Management/Networking Professional

Name
Street Address
City, State, Zip
Telephone Number

EXPERIENCE:
- ❏ More than 12 years in the design, management and updating of networking and data communications systems.
- ❏ Hire, train and supervise staff in system use and troubleshooting; coordinate programmers and technical personnel for custom configurations.
- ❏ Proficient in Novell/Netware, IBM/Lan Server 2.0, UNIX, Ethernet, Token Ring, IPX, TCP/IP and 10BaseT; OS2 (all levels), DOS, Macintosh, Lotus 1-2-3, WordPerfect, MS Word, Excel and Paradox.
- ❏ Well-versed in Codex DSUs, AT&T 3500s & 3600s, Datatel, Micom and Tellabs equipment, WellFleet LNs/FNs & Cisco Routers.

EMPLOYMENT:

Glass & Bingham, Inc., Chicago, IL   1981–Present
Network Manager   1987–Present
Perform all networking and data communication system design and installation, including full Netware and LAN/WAN applications.
Effectively hire, train and supervise up to eight employees, including software/hardware technicians and network managers.
Manage a network of 450 nodes; oversee and assist in all hardware and software selection & updating; manage T1s, leased lines and dial ups.
Design and troubleshoot wiring and systems to board level; configure hard drives, backup devices, NICs and all other systems listed above.
- ❏ Utilize Synoptics Hubs & Lattisnet Management Systems.
- ❏ Implemented a Token Ring Network linked with a Netware MPR Router.
- ❏ Designed/implemented a TCP/IP Network to interface with an RS 6000.
- ❏ Assisted in designing and building an entire computer room.

Assistant Operations Manager   1984–1987
Performed all scheduling and supervision of up to eleven operators on three shifts and a 24-hour/six-day schedule.

Computer Operator   1981–1984

EDUCATION:

Elmhurst College, Elmhurst, IL   Graduation: 5/93
B.S. Degree: Business Administration

LAN-Mind, Chicago, IL   CNE Classes: 1991

Triton College, River Grove, IL   Graduation: 5/84
A.A.S. Degree: Computer Science

Occupational Health Specialist

Name
Street Address
City, State, Zip Code
Telephone Number

KEYWORD SUMMARY: Occupational Health Specialist. Public Health. Alcohol Technician. Bachelor of Science in Community Health. Department of Health. BAT. Breath Alcohol Technician. Environmental Control. Food Inspector. Works Effectively with Public. Organized. Strong Work Ethic. IBM. Apple. Pagemaker. WordPerfect 6.0. Word. Excel. Powerpoint.

OBJECTIVE: A position in a health care setting with a focus on community health education and awareness.

EXPERIENCE: **Occupational Health Specialist,** Pulaski Community Hospital. Pulaski, Virginia. 1995.

Responsible for the employee drug screening procedures of 30 industrial facilities.

❏ Includes urinalysis and alcohol testing.
❏ Effective interpersonal skills.

Assistant, South Carolina Department of Health and Environmental Control. Aiken, South Carolina. 1994.

Served as student intern completing 400 hours of work focused on environmental health issues.

❏ Food Protection Permits.
❏ Rabies Control, Lead Poisoning, Septic Tank Inspections.
❏ Health Education and Health Promotion.
❏ Nutrition, Smoking Cessation, STD's.

Assistant to Volunteer Coordinator, Pulaski Community Hospital. Pulaski, Virginia. 1993–1995.

Planned holiday activities for hospital employees and their families.

❏ Worked extensively with computer systems.
❏ Learned time management and workplace communications.

EDUCATION: **Bachelor of Science,** Radford University, Radford, Virginia. 1994.

Major: Community Health.

Pilot/Aircraft Mechanic

Name
Street Address
City, State, Zip
Telephone Number

OBJECTIVE: *Aircraft Mechanic/Pilot*
A position where demonstrated flying skills and/or mechanical expertise would be utilized.

PROFILE:
- ❑ Licensed as Private Pilot, single and multi-engine land/instrument planes, Commercial Pilot, Airframe Mechanic, Powerplant Mechanic and Certified Flight Instructor.
- ❑ Experience in flying instruction, including experience with the Cessna 150, 152, 172, 172RG, Piper Warrior, Piper Aztec and Turbo Arrow.
- ❑ Skilled in the use of lathes and standard shop equipment, as well as:
    - ❑ Weighing & balancing of control surfaces
    - ❑ Removal & replacement of skin panels & aircraft fasteners
    - ❑ Manufacture and testing of control cables
    - ❑ Comprehensive modification of aircraft structures
    - ❑ Corrosion control and aircraft painting
    - ❑ Power shears, band saws and the Conrac Synchrobender
    - ❑ Ecro sheet metal formers and the Di-Arco turret punch
    - ❑ Hand and power rollers, belt sanders, drill presses, lathes & mills

EDUCATION:
Northern Maryland University, Carbondale, MD

Bachelor of Science Degree—Aviation Management	12/92
Associate Degree—Aviation Maintenance	8/92
Associate Degree—Applied Sciences	8/90

- ❑ Overall GPA: 3.0/4.0

EMPLOYMENT: Self-funded college costs through employment at:

Blue Jay Construction Company, Bloomingdale, MD
Apprentice   Summers/Breaks, 1990–Present
Responsible for electrical, plumbing and carpentry work on office buildings, townhomes, single-family homes and warehouses.

Ronnie's Office Furniture Warehouse, Itasca, MD   Summers, 1988–1989
Forklift Driver/Order Puller

Federal Express, Addison, MD   1/86–7/87
Customer Service Representative
Performed shipping/receiving and truck loading & unloading on a daily basis.

Product Design/Development

Name
Street Address
City, State, Zip
Telephone Number

PROFILE:

- ❏ More than ten years in drafting and CAD systems, including product research, design, development, and testing.
- ❏ Utilize Windows and AS400 for customizing CAD applications; skilled in Rasterex, Automanager, and Teradyne on System 38s and PCs.
- ❏ Handle sourcing and purchasing of parts and components, as well as inventory control, production scheduling, project tracking/documentation, and technical staff training.

EMPLOYMENT:

Evanston/Rogers Corporation, Addison, IL   4/85–Present
Mechanical / Electrical Draftsman   5/88–Present
Perform all aspects of product design and development from blueprints, requiring constant communications with electrical/mechanical engineers, production supervisors, and customers.
Design, update, and troubleshoot prototypes for sheet metal and electrical control panels, used primarily in industrial and commercial refrigeration units.
Provide instructions for brazing, soldering and welding; materials include steel & copper tubing, steel and aluminum.
Interpret blueprints for wiring to customer specs; utilize ohmmeters and ensure accuracy and feasibility of all wiring and related systems.
- ❏ Directly involved in production line setup and streamlining.
- ❏ Major accounts include Hussman, Baxter, the Shedd Aquarium, and major supermarket chains.

Electrical Assembler/Department Supervisor   4/85–4/88
Established production schedules and performed wiring, assembly, and testing of electrical control panels.
Coordinated stock levels to correspond with demand, resulting in major savings.
Trained and supervised five employees in procedures and operations.

Rockwell International, Downers Grove, IL   9/79–3/85
Electrical Repair/Troubleshooter
Operated a Teradyne system and ohmmeter
Responsible for electrical troubleshooting and repair of telecommunication systems, including wiring and soldering backplates.

EDUCATION:

MIMA: Midwest Industrial Management Association, Westchester, IL
Completed training in Supervision, Supervision Psychology, and Basic Electricity.

Hussman Institute, Bridgeton, MO
Trained in various state-of-the-art engineering applications.

Production/Distribution Management

Name
Street Address
Telephone Number/Day   **City, State, Zip Code**   Telephone Number/Evening

OBJECTIVE   Production/distribution management.

PROFILE   Determined professional with extensive, progressive manufacturing and distribution experience. Major strengths in areas of Quality Control, Finished Goods and Warehouse Supervision. An innovative, results-oriented problem solver with strong analytical, conceptual and design skills.

SPECIALIZED EXPERTISE and EXPERIENCE

❏ PRODUCTION
Production planning
Improve line flow efficiency
Create engineering modifications
Packaging technology improvements
Computer systems
Purchasing

❏ HUMAN RELATIONS
Supervision
Train prod. and whse. supervisors
Create training manuals
Create efficient work procedures
Customer service
Developed work teams

❏ QUALITY
Develop quality standards
Monitor quality standard compliance
Packaging technology quality
Cost reductions

❏ WAREHOUSE / DISTRIBUTION
Initiate JIT
Design warehouse layout
Space utilization
Inventory control
Negotiate freight contracts

SELECTED ACCOMPLISHMENTS

Examined line moving bottles through annealing oven (lehr). Any falling bottle tipped others producing breakage, line jams, and safety hazard. Suggested tightening spacing to prevent falling bottle from causing a chain reaction. This increased density and also reduced electricity expense by 25%. Rewarded for "Best Employee Idea of the Year."

Initiated time study program that created efficient work procedures increasing production by 20%.

Increased production and improved the line flow efficiencies by isolating "bottlenecks" and taking corrective action on machine speeds, conveyor speeds, transfer alignments, set-up specifications.

Created engineering modifications to eliminate falling bottles at conveyor transfer points.

Showed continued improvement in quality as the complexity of the operations increased from 20 to 40 different packages.

Trained three production and two warehouse supervisors.

Continued

Production/Distribution Management

Name
Street Address
Telephone Number/Day   **City, State, Zip Code**   Telephone Number/Evening

As part of a plant start-up team, wrote training manuals and established departmental standards. Insured smooth start-up of two new manufacturing facilities and the proper training of its employees including launching a Finished Goods Department.

Attained a record shipping volume during JIT implementation and colleague's vacation. Brought down warehouse inventory to record lows and assured on-time delivery to each of Miller's six breweries.

Analyzed loading pattern of empty bottles that caused shifting and disrupted depalletizing. Worked with receiving supervisors, forklift drivers, and drivers to determine that crown of road caused shifting. Devised a new trailer loading diagram to end shifting. In addition loaded more product on trailer saving $100,000 a year.

EXPERIENCE

1995–Present Distribution
    Ben Dover Distribution Statos, PA

1994–1995 Distribution/Production
    American Nudnicks Statos, PA

1994 Distribution/Production Consultant
    Wetness Plastics Topsville, NY
    Tweedle Plastics Oldeboro, NY
    Roadshow Plastics Gummit, NY

1985–1993 Warehouse Supervisor
    Duff Brewing Company Springfield, NY (Glass Manufacturing Division)

1977–1985 Finished Goods Supervisor
    Duff Brewing Company Springfield, NY (Glass Manufacturing Division)

1975–1977 Laboratory Technician
    Vesuvious Crucible Research Laboratory Pittsburgh, PA

EDUCATION and TRAINING

B.A. Papermill State College, Gunsnroses, UT Biology Major-Chemistry Minor

Company sponsored training includes:
    American Management Association Training for Firstline Supervisors
    Advanced Management Skills & Techniques for Firstline Supervisors
    Symphony computer training   Dimensional Management Training
    Understanding People   Assertiveness Training for Managers
    Human Relations Seminar   Increased Managerial Effectiveness
    Managerial Effectiveness Course

Public Relations Specialist

Name
Street Address
City, State, Zip Code
Telephone Number

KEYWORD SUMMARY: Experience in Telecommunications Field. 5 Years. Radio. Television. Production Assistant. Editing. Video Programs. Master Control Switcher. News Department. Layout. Design. Print Advertisements. Photographer. Excellent Written and Oral Communication Skills. Bachelor of Arts in Mass Communications. Computers. Desktop Publishing. Internet. Works Well in Variety of Environments. Can Handle Pressure. Meets Deadlines.

PROFESSIONAL SUMMARY:
- ❏ 5 Years Experience in Communications Field.
- ❏ Familiar with Radio, Television, and Print Media.
- ❏ Strong Work Ethic.
- ❏ Excellent Interpersonal Skills.

OBJECTIVE: A public relations position with particular interest in sports promotion.

EDUCATION: **Bachelor of Arts,** University of Southwestern Louisiana.
Lafayette, Louisiana. 1992.
Major: Mass Communications.

EMPLOYMENT EXPERIENCE: **Production Assistant,** Video Design Associates. Lynchburg, Virginia. 1994–Present.
Responsible for shooting and editing of video productions. Handled layout and design of print advertisements.

Board Operator and DJ, KRVS-FM. Lafayette, Louisiana. 1989–1994.
Responsible for production of weekly program. Included recording satellite feeds and board operation.

Master Control Switcher, KATC-TV3. Lafayette, Louisiana. 1992–1994.
Handled on-air signal, maintained a program log, set up live remote shots, and recorded satellite feeds.

Assistant, The Cajundome. Lafayette, Louisiana. 1981–1994.
Worked with setup of major entertainment and concert events including lights, sound systems, and staging.

News Intern, KATC-TV3. Lafayette, Louisiana. 1991–1992.
Assisted news department in shooting, editing, and writing news packages for nightly newscasts.

Quality Management Specialist

Name
Street Address
Telephone Number/Day   **City, State, Zip Code**   Telephone Number/Evening

OBJECTIVE

Lead an organization to technological excellence and competitive advantage using Total Quality Management, the Quality Sciences and Applied Statistics.

SUMMARY OF QUALIFICATIONS

BSME, MS Applied Statistics, CQE. Eighteen years in quality and engineering. Proven ability to apply quality principles to manufacturing and design. Results-oriented and detail-minded.

AREAS OF EXPERTISE AND EXPERIENCE

- ❏ Trained as ISO 9000 Lead Assessor
- ❏ Team-Oriented Problem Solving
- ❏ Statistical Process Control
- ❏ Total Quality Excellence
- ❏ Leaded Component Insertion
- ❏ Personnel Training
- ❏ Pennsylvania Quality Leadership Award Examiner
- ❏ Supervision of Engineers, Operators and Skilled Trades
- ❏ Self-Managed Work Groups
- ❏ Quality Function Deployment
- ❏ Design of Experiments
- ❏ Deming Philosophies
- ❏ Surface Mount Technology
- ❏ ASQC Certified Quality Engineer

PROESSIONAL DEVELOPMENT AND SELECTED ACCOMPLISHMENTS

Grace L. Krebople Electronics and Screen Door Corp.   **1990–Present**
Lead Engineer—Leaded Component Insertion
Electronic Engine Controls (EEC) Manufacturing, 1994–Present

Supervise two-shift operation responsible for inserting 10 million electronic components per month. Team includes 4 engineers, 42 operators and 15 skilled tradespersons on 28 insertion machines.

Statistical Methods Facilitator, 1992–Present

Train supervisors, engineers, operators and skilled tradespeople in use of statistical methods. Performed internal quality audits in support of Krebople's Total Quality and Excellence (TQE) Award program. Design procedures for acceptance testing of manufacturing equipment and gages, and for new product and process qualification in accordance with Krebople and Automotive Industry Action Group (AIAG) standards. Provide data analysis for multiple machine acceptance tests. Serve as local training resource and internal consultant for Root Cause Analysis and 8-Discipline Problem Solving Process.

- ❏ Worked with engineers and operators to redesign an SPC application. Achieved 60% reduction in defect rates within 18 months.
- ❏ Used non-parametric statistical methods to develop a test procedure for objectively determining "best" of 4 epoxies using 5 evaluation criteria.
- ❏ Selected as examiner for inaugural 1994 Pennsylvania Quality Leadership Awards.

Continued

Quality Management Specialist

Name
Street Address
Telephone Number/Day   **City, State, Zip Code**   Telephone Number/Evening

Manufacturing Engineer, Printed Wiring Board Assembly
Surface Mount Electronic Component Technology, 2 years

Responsible for placement of 50–60 million electronic surface mount devices (SMDs) per month. Included 'solder side' (save solder) and 'top side' (reflow solder) SMDs. Participated in development and launch of factory floor self-managed work groups. Interacted with skilled tradespeople and operators to reinforce Total Quality Management techniques for processes and procedures. Established procedures and training for supervisors, operators and skilled trades and directed maintenance of equipment to achieve required throughput. Designed and managed data collection system, based on Deming and CQE principles, to monitor processes and prioritize corrective actions.

❏ Developed a procedure for using existing X-ray machine to inspect finished goods for potential defects. Created first-year savings of $200,000.

❏ Designed and developed an inspection procedure to efficiently screen 10,000 modules for defects. Protected the customer from potential poor quality.

❏ Supervised relocation and setup of complex surface mount equipment. When complete, equipment ran more efficiently.

Krebople Motor Company   1977–1990
Powertrain Planning and Engineering Div.
Powertrain Electronics Development Department, 3 years

Revised and updated Subsystem Design Specifications (SDS) for Electronic Engine Control (EEC) Systems. Designed and analyzed control systems and components within the Engine Control System. Designed and performed experiments and regression analyses as Statistical Methods Consultant for a department of 225 people. Participated in and/or led three different Quality Function Deployment (QFD) teams.

❏ Developed a test plan to convince Hertz that we fixed a potentially fatal problem with thousands of our cars. Prevented the loss of a multi-million dollar contract.

Quality Support Department, 2 years

Planned, organized and scheduled quality reviews as part of Total Quality Management implementation. Designed and developed quality reporting formats for the division. Analyzed and reported on warranty data.

V6/V8 Engine Development Department, 6 years

Calibrated mechanical and electronic engine control systems to meet customer expectations for performance and federal government standards for exhaust emissions and fuel economy. Worked in initial design and development stages for Krebople's 3.8L Supercharged Engine. Designed and performed experiments and analyzed exhaust emissions data. Served as department Statistical Methods Coordinator.

❏ Designed electric circuit to reduce risk of catalytic converter fires on police cars.

❏ Simplified and combined 3 engine calibrations into 1. Resulted in company savings of $200,000.

Continued

Quality Management Specialist

Name
Street Address
Telephone Number/Day   **City, State, Zip Code**   Telephone Number/Evening

❏ Worked with my partner to perform detailed diagnostics and repair of engine control system on one-of-a-kind test car. Completed work in just 10 minutes.
❏ Produced mileage calibration for California which resulted in values 1 mile per gallon better than those for other states.

Product Analysis Department, 2 years

Analyzed automotive exhaust emissions data to determine confidence of meeting federal regulations. Reviewed proposed regulations and analyzed data for compliance to proposed emission and fuel economy levels.

Doubletalk and Co., Inc.   **1976–1977**

Manufacturing Engineer, 1 year

Responsible for printing and binding operations in hardcover book manufacturing. Responsible for installation and test of and operator training on relocated machinery.
❏ Reacted quickly and led a team to save the life of an operator caught in a machine.

EDUCATION

M.S., Applied Statistics, San Leandro University, 1989
B.S., Mechanical Engineering, Sohigh University, 1976
Additional Quality-Related Courses:
❏ "ISO-9000 Lead Assessor Training," Stat-A-Matrix Institute
❏ "Salaried Supervisor Institute," Krebople Motor Company
❏ "Pennsylvania Quality Leadership Award Examiner Training"
❏ "Root Cause Analysis," Train-the-Trainer
❏ "QFD Phase I"—Product Planning; "QFD Phase II"—Parts Deployment
❏ "TOPS"—Krebople's 8-Discipline Problem Solving Program
❏ "Quality, Productivity and Competitive Position," W. Edwards Deming
❏ "Effective Speaking and Human Relations," Dale Carnegie

CERTIFICATIONS

American Society for Quality Control Certified Quality Engineer (CQE), since 1989
Engineer-in-Training (EIT), Pennsylvania

MEMBERSHIPS

American Society for Quality Control

PERSONAL

Married, one child. Excellent health.

Real Estate Appraiser

Name
Street Address
City, State, Zip
Telephone Number

PROFILE:
- ❏ Trained in full property assessment including measuring, picture taking, evaluation of comparative properties, and the preparation of final reports.
- ❏ Completed studies in Real Estate Appraisal Principles at The Appraisal Institute in Chicago; currently working toward SRA designation.

EMPLOYMENT:

<u>Eichmann & Associates,</u> Westchester, CT
Research Assistant   1991–Present
Maintain thousands of files and a computer-based employee tracking system for the M.I.S./Mainframe Division.
Independently research accounts and provide administrative support to data entry staff.

<u>Grover Place Restaurant,</u> Bloomingdale, IL
Waiter   1990–1991
Coordinated side-station duties, assisted in problem solving and served as host.

<u>Barnum Clothiers,</u> Bloomington, IL
Sales Associate   1986–1989
Employed aggressive sales techniques to consistently achieve or exceed weekly goals. Handled nightly department closings and provided direct customer service.

<u>White Hen Pantry,</u> Hinsdale, IL
Assistant Manager   1985–1986
Trained, scheduled and supervised up to 10 employees.
Responsible for inventory control, purchasing and cash management.

EDUCATION:

<u>Illinois State University,</u> Normal, IL
Bachelor of Science Degree: Political Science   Graduated 1990
Minor in Criminal Justice Sciences

- ❏ Delta Chi Fraternity: GAMMA Committee Representative and PR Committee, Fall 1988 to Fall 1990
- ❏ Illinois State University Law Club, Fall 1988 to Spring 1989
- ❏ Illinois State University Tae Kwon Do Club, Fall 1985 to Spring 1987

With the Risk Management Committee under GAMMA:
- ❏ Implemented and organized the Greek Designated Driver Program in conjunction with local drinking establishments.
- ❏ Developed and designed pamphlets to provide necessary information and promote responsibility in planning social gatherings.

Retail Sales

Name
Street Address
City, State, Zip Code
Telephone Number

KEYWORDS

Motivated. Able to Work Independently. Leader. Honor Student. Dean's List. National Honor Society. Junior at William and Mary. Radford High School Graduate.

OBJECTIVE

A sales position for a retail operation in the Williamsburg or Tidewater area.

EDUCATION

College of William and Mary, Williamsburg, Virginia, 1994–1995.
   Major: Political Science
   Minor: English
   GPA: 3.2 on 4.0 index

EMPLOYMENT HISTORY

Radford University, Radford, Virginia. May, 1994 to August, 1994.
Summer Assistant, University Development Office.

Worked with annual phonathon effort. Tracked donations and helped maintain computer database of fundraising efforts.
❏ Excellent oral communication skills.
❏ Computer literacy.
❏ Functioned as part of fundraising team.

Radford University, Radford Virginia. June, 1993 to August, 1993.
Summer Assistant, Housekeeping Staff.

Worked as part of team performing summer maintenance chores in a series of residence halls.
❏ Learned value of hard, physical labor.
❏ Able to fulfill work orders and follow directions.

VOLUNTEER EXPERIENCE

President, Earthbound Environmental Group, Roanoke College.
Roanoke, Virginia, 1993–1994.
❏ Developed recycling program for college.
❏ Worked with college administrators to implement program.

Residence Hall Representative, Roanoke College.
Roanoke, Virginia, 1993–1994.
❏ Elected as representative to Residence Hall Council.

Member, Delta Gamma Sorority, College of William and Mary.
Williamsburg, Virginia, 1994–1995.

Risk Management

Name

Street Address • City, State, Zip • Phone Number

PROFILE

❑ *Experienced as a Risk Manager and sales professional, with highly successful track record in market development, program management, and finding solutions to complex situations.*

❑ *Proven abilities in sales, with excellent skills in contract and price negotiations, as well as technical knowledge. Capable of developing products to meet the risk management needs of large firms due to extensive command of the overall concept of risk management, and all the technical/procedural details.*

RELATED PROFESSIONAL EXPERIENCE

NEVILLE RISKER & ASSOCIATES, INC.—Houston, Texas

Consultant   Feb/1993–present

Insurance: ABC Company purchased client base. Provide assistance for former clients and assist with the transition.

Agent/Owner   Dec/1988–Feb/1993

Agent for International Insurance Company. Started the agency from scratch, and over a seven-year period created premium volume totaling $6.8 million annually. Managed fully-automated agency with ten administrative support personnel. Terminated contract February, 1993.

❑ *Handled sales and renewals: emphasis on casualty commercial insurance products for medium to large businesses.*

❑ *Advised customer regarding risk management needs related to employee safety, property and business losses, including nonsubscription as an alternative to worker's compensation.*

❑ *Negotiated contracts and functioned as liaison between company and clients.*

INTERNATIONAL INSURANCE COMPANY, Houston, Texas

Business Sales Agent   Jul/1986–Dec/1988

As in-house agent, developed solid account base in two years, qualifying for independent contractor status one year early.

FIRST MUTUAL INSURANCE COMPANY, Little Rock, Arkansas

District Sales Manager   Jul/1985–Jul/1986

Managed three offices in three cities. Recruited and supervised ten Business Sales Representatives, and conducted weekly sales meetings. Assisted agents in sales and service for larger clients.

AFFILIATIONS/AWARDS

National Award, President's Conference Qualifier, 1989, 1990, 1991, 1992
Agent of the Year for the Southwest Region, 1991
Member: Houston Chamber of Commerce, Professional Insurance Agents

EDUCATION

B.S., Management, Business minor, Austin Technological University, Austin, Texas 1981

Sales/Customer Service

Name

Street Address • City, State, Zip • Phone Number

OBJECTIVE

A position in sales/customer service where experience as a top producer, customer-driven professional and account manager have been developed through increasingly responsible positions.

PROFILE

❑ Highly motivated and goal-oriented sales professional with 13 years sales experience and an excellent record of achievements and new business development.

❑ Excellent communicator able to promote confidence with customers because of a thorough product knowledge. Able to communicate in a multicultural, worldwide environment.

❑ Effective interpersonal skills building rapport with customers, able to develop new sales territories, while continuing to service existing accounts.

❑ Excellent organizational and administrative skills. Able to coordinate priorities and provide support as required.

❑ Computer literate. Proficiency in WordPerfect 5.1 for Windows, Lotus 1-2-3, and email systems.

SKILLS

Territory Development	Niche Marketing	Trade Shows
Account Management	International Markets	Customer Relations

ACHIEVEMENTS

❑ Assisted a customer unfamiliar with a product make a sales presentation to a prospective buyer. By providing technical support and assistance demonstrating the product, the customer landed the largest account ever sold.

❑ Managed a sales office in the absence of the Sales Manager injured in an accident. By providing extra support to the sales representatives and making necessary decisions based on interaction with the European office, a replacement manager was deemed unnecessary.

❑ Hired and trained administrative support to free up time to assist customers with problems and questions. Improved communications between corporate office, sales representatives and customers.

❑ Set up Santa Clara, California office. Purchased phone system and furniture and fixtures. Hired and trained support staff and had office up and running in record time.

EDUCATION/TRAINING

Course work in Marketing/Communications, San Jose State University, San Jose, California, 1993–1994.

Continued

Sales/Customer Service

Name

Street Address • City, State, Zip • Phone Number

PROFESSIONAL EXPERIENCE

ZERSONS PRODUCTS, Austin, Texas

Sales Associate   **Aug/1992–present**
Account management and sales responsibility for 3 major customers totaling over $1 million in revenues, and other smaller accounts.
Liaison with: management in Liechtenstein and Munich, Germany; distributors and representatives in the United States.

Products include: sun filters, hot combs, computer chips, etc.

Responsibilities: account management … trade shows … marketing … international liaison.

Customer Service Representative   **Feb/1992–Aug/1992**
Supported the United States Sales/Marketing Manager.
Responsibilities: customer service, administrative, inventory control, communications for manufacturing in Leichtenstein, and trade show development and implementation.

XYZ CORPORATION, Austin, Texas and San Francisco, California
XYZ COMPANY, Santa Clara, California

Customer Service Representative   **Mar/1988–Feb/1992**
Transferred to Customer Support Center for company in Santa Clara.
Responsibilities: troubleshooting … customer relations … computer training … communications.

Administrative Support   **Apr/1981–Mar/1988**
XYZ Company, Santa Clara:
Transferred to provide executive administrative support to Vice President of Manufacturing and staff of 6 employees.

XYZ Corporation, San Francisco:
Transferred to Back Up Operator for XYZ 50 System which included maintenance of system.

XYZ Corporation, Austin:
Promoted to Back Up Operator for XYZ 50 System which included: text and graphics, training other users, installing hardware and software, and troubleshooting.
Promoted to senior position supporting Vice President of Manufacturing and staff of 5.
Hired as Administrative support to Manager of Design Technology and staff of 36.

Sales Director

Name • Street Address • City, State, Zip • Telephone Number

PROFESSIONAL EXPERIENCE

BIG FOREIGN AIRLINE—New York, New York • 1975–Present

DIRECTOR OF INTERNATIONAL SALES • JOINT VENTURES · 1994–Present

Spearhead this first joint venture for both airlines. Provide leadership in strategic planning and creative development of initiatives targeting the transatlantic market. Direct and implement joint sales programs; monitor benchmarks and keep programs on target to revenue / market share goals and highest possible quality performance.

❑ *Prepare, control and administer a $500,000,000 annual sales budget.*
❑ *Foster clear inter-organizational communications and maintain excellent working relations.*
❑ *Ensure consistency between the separate organizations.*

DIRECTOR OF AREA MANAGEMENT SERVICES · 1993–1994

Conducted a comprehensive needs analysis and implemented an information technology infrastructure maximizing productivity, efficiency and accuracy critical to transport operations, commercial services and corporate administrative elements linking 25 gateway cities.

❑ *Sourced, customized, implemented and supported all hardware and software controlling internal/ external electronic information distribution channels.*
❑ *Provided leadership in areas of creativity, technical expertise, quality assurance and project management.*
❑ *Ensured highest possible performance standards for all products and systems.*

DIRECTOR OF PASSENGER MARKETING · 1992–1993

Designed and oversaw the implementation and effectiveness of passenger-oriented marketing programs, promotions for Corporate and Leisure Products. Developed concepts and approved all advertising and promotions. Guided and supervised the consumer relations function.

❑ *Spearheaded negotiations with corporations, incentive houses and national accounts.*
❑ *Made policy decisions at the International Air Transport Association, International Travel Agents Network and Travel and Tourism Association conferences.*

ACTING DIRECTOR OF PASSENGER SALES AND SERVICES · 1990–1992

Provided critical leadership through a period of company restructuring. Directed the Sales, Marketing and Operations Division with responsibility for the performance of nine gateway cities and five regional offices.

❑ *Effectively administered an annual sales revenue budget exceeding $500,000,000.*
❑ *Assigned, supervised and evaluated the performance of 800 personnel.*

DIRECTOR OF INDUSTRY AFFAIRS & PASSENGER MARKETS · 1987–1990

Drove revenue enhancement efforts targeting improvement of yield per seat to 145 destinations worldwide. Controlled an annual budget of $10,000,000; directed the performance of 40 headquarters personnel in maintaining $50,000,000 in national account sales.

❑ *Negotiated sales budgets with regional sales offices, USA management and headquarters.*
❑ *Calculated and established commission levels to agencies, corporate and national accounts.*

Continued

Sales Director

Name • Street Address • City, State, Zip • Telephone Number

DIRECTOR OF PRICING & INDUSTRY AFFAIRS 1985–1987

Energized business development activities and motivated a staff of 20 in passenger pricing and sales support activities. Conducted market research; monitored competition and made contributions to pricing policy.

ASSISTANT MANAGER: Office Automation • SYSTEMS ANALYST 1983–1985
MANAGER OF INDUSTRY TRAINING • PRICING ANALYST 1979–1983
RATE DEPARTMENT SUPERVISOR • ANALYST • SALES AGENT 1975–1979

EDUCATION

MASTER OF BUSINESS ADMINISTRATION: International Business and Management
PACE UNIVERSITY LUBIN GRADUATE SCHOOL OF BUSINESS New York, New York

REFERENCES & FURTHER DATA AVAILABLE UPON REQUEST

Sales Management

Name
Street Address
City, State, Zip
Telephone Number

OBJECTIVE: A position utilizing extensive experience in Sales or Sales Management, preferably in the sale of equipment and supplies to the food service industry.

EXPERIENCE:
- ❏ More than 15 years in food service, including full responsibility for equipment sales, restaurant management and the setup and operation of new locations; M.B.A. Degree, DePaul University.
- ❏ Experience in budget planning and sales forecasting, as well as market research and new product introduction.
- ❏ Plan and conduct sales presentations in a professional manner; design and utilize sales support materials including videotapes, brochures and detailed user guides.
- ❏ Skilled in executive-level contract negotiations; utilize CAD systems and SmartCom to develop equipment configurations and meet specific client needs.
- ❏ Effectively hire, train and supervise sales personnel; interface with senior-level executives in the planning and implementation of sales incentive programs.

MAJOR ACHIEVEMENTS:

Management
Reduced turnover of Sales Representatives by 22 percent at most recent position by improving training program and compensation structures. Hired and trained an inside sales force of 21, exceeding all previous annual sales records in the Midwest for a leading food service firm.

Administration
Provided full interface between accounting and executive personnel in the design of a computerized order entry and billing system.
Reduced delinquent accounts by 19 percent.

Marketing
Conducted in-depth regional market research and acquired exclusive rights to supply ovens, freezers, and dishwasher equipment to a rapidly expanding chain of pizza stores. Sales exceeded $1 million in the first six months. Projected sales for 1991: $4 million.

EMPLOYMENT: So-Cool Products, Washington, DC   **Sales Manager** 1983–Present

Litton Corporation, Los Angeles, CA   **Sales Representative** 1980–1983

EDUCATION: DePaul University, Chicago, IL
M.B.A. Degree   1977

Sales Operations Management

Name
Street Address
Telephone Number/Day   **City, State, Zip Code**   Telephone Number/Evening

OBJECTIVE   Sales, Operations, Management, Distribution, Administration

SUMMARY OF QUALIFICATIONS

Excellent at building rapport with customers and leading product, delivery and customer service teams to satisfy customers … Finance, CPA, and broad business background … Strong administrative and analytical skills … Effective communicator and negotiator … Strong people skills and a commitment for success … Self-motivated and dedicated … Mindful of details and the bottom line … Computer literate … Team oriented and effective problem solver.

AREAS OF EXPERTISE AND EXPERIENCE

❏ Sales	❏ Transportation	❏ International
❏ Contract Administration	❏ Finance	❏ Customer Service
❏ Negotiations/Trading	❏ Planning/Scheduling	❏ Quality Control
❏ Customer Relations	❏ Project Management	❏ Market Analysis
❏ Distribution/Logistics	❏ Operations	❏ Sales Planning & Strategy

SELECTED ACCOMPLISHMENTS

SALES OPERATIONS—INTERNATIONAL AND DOMESTIC

❏ Coordinated and supervised the export in regard to distribution, logistics, transportation, inventory/quality control, for over 6 million tons annually. Annual sales revenue in excess of $180 million.

❏ Managed the sales planning and strategy for the United Kingdom and Ireland. Instrumental in selling and maintaining accounts with over 1 million tons resulting in revenues of over $30 million annually.

❏ Planned and scheduled all logistic movements for rail and ocean transportation, including domestic and foreign terminals. Scheduled all logistics and managed inventory to run terminal at near 100% capacity.

❏ Negotiated vessel charters, railroad contracts, and terminal services in accordance with the economic plans developed for the movements. Negotiated favorable contracts increasing revenue by 5% or $6,000,000.

❏ Procured materials needed to maintain proper quality and quantity by negotiating with producers and trading companies. Consistently achieved over 98% in maintaining quality and integrity of the finished product. Averaged 10% return in the trading function.

❏ Scheduled and managed fleet of company-owned railroad cars. Consistently produced $1 million net income annually with creative trading and rebates.

DISTRIBUTION

❏ Planned, organized, controlled and coordinated the distribution function. Daily liaison between sales and production. Increased operating efficiency and minimized downtime with tenacious communication style.

❏ Developed sales projections and production reports to capture sales opportunities for maximizing corporate realization. Chaired quarterly strategic planning meetings with functional heads of all divisions and sales force for the purpose of variance reporting and strategic planning. Participated in the preparation of 5-year business sales and production plans.

Continued

Sales Operations Management

Name
Street Address
Telephone Number/Day   **City, State, Zip Code**   Telephone Number/Evening

TERMINAL OPERATIONS

❏ Supervised Customer Service Department. Controlled inventory, distribution, transportation, and billing.

❏ Interfaced with both marine and terminal personnel to coordinate terminal and warehouse activities. Controlled all rail truck ingress and egress for the terminal and developed standard operating procedures for the department.

CONTRACT ADMINISTRATION

❏ Negotiated pricing terms on all base price cost escalating contracts. Negotiated and resolved disputes between 3rd-party producers and customer. Maintained contract administrative controls and price adjustments on all producer contracts.

FINANCIAL

❏ Audited and verified the fairness of financial statements. Prepared income tax returns (Individual, Partnership, Corporation). Prepared financial statements, budgetary planning, and consolidations. Evaluated the adequacy of internal control and the extent of compliance.

CAREER HISTORY

DROOPY TERMINALS INC., Endodaline, PA   1993–1995
Manager—Customer Service

BLACKLUNG COAL COMPANY, Philadelphia, PA   1980–1993
Director—International Sales Operations   1989–1993
Manager, Distribution   1987–1989
Senior Tax Accountant   1984–1987
Senior Contract Administrator   1980–1984

SACROSANCT SPIVEY & CO., C.P.A., Philadelphia, PA   1978–1980
Auditor/Accountant

SWILL BEVERAGES, INC., Pottersville, PA   1975–1978
Controller/Manager

GRAZINGLAND SCHOOL DISTRICT, Grazingland, PA   1973–1975
Teacher

EDUCATION and LICENSE

B.S. Business, University of Hardknocks, 1973
C.P.A., Pennsylvania, 1984

PROFESSIONAL AFFILIATIONS

American Institute of Certified Public Accountants
Pennsylvania Institute of Certified Public Accountants

PERSONAL

Married, two children. Excellent health. Enjoy all sports. High school football referee for past 20 years.

Sales Representative

Name
Street Address
City, State, Zip
Phone Number

JOB TARGET: Sales Representative

EDUCATION

1994   IOWA STATE UNIVERSITY   Cedar Rapids, IA
            B.A.—Communication Arts

CAPABILITIES

❑ Sell and promote a variety of products to individuals or companies on cold-call basis.
❑ Establish customer base in a familiar or unfamiliar territory within a short period of time.
❑ Instruct and train new employees.
❑ Exhibit leadership and motivational abilities.
❑ Communicate effectively with people in a sales and customer relations atmosphere.
❑ Work on IBM-PC or Macintosh computers; operate word processing, database, and spreadsheet programs.
❑ Speak semi-fluently in Spanish.

ACCOMPLISHMENTS

❑ Sold educational books on a door-to-door basis; placed orders, handled cases, and delivered. Grossed $7,600 in sales in a 2-month period.
❑ Ranked 18th nationally out of over 2000 first-year dealers.
❑ Won Gold Seal Award for dealer who averaged 80 hour workweek.
❑ Sold/rented water treatment systems to homeowners and commercial businesses.
❑ Contacted business leaders throughout Iowa as part of marketing services of the International Business Club to promote cooperation and fellowship between Iowa and foreign businesses.

WORK HISTORY

1989–present   SALTWATER SYSTEMS, INC.   Cedar Rapids, IA
               Salesperson/Service Representative

1994   A.J.'s RESTAURANT   Cedar Rapids, IA
               Waiter

1992–1993   SOUTHEASTERN PUBLISHING CO.   Atlanta, GA
               Salesperson

Software Programming

Name
Street Address
City, State, Zip
Phone Number

JOB TARGET: Software Programmer

CAPABILITIES

❑ Program IBM PC and compatibles in DOS and Windows environments.
❑ Design user interface in software programs which incorporate easy-to-follow, logical progression of steps.
❑ Program software in C, C++, Visual BASIC, and Pascal.
❑ Design and produce computer generated graphics.
❑ Operate DOS machines and peripherals; diagnose and fix hardware problems.
❑ Operate a variety of software programs including most major authoring systems, word processors, data base programs, spreadsheet, and graphics packages.

ACCOMPLISHMENTS

❑ Designed and programmed an attendance/registration database program for the Ohio School of Electronics.
❑ Created six utility programs which have been distributed through the shareware network; received over two thousand registrations from satisfied users.
❑ Won Golden Disk Award (utilities category) for 1991.
❑ Established the Central Ohio PC User's Group; increased membership from 10 to 235 individuals in four years.
❑ Created and maintained an on-line, 24-hour bulletin board for the PC user's group.

WORK HISTORY

1989–present   WAYLAND PLASTICS, Inc.
                Assistant Manager—Quality Control

1986–1989   OHIO SCHOOL OF ELECTRONICS
                Registration Clerk (work-study)

EDUCATION

1989   OHIO SCHOOL OF ELECTRONICS

Technical Writing/Editing

Name
Street Address
City, State, Zip
Phone Number

TECHNICAL WRITING:

- ❏ Provided article for *Values Forum,* an in-house magazine for The American Family Association.
- ❏ Wrote and edited nutrition column in newsletter for Bayou County Foster Parents' Association.
- ❏ Wrote, revised, compiled and developed instructional materials for guitar students while serving as guitar instructor at Louisiana State University.
- ❏ Wrote individual educational plans; composed progress reports; created lesson plans; recorded observations and parent conferences while employed as an educator.

EDITING:

- ❏ Served as editor for LSU's student literary magazine, *Chrysanthemum.*
- ❏ Created office manual, conducted correspondence, recorded meetings and other business as an administrative aide.
- ❏ Served as secretary for the Louisiana Multiple Sclerosis Association.

WORK HISTORY:

1980–Present   Independent editing and administrative assignments in Bayou County and LSU departments on a contract basis.

1988–Present   Self-employed as a family day-care provider
Licensed as a Bayou County Foster Parent

1982–Present   Guitar Instructor—Louisiana State University

1982–1986   Group Leader—Sunburst Childcare Center

EDUCATION:

1980–Present   LOUISIANA STATE UNIVERSITY
Classes in technical writing and editing, desktop publishing, early childhood courses.

1978   UNIVERSITY OF TEXAS—AUSTIN—B.A. English Lit

Truck Mechanic

Name

Street Address • City, State, Zip • Phone Number

Expert mechanic on gasoline and diesel engines with over fifteen years of experience as a self-employed contractor working with small to medium companies.

Proven record maintaining 1 1/2 ton dual wheel trucks to 80,000 GVW vehicles. Able to repair or replace clutch … drive axle … transmission … air brake components … suspension components … truck cab and cab parts … wiring.

Excellent diagnostic skills with the ability to troubleshoot all types of vehicles. Possess own tools and have service truck available.

CAREER HISTORY

Hired in March, 1993, as **Shop Mechanic** for San Marcos Rental, San Marcos, CA, and currently employed.

Responsible for overseeing the good working condition of trucks from 3/4 ton and up with a fleet of approximately 80 trucks.

❑ Diagnose poorly operating engines and by removing and sending the engines to a rebuilder to repair, I have been able to keep trucks running with rebuilt engines and have reduced the capital expenditure necessary to replace trucks.

❑ Research available vendors in the area able to repair and/or rebuild parts of the fleet. The research has saved money for the company by soliciting competitive bids.

Relocated from Nebraska and as **Owner, Operator,** I established General Engine Service in 1983, in the Phoenix metropolitan area.

Responsible for marketing services to new customers … providing customer service to existing customers … billing for A/R … hiring and training employees … responding to emergency road calls.

❑ Converted truck tractors to dump trucks by installing complete hydraulic systems making the old truck tractors that had no more road use, roadworthy as dump trucks. This allowed companies to save thousands of dollars in recycling equipment instead of junking the truck tractors.

❑ Knowledge of the parts required to stock on my truck allowed me to service trucks on site which saved the companies towing charges and unnecessary downtime.

❑ Knowledge of the different engines in various trucks allowed for conducting proper diagnostic research before responding to a call so that the parts identified from the <u>control parts list</u> were taken to the service site.

In 1979 established a contractors business as **Owner, Mechanic** assembling and wiring irrigation systems, both water and electric driven.

❑ Repaired and maintained older irrigation systems by reading wiring schematics when necessary and troubleshooting engine related and/or system related problems.

❑ Repaired and maintained gasoline and diesel engines, other power supplies, pumps, generators, and electric and electronic components of irrigation machinery.

Warehouse Management

Name
Street Address
Telephone Number/Day   **City, State, Zip Code**   Telephone Number/Evening

---

OBJECTIVE   Management position which utilizes my motivation, innovation, distribution, and warehousing skills.

PROFILE

Innovative, effective distribution and warehousing professional with excellent interpersonal skills ... self-motivator ... people motivator ... team player ... problem solver.

AREAS OF EXPERTISE AND EXPERIENCE

- ❏ Cost Reductions
- ❏ Team Development
- ❏ Computer Systems
- ❏ Inventory Control
- ❏ Space Planning
- ❏ Budget Control
- ❏ Freight Rate Negotiations

- ❏ Human Resources Functions
- ❏ Customer Service
- ❏ Receiving Procedures
- ❏ Shipping Procedures
- ❏ Purchasing
- ❏ Logistics Planning
- ❏ International Shipping

EDUCATION

Pine State University, Buck Campus, Major: Business, GPA: 3.6.
B.S. Business Administration expected 5/96.

EXPERIENCE

11/94–Present BUZZ CITY, **Sales Associate,** Computer Department

8/80–10/94 VIRTUAL CORPORATION

10/90–10/94 **Regional Distribution Manager** (Central, Northeastern, and Southeastern regions) RESPONSIBILITIES: Control of $14 million in annual inventory. Organize and maintain the distribution and warehousing of Virtual products to a retail and corporate customer base. Budgeting, forecasting, inventory control, staff maintenance, human resources, space planning, vendor/transportation selection, negotiations and purchasing.

- ❏ Sourced and worked with a domestic vendor to manufacture printer ribbon. Solved low availability problem and saved $181,000/year. Won Unisys achievement award.

- ❏ Worked with MIS to design and implement a locator and bar code system for use on mainframe. Was instituted in my location as a test site to confirm accuracy and efficiencies before being adopted by the entire division.

- ❏ Designed and implemented a PC-based address download program from mainframe to provide shipping system with the addresses for orders. Created 70% time saving per shipment while improving address accuracy.

- ❏ Designed and implemented a new product return procedure for use by customers, resulting in a faster, simpler, and more cost-effective method of returning product. Savings per year $10,000 plus customer service improvements.

Continued

Warehouse Management

Name
Street Address
Telephone Number/Day   **City, State, Zip Code**   Telephone Number/Evening

❏ Planned and implemented the closure and relocation of 80,000 sq. ft. facility. With 30 days notice and demoralized workforce, orchestrated notifications to vendors, lessor negotiation, and selling of equipment, and transferred distribution function to West Virginia.

5/87–10/90 Inventory Control Supervisor

RESPONSIBILITIES: Cycle counts, organization/implementation of physical inventories, oversee administrative functions: receipts, disbursements, expedition of supplies to customers via diverse distribution services. International export and domestic distribution activities.

❏ Created a PC-based locator system to improve effectiveness and efficiencies in our warehouse. Resulted in a 25% improvement in cycle counts and a 25% decrease in missing stock problems. Adopted by my division for use in all five facilities.

❏ Headed up an improvement team which recommended customizing software for our new mainframe computer. Savings to the company estimated at $52,000 per year.

9/84–5/87 Materials Control Planner

RESPONSIBILITIES: Set up and operate in-house refurbishment center. Control the return of parts from field locations to ensure proper credit, control the return of parts to vendors for warranty and return credit, provide logistics support to refurbishment center, expedite parts and materials for site-down and routine replenishment orders.

❏ Set up in-house refurbishment center. Received defective components from field, diagnosed problem, claimed warranty from vendor, repaired component and returned it to field for reuse. Set up all systems and procedures with branches, inventory, material planning, vendors, manufacturing and warehousing. Savings plus revenue generated $500,000 per month.

10/81–9/84 Inventory Control Analyst

RESPONSIBILITIES: Provide Customer Service and support to service staff of over 1,500 engineers, expedite parts from manufacturing and vendors' emergency needs. Control the replenishment of inventory to field locations.

❏ Saw opportunity to combine purchasing and distribution of shipping and office supplies to our 65 branches. Absorbed purchasing function. Savings from consolidation and other efficiencies saved 15% on these supplies.

❏ Created PC-based inventory control system to replace cardex method. Designed pick lists with locator. Set up inventory levels and automated back ordering procedure. This permitted consolidated orders with a 20% decrease in freight costs. Overall resulted in a 35% decrease in processing time.

❏ Discovered that our customers were cleaning tape drives with damaging solvents. Worked with our test lab and vendors to develop new cleaning kit that worked with all types of drives. Prevented $31,000 of warranty expense for our customers. Kit created $5,600 in profit.

8/80–10/81 Senior Material Handler

RESPONSIBILITIES: Shipping and Receiving in a warehouse environment, pick and pack operation, forklift experience, experience in shipping systems.

Writing and Communications Specialist

Name • Street Address • City, State, Zip • Telephone Number

TECHNICAL WRITING • COMMUNICATIONS • DESIGN

OFFER ENERGY, ENTHUSIASM AND COMPREHENSIVE EXPERIENCE IN ALL PHASES OF PROJECT MANAGE-MENT WITH EXPERTISE ENCOMPASSING WRITING, RESEARCH, EDITING, DESIGN, GRAPHICS, PROOFING, PRODUCTION AND TRAINING IN COMMUNICATIONS AND MANAGEMENT TOPICS

QUALIFICATIONS HIGHLIGHTS

❏ **Project Management Skills:** Utilize strong planning, controlling, organizing and leadership skills to make needs assessments, set priorities and establish project benchmarks to consistently meet deadlines, budget and deliver high-quality performance.

❏ **Publications:** Include how-to guides and manuals, reference guides, tips, shortcuts and information updates and user aids on topics including Adult Learning Principles, Creative Thinking, Business Communications Skills, Problem Solving and Leadership.

❏ **Industry Specific Knowledge:** Includes Administration, Communications, Education & Training, Entertainment & Arts, Finance/Banking, Human Resources Development, Medical/Health, Science, Publishing, Transportation, Travel and Hospitality fields.

❏ **Computer Proficiencies:** Skilled in sourcing, purchase negotiations, installation, administration and technical support for Apple / Macintosh and IBM PC systems including PC-based Local Area Networks.

Hardware: Graphics ICR & OCR scanners

Software: Excel • FileMaker Pro • Freehand • Gram-mat-ic • HPDesk • Hypercard • Lotus • MacDraw • Paint • Malcolm Baldridge Awards Program • Microsoft Office / Project / Word • Multimate • Norton Utilities • PageMaker • Paradox • Persuasion • Photoshop • PowerPoint • QuarkXpress • SABRE

PROFESSIONAL EXPERIENCE

INSTRUCTIONAL DESIGN TEAM: **Corporate Training & Development**   1989–Present
FIELD CONTROLLER AND METHODS & STANDARDS: **Field Services**   1986–1989

BIG CORPORATION   Clarity, Pennsylvania
Spearhead creation of instructional programs and materials used by corporate trainers. Make key contributions in design, development and technical writing. Plan, schedule, budget and track multiple project assignments; source and negotiate capital, supply and service purchases. Execute research, editing, desktop publishing and prop production.

❏ *Plan and facilitate project and program development meetings.*
❏ *Develop text for publications, reference materials, speeches, on-line products.*
❏ *Devise line drawings, graphs, flow charts, graphics / data illustrations and diagrams.*
❏ *Produce visual aids: vinyl wall murals, slides, transparencies, audio and video tapes.*
❏ *Edit copy, graphics / illustrations and design for accuracy, audience and appropriateness.*

Continued

Writing and Communications Specialist

Name • Street Address • City, State, Zip • Phone Number

CONSULTANT • CURRICULUM DESIGNER •TRAINER • FACILITATOR   1992–1994
CONSULTING AND TRAINING COMPANY   Clarity, Pennsylvania
Rendered project management and specialized expertise for production and delivery of effective teaching and training programs for this management consulting firm. Established relationships with client representatives; drafted and edited copy, designed and produced illustrations and quality product.

❏ *Produced highly effective classroom and conference materials, self-study workbooks, training / technical guides and support documentation.*
❏ *Articulate and expressive, able to explain complex concepts in a clear fashion.*
❏ *Controlled project budget to meet or exceed profit goals.*

ASSISTANT MANAGER   1987–1989
SYMPHONY ASSOCIATION   Clarity, Pennsylvania
Provided financial management services to this arts organization. Contributed strong marketing capabilities and excellent written and verbal communications abilities to fundraising efforts.

❏ *Fostered and maintained excellent client and community relations.*

DARLA SHEDRON, COMMUNICATIONS CONSULTING   1987–1992
Analyzed client needs and resources, made presentation of qualifications and services; negotiated and secured contract work. Developed technical training programs and did extensive desktop publishing involving research, writing, illustration and design expertise.

❏ *Drew on resource networks in related industries and professional organizations to meet specialized client needs.*
❏ *Created brochures, annual reports, newsletters, promotional packets, marketing and advertising pieces and special events flyers.*
❏ *Record for maintaining high level of customer satisfaction.*

ADMINISTRATIVE ASSISTANT TO THE DEAN OF EDUCATION   1983–1984
TEXAS WESLEYAN UNIVERSITY SCHOOL OF EDUCATION   Clarity, Pennsyvlania

---

EDUCATION

BS IN COMMUNICATIONS AGREAT UNIVERSITY   Clarity, Pennsylvania

---

REFERENCES & FURTHER DATA AVAILABLE UPON REQUEST

Acknowledgments

The authors gratefully acknowledge these experts for contributing the following resumes:

Resumes written by Kathryn Jordan

Occupational Health Specialist
Business Manager
Environmental Manager
Retail Sales
Administrative/Clerical Position
Clothing Manufacturing Administrator
Career Guidance/Counseling Specialist
Human Resource Management
Laboratory Technician
Public Relations Specialist

Resumes written by Steven Provenzano

Sales Management
Administration/Management
Elementary Teacher
Credit/Collections Management
Legal Secretary
Engineering/Facility Management
Computer Aided Design/Manufacturing Programmer
Pilot/Aircraft Mechanic
Chef
Real Estate Appraiser
MIS Management/Networking Professional
Product Design/Development

Resumes written by John Bakos

Banking and Financial Development Specialist
Educational Psychology / Human Development
Financial Operations Management
General Management
Sales Director
Finance/Investments Management
Insurance Professional
Writing and Communications Specialist
Marketing and Sales Management

Resumes written by Gary Ames

Association Management
Information Technology Manager

Warehouse Management
Quality Management Specialist
Production/Distribution Management
Sales Operations Management
Logistics Management

Resumes written by Tom Jackson

Health Care Operations Management
Geologist
Technical Writing/Editing
Advertising Manager
Software Programming
Sales Representative

Resumes written by Timothy Gibson

Accounting/Financial Analyst
Athletic Director/Coach

Resumes written by Debarah Wilson

Marketing Professional
Management
Customer Service
Risk Management
Truck Mechanic
Electronics Technician
Health Care Sales and Marketing
Air Conditioning and Refrigeration Technician
Sales/Customer Service

12
Sample Cover Letters

When distributing your electronic resume, either the online searchable database or the multimedia version, it is wise to include a standard cover letter. For example, when posting your electronic resume in an online searchable database, you can—and you are encouraged to—include a one-page cover letter, at either the beginning or end of your resume. The single file that you upload to an online service could include both your cover letter and resume. Also, when you distribute your multimedia resume, a cover letter can be included in the introduction section of your resume.

While a cover letter, when used in this manner, must remain somewhat generic and nonspecific to a particular employer's needs and business interests, it is nonetheless a good strategy to help employers and employment recruiters assess your employment potential and application.

In this chapter you will find a number of sample cover letters written by our team of resume writing experts. You are encouraged to review these cover letters to discover clues regarding how you can prepare your own letters. For information on additional cover letter resources, see Appendix B.

The cover letters found in this chapter include:

Account Management
Administrative Assistant
Administrator
Boiler Plate Cover Letter
Business and Facility Operations
Cost Accountant
Electric Engineer
Electrical Engineering
Executive
Inquiry Regarding Meeting to Discuss Employment
Laboratory Technician
Outside Sales
Public Relations
Sales Administration
Sales Management
Sales Marketing and Staff Training
Statistician
Teaching
Training

Account Management

Ms. Shelly Cloud
Cloud Marketing, Inc.
1135 Washington Drive
Chicago, IL 60690

Dear Ms. Cloud:

Given the excellent reputation of your firm *(or Cloud Marketing/company name)*, I am submitting my resume in application for an Account Management position. Specifically, I am seeking to utilize my profit-building skills in account prospecting, acquisition and management to expand your company's profitability.

❏ In my position with Arty Incentives, I have proven my ability to create highly profitable, personalized relationships with key clientele at hundreds of companies. I've executed complex sales with a strong knowledge of product lines *(you could list several here)*, industry trends and of course, the customers' specific needs.

❏ My success thus far is the result of comprehensive research and taking an interactive role in a client's business. This allows me to design and implement customized incentive programs while always keeping a sharp eye on bottom-line results.

I am willing to travel *(and/or relocate)* for the right opportunity, and can provide excellent references at your request. Please let me know as soon as possible when we may meet for a personal interview *(or: I will be contacting you soon to arrange a personal interview)*. Thank you for your time and consideration.

Sincerely,

Jeffrey H. Crockett

Encl.

Administrative Assistant

Cooper Norman, Vice President
Total Power Corporation
1400 S. Madison Street
Burr Ridge, IL 60521

Dear Mr. Norman:

I am exploring opportunities as Administrative Assistant and heard about your company through Jennifer Leigh, who suggested I send you my resume.

- ❏ I am a skilled typist, and proficient in WordPerfect 5.1 and Lotus 1-2-3. As my resume indicates, I have highly successful experience in the medical field and with Montgomery Ward's insurance division.
- ❏ Throughout my career, I've proven my ability to work effectively with management and staff at all levels of experience. Most importantly, I can ensure high customer satisfaction through personalized, yet highly effective communications.
- ❏ I thrive in the type of fast-paced environment where attention to detail and composure are essential to customer satisfaction and referral business.

I am eager to join your highly successful team of professionals. Please let me know as soon as possible when we may meet for an interview and discuss mutual interests. I look forward to your response.

Thank you for your time and consideration.

Sincerely,

Shirley Monroe

Encl.

Administrator

123 Paper Court
Document, Massachusetts 12345
(123) 456-7890

April 1, 1995

Dear Sir or Madam:

I am a seasoned administrator with a comprehensive background encompassing both public relations and organizational communications. You will note from my enclosed resume that my background conforms to the demands of the Communications and Marketing position advertised by the Executive Office of Economic Affairs.

As a retired Manager for the Commonwealth's Department of Public Whatever I have knowledge of all state law, regulations and administrative protocol, and, additionally, as former educator and leader within the Western Massachusetts Ethnic-American community, I have extensive experience in developing public information and in publicizing community service programs. I am convinced that I offer a unique blend of skills and experience which will guarantee success in promoting the new career centers.

To illustrate:

- ❏ I hold masters degrees in literature and education and have a decade of college-level teaching experience. I am an articulate and accomplished public speaker, and have dealt with the print and broadcast media as spokesperson for the Ethnic-American community. I am tactful in charged and sensitive situations.

- ❏ I have a solid record of advocacy in areas of education, social services, housing, and employment and have special sensitivity regarding the needs within the immigrant community. I also spearheaded the design, development and implementation of numerous programs.

- ❏ I'm a self-starter with strong planning, controlling, organizing and supervisory skills. My management talents encompass strategic planning, budget controls, establishing performance benchmarks, assigning, developing and evaluating staff.

Additionally, I have a strong grasp of marketing techniques, solid problem solving skills and a proven ability to motivate others.

If my qualifications meet your needs, I would look forward to a personal meeting. I will call to arrange a time for us to get together. I look forward to meeting with you.

Very truly yours,

Joseph P. Administrator

Boiler Plate Cover Letter

(**Note:** If name or title is not available,
you may use Ladies/Gentlemen, Dear Hiring
Manager or Dear Prospective Employer)

Mr. Bart Dennison
Director of Product Development
Snicker Corporation
129 LaSalle Street, Suite 12
Chicago, IL 60606

Dear Mr. Dennison:

The position of *(position name)* advertised in last Sunday's *(newspaper name)* seems tailor-made for me. My experience with *(last or current employer)* involved responsibility for *(several duties listed in the ad)*, and my efforts resulted in a 20 percent reduction in overhead for 1989. The enclosed resume outlines my qualifications and accomplishments.

I now wish to apply my *(supervisory/design/organizational, etc.)* skills with an industry leader such as *(company name, if applicable)*. I am willing to travel or relocate and my salary requirements are negotiable. *(You may omit "negotiable" and give a range, such as "upper $40s per year" if requested in the ad.)*

I will contact you during the first week of August *(or soon)* to arrange an interview. Meanwhile, please feel free to give me a call should you require any further information on my background.

Sincerely,

Job Seeker

Encl.

Business and Facility Operations

Good Morning:

I am a dedicated, competent and high-energy individual with a sound foundation of comprehensive training, education and hands-on experience in business and facilities operations. From my enclosed resume, you will find that my experience and background run parallel to the demands of your company.

Of special interest is the knowledge and experience I gained as a proprietor and general manager of a landscaping business and while working for the MajorNational organization. The work and education were demanding, requiring dedication and a commitment to quality. My capabilities have outpaced the challenges currently available to me, and I am now prepared to accept new responsibilities. With my achievements and abilities, and with my commitment to my work, I am confident I can make a positive contribution to your organization.

If you wish to contact me, I can be reached at (123) 345-6789 during the day. Thank you for your time and consideration.

Sincerely yours,

Humble Job Seeker

Enclosure

Cost Accountant

Inside Address

March 30, 1995

Name of Specific Individual
Company Name
Street Address
City, State, and Zip Code

Dear *(Specific Individual)*:

I am an accountant with several years of experience working for a business in the New River Valley area. I have learned there is a position as cost accountant currently available at *(Name of Organization)* and would like to be considered. Enclosed is a copy of my resume for your use. My interest is in locating a position with opportunities for additional growth and skill development in the accounting field.

My background does include a Bachelor of Business Administration with a major in Accounting. In my most recent position, I have been involved in learning the practical applications of the field and am now ready for increased responsibilities. I am experienced in many phases of accounting including accounts receivable, bank reconciliations, sales tax reports, month end reports and others. Additionally I have a strong work ethic, excellent interpersonal skills, office management, and administrative experience.

If there is additional information you require, you can reach me at *(Telephone Number)*. I do plan to contact you in approximately 10 days to arrange a time to discuss the position of cost accounting, and I look forward to talking with you.

Sincerely,

Name of Job Seeker

Electric Engineer

Address
Date

Name of Individual
Title
Organization
Street Address
City, State, Zip Code

Dear (Specific Name):

I enjoyed getting to know you two years ago when you were a student in a class I taught at New River Community College. Since that time I have been working at XYZ Corporation in Radford; however, I am very interested in exploring a position as an electric engineer at *(Name of Organization)*. I would like to meet with you to discuss how my skills and background might fit into the organization.

I am interested in *(Name of Organization)* because of the excellent manufacturing environment and the high degree of automation in the facility. My previous experiences with PLC system design and programming would be a definite asset to the organization. During the expansion phase you are presently experiencing, I believe my background in project engineering and construction would also be valuable. I have worked in a variety of manufacturing plants for over 15 years and have enclosed a resume to give you additional information about my work history and experience.

Please feel free to call me at my home. The telephone number is *(Insert)*, and you can reach me any evening after 4:30 p.m. If I have not heard from you in 10 days, I will contact you to set up a time to talk. I look forward to hearing from you.

Sincerely,

Name of Job Seeker

Electrical Engineering

March 7, 1995

Ms./Mr. Hiring Authority
Full Title
ABC Corporation
123 Opportunity Street
Contribution, Massachusetts 99999

Dear Ms./Mr. Hiring Authority:

I am a dedicated, competent and high-energy individual with a sound foundation of comprehensive training, education and hands-on experience in Electrical Engineering. From my enclosed resume, you will find that my experience and background run parallel to the needs of your organization.

Of special interest is the knowledge and experience I gained in the Polytechnic University's Electrical Engineering program which ranks as one of the country's best. The program was demanding, requiring dedication and a commitment to quality. I also have practical experience in the construction field where my capabilities have outpaced the challenges currently available to me, and I am now prepared to accept new responsibilities. With my achievements and abilities, and with my commitment to my work, I am confident I can make a positive contribution to your organization. I will be calling you next week to arrange a meeting.

If you wish to contact me, I can be reached at (123) 345-6789 after 5:30 in the evening. Thank you for your time and consideration.

Sincerely yours,

Hopeful Techie

Enclosure

Executive

April 1, 1995

Dear Mr./Ms. Hiring Authority:

I have more than 20 years of diverse international sales, marketing and management experience in the airline industry, establishing a track record of consistently superlative performance. You will note from my enclosed resume that my background will suit a need within your organization for a professional International Sales, Marketing and Management executive.

Accustomed to multimillion dollar responsibilities, I am now postured for a new position offering me broader opportunities in executive management. I can bring dynamic leadership, technical acumen and decisive management skills to your firm.

To illustrate:

❑ Spearheaded a 500% traffic increase within 12 months; optimized sales by 65% over 4 years, focusing on a commitment to customer satisfaction.

❑ Utilized highly effective negotiations abilities to broker the first ever international marketing agreement for MyBigCompany.

❑ Possess multilingual talents, with fluency in English, French, Italian and Spanish; also have a working knowledge of Dutch.

These are but a few highlights. I have a strong grasp of all team management concepts, sales and marketing techniques, solid problem-solving skills and a proven ability to motivate others.

If my qualifications meet a need in your company, I would look forward to a personal meeting.

Very truly yours,

A. Proven Executive

Enclosure

Inquiry Regarding Meeting to Discuss Employment

Dear Hiring Manager:

With more than 12 years in Manufacturing and Design Engineering, I would like to discuss how my experience can benefit your company. I most recently read about your company's acquisition of Dilmer, Inc., a former client of my employer, GS Gibson.

❏ I currently manage a design and manufacturing engineering team in state-of-the-art product and process development for a wide range of applications. I would be most valuable in a position requiring greater innovation and creativity, that offers the potential for career advancement.

❏ My efforts have resulted in major cost reductions and quality improvement for key customers, as well as for in-house operations. I can now assist your technical staff in virtually all stages of process and product development.

There is much more information I could provide, including a portfolio of photographs of my most important work. I look forward to hearing from you soon so we can discuss mutual interests.

Sincerely,

Edward R. Hound

Encl.

Laboratory Technician

Date
Address

Name of Specific Individual
Title
Organization
Street Address
City, State, and Zip Code

Dear (Specific Name):

A recent relocation to the Roanoke—New River Valley Area has me actively involved in a job search to find a position as a laboratory technician which would utilize my 12 years of laboratory experience. Your *(office / laboratory)* was recommended to me by *(health department, state, individual, chamber of commerce, etc.)*. I am very interested in pursuing a position with your organization.

As an experienced laboratory technician and laboratory manager, I feel my background would be of interest to you. My qualifications include:

- ❏ 12 Years of Progressively Responsible Work in a Laboratory
- ❏ Analytical Testing. Endocrine Hormones. Esoteric Test. Viral Hepatitis. Estrogen. Progesterone Receptors.
- ❏ Environmental Testing.
- ❏ Bachelor of Arts & Sciences and an Associate Degree in Laboratory Technology.

I would like an opportunity to discuss possible opportunities at *(Name of Organization)* and plan to call your office in 10 days to arrange a time to talk with you. If you would like to reach me, please do not hesitate to call my home telephone number, *(Insert Number)*. I look forward to hearing from you.

Sincerely,

Name of Job Seeker

Outside Sales

123 Prospect Boulevard • Huge Revenues, New York 12345
(123) 456-7890

April 3, 1995

Dear Sir or Madam:

I am an executive sales manager who has provided effective leadership to multimillion dollar operations. You will note from my enclosed resume that my background runs parallel to the needs of your organization.

Of special interest is my facility in communication encompassing client relations, business negotiations and staff motivation. I am now ready to assume new challenges and responsibilities. With my knowledge and experience in these areas, I am confident that I can make an immediate and positive contribution to your company. I offer dynamic and innovative marketing ideas and decisive management abilities.

To illustrate:

❏ I successfully developed and maintained MyCompany's $50,000,000 in annual revenues through a ten-year tenure by identifying and responding to consumer trends. Averaged more than $5,000,000 in yearly sales for start-up company, TheOtherCompany, implementing aggressive and highly effective sales methods.

❏ Made key customer service contributions to MyCompany serving as the sole troubleshooter for customer problems, generating goodwill and client loyalty. Established a solid client base for TheOtherCompany.

❏ Achieved outstanding improvements in productivity at MyCompany demonstrating outstanding skills in operations planning, purchasing, inventory control, distribution, personnel and organizational administration.

If you wish to contact me, I can be reached at (123) 456-7890. Thanking you in advance and counting on your interest, I remain,

Very truly yours,

Outside Sales

Enc.

Public Relations

Name of Specific Individual
Title
Company
Street Address
City, State, Zip Code

Dear Specific Name:

After several years working out of the state, I am interested in returning to Louisiana and would like to locate a public relations position in the Lafayette or Baton Rouge vicinity. I am an experienced communications professional with a background in television, radio, and print media and am looking for an organization with which I can utilize my previous work experiences. I believe public relations and marketing work is the next logical extension for my skills. Your organization was recommended to me by the Sports Information Office at Southwestern Louisiana University, my alma mater.

Enclosed is a resume with additional details of my academic and employment background. I am familiar with all phases of radio and television broadcasting and production. In addition I am an accomplished photographer, experienced in print media layout for advertisements, and particularly interested in the sports promotions field.

If you require additional information, please do not hesitate to contact me. I do plan to be in Louisiana soon and will contact you to discuss possible opportunities with your organization.

Sincerely,

Name of Individual

Sales Administration

76 Club Tree
Greenwood, IL 60107
708/555-9256

Dear Hiring Manager:

In the interest of helping your company achieve greater sales and customer satisfaction, I am enclosing my resume. Specifically, I am seeking to better utilize my skills in sales, administration and customer service to expand the profitability of your operation.

My position at Lawrence & Fredrick requires extensive product knowledge and sales skills. Most importantly, I feel it is my ability to communicate well with clients that has resulted in high customer satisfaction and repeat business.

I've proven my ability to handle numerous sales calls and quickly solve problems in this fast-paced environment, all while establishing an excellent record of sales and success. This is the kind of experience I can now bring to your company, along with a strong ability to learn new systems and procedures.

Because my resume is only a summary statement of my abilities, I would welcome the chance to meet with you personally to discuss the needs of your company. I can provide excellent references on request, and look forward to hearing from you soon.

Sincerely yours,

Maureen Janus

Encl.

Sales Management

123 Long Road • Somecity, Massachusetts 12345 • (123) 456-7890

April 1, 1995

Dear Ms./Mr. Authority:

I am a dynamic goal and profit oriented professional with 18+ years progressive achievement in Sales and Management. You will note from my enclosed resume that my background will suit a position of Sales Manager and allow me to make a positive and mutually beneficial contribution to your company.

Accustomed to multimillion dollar sales responsibilities, I am now postured for a new position offering me broader opportunities in Sales Management. I can bring dynamic leadership, technical acumen and decisive management skills to your firm. To illustrate:

- ❏ I spearhead sales and marketing initiatives for more than 2500 regional and national client accounts.
- ❏ I have generated in excess of $50,000 in annual savings through leadership in successful freight rate negotiations.
- ❏ I offer a track record of management success including skill in strategic planning based on thorough knowledge of prevailing market and consumer trends.

If my qualifications meet a need in your company, I would look forward to a personal meeting.

Very truly yours,

P.L. Manager

Enclosure

Sales Marketing and Staff Training

Dear Hiring Executive *(or Manager)*:

I am exploring the possibility of joining your staff and have enclosed my resume for your review. Specifically, I would like to better utilize my talents in *(sales/marketing, staff training, general accounting, production operations, etc.)*.

Throughout the challenges of my career, I've worked effectively with management and staff at all levels of experience. Most importantly, I have demonstrated my ability to determine and meet the needs of the customer with tact and professionalism.

My background includes full responsibility for *(account prospecting, sales presentations and effective client relations)*, and this is the type of experience I can now bring to your company. I've developed excellent contacts at hundreds of large and small businesses, and I feel this can be extremely valuable to your firm.

I am available for an interview at your convenience to discuss how my education and experience could benefit you. Please contact me at the above number or address in order to arrange a meeting. I am looking forward to meeting you and discussing mutual interests.

Thank you for your time and consideration.

Sincerely,

Thomas D. Flanders

Encl.

Statistician

Name of Individual
Title
Organization
Street Address
City, State, Zip Code

Dear *(Specific Name)*:

   I am actively involved in a job search for a statistically related position in the *(insert the geographic area)*. Enclosed is my resume with an outline of my academic background. This Spring I will finish my second degree at Virginia Tech in Statistics, and I would like to locate a position in the *(manufacturing sector or insurance industry or research areas)*. Your firm was brought to my attention by *(name of individual, or cite specific advertisement)* and my research into the field.

   As you can see, I have a solid academic background with degrees in both mathematics and statistics. I am also equipped to utilize a variety of computer applications in statistical analysis. Throughout high school and college, I have worked to supplement my income through a variety of positions and am now very eager to begin work in my field. Although these work experiences were not related to statistical analysis, they did help me develop excellent communications skills, the ability to work in a variety of settings, and a respect for hard work. I am confident the combination of my work ethic and familiarity with statistics would be of value to *(insert name)* company.

   If you are interested in additional details about my background or if you require references, please do not hesitate to call. I do plan to contact you myself in about 10 days to arrange a time to talk with you further.

                    Sincerely,

                    Name of Job Seeker

Teaching

Ladies/Gentlemen:

(1)   In the interest of seeking a position as teacher with DePaul Language Academy, I have enclosed my resume for your review. It outlines my Teaching experience with learning disabled and mainstream students in Chicago and the suburbs.

(2)   As a mother of an LD student and two college-bound students, I have proven my ability to work effectively with parents of students at virtually all aptitude levels.

(3)   Throughout my career, I've demonstrated a strong devotion to teaching and my desire to work with students on a daily basis has never been greater. Former class activities have included full production supervision for the Rolling Knolls High School Year Book and I would be very interested in volunteer work with DePaul's After School Program.

Please contact me directly to arrange an interview, or for further information. Thank you for your time and consideration, and I look forward to great success with the students at DePaul.

Sincerely,

Mary Rodriquez

Encl.

NOTE: (1) This is a unique letter because Mary was presenting her qualifications directly to a committee for full-time status where she was currently a substitute. She was applying in Chicago where she had very little work experience, so I listed Chicago before suburbs. (2) It's alright to use LD after spelling out learning disabled in the first paragraph. Mentioning her children shows she has actual experience raising an LD child. (3) This shows a genuine interest in extra-curricular activities and a familiarity with the school's proposed program.

Training

1121 Wicka Road
Heartland, WI 53029
414/555-5892

Dear Hiring Manager:

I am exploring opportunities with your company. Specifically, I am seeking to better utilize my ability to train, motivate and energize both groups and individuals in successful endeavors.

❑ During various volunteer positions in college, I was highly successful in training and co-ordinating individuals with a wide range of backgrounds. My hands-on work experience includes customer service, sales and business administration, all with a highly positive attitude.

❑ I've proven my ability to work effectively with management and staff at all levels of experience. Most importantly, I have demonstrated my ability to determine and meet the needs of the customer in a professional, yet personalized manner.

I can provide excellent references upon request, and am willing to travel for the right opportunity. Please let me know as soon as possible when we may meet for an interview and discuss mutual interests. I look forward to your response.

Thank you for your time and consideration.

Sincerely,

Gary L. Larson
Encl.

Acknowledgments

The authors gratefully acknowledge the experts who contributed the cover letters found in this chapter.

Letters written by Kathryn Jordan

Statistician

Electric Engineer

Laboratory Technician

Cost Accountant

Public Relations

Letters written by Steven Provenzano

Application for Account Management

Meeting to Discuss Employment

Inquiry Regarding Sales Administration

Administrative Assistant

Teaching

Training

Sales Marketing and Staff Training

Boiler Plate Cover Letter

Letters written by John Bakos

Electrical Engineering

Business Facility Operations

Executive

Administrator

Sales Management

Outside Sales

APPENDIXES

A

Registering with the Worldwide Resume/ Talent Bank

One of the most popular online resume database services available today is the Worldwide Resume/Talent Bank offered by Gonyea & Associates, Inc. As of the date of the writing of this book, it contained over 20,000 resumes from job seekers and career professionals worldwide. The Worldwide Resume/Talent Bank is the largest collection of online resumes open to the general public available on any commercial computer network service in the United States. On any given week, hundreds of thousands of employers, employment recruiters, and other folks access this database looking for people to satisfy their employment needs. In only a few hours from now, your resume can be part of this database!

Resumes contained within the Worldwide Resume/Talent Bank appear (and may be viewed) on the following computer online services:

Computer Online Service	Location online
America Online	Use keyword "career center" to go to the Career Center, or from the Welcome screen, select Main Menu, then Education, then Careers, then Career Center. Once at the Career Center, select the Talent Bank menu item. Then select Search the Talent Bank to view resumes.
Internet/ICC	If you have Web access, use the following URL address: http://iccweb.com to access a site called the Internet Career Connection.
	Once you arrive at the Internet Career Connection, select the Resumes menu item.

If you are a member of CompuServe, Prodigy, GEnie, or Delphi, use the Web browser that is provided by any of these services and the Web URL address above to access the Worldwide Resume/Talent Bank resumes at our Internet site.

As reviewed in Chapter 4 in depth, you should consider posting your resume in an online resume database for several reasons, including:

❏ *Speed of delivery.* Your resume gets into the hands of employers faster!

❏ *Cost savings.* You save money!

❏ *Extended presence in the marketplace.* You're always out there!

❏ *Global access.* Employers worldwide can find you!

❏ *Powerful first impression.* It demonstrates you're on the leading edge!

Note: If you wish to post your resume in the Worldwide Resume/Talent Bank service, you *must* use the *Resumes Online* software program bundled with this book to produce a text copy of your resume.

Directions

To forward your electronic resume to Gonyea & Associates for posting in the Worldwide Resume/Talent Bank service, please follow *one* of the following two options:

Option 1: Forwarding via Email on America Online

If you are a member of America Online and wish to forward your resume via AOL:

1. Sign onto America Online.
2. Select Compose Mail from the Mail menu.
3. In the To box, enter "CareerDoc."
4. In the Subject box, enter "Resume for WR/TB."
5. In the Message box, enter:

    Your name

    Your mailing address

    Your home phone number with area code

    Your credit card number and expiration date

    The following statement:

    > Please enter my resume (see attached file) into the Worldwide Resume/Talent Bank service. I understand the cost is $39.95 for a one-year posting.

6. Click on the Attach File icon, and select the file that contains your electronic resume (the file created with the use of the *Resumes Online* software program).
7. Click on the Send button.

You will receive confirmation via email from Gonyea & Associates when your resume is received and posted into the Worldwide Resume/Talent Bank.

Option 2: Forwarding via Diskette

If you are not a member of America Online, or if you simply prefer to send your resume on diskette:

1. Copy your electronic resume file (the file created with the use of the *Resumes Online* software program) onto an *empty* 3.5-inch diskette.
2. Attach a disk label containing the following information:

    Your name

    File name

    Date

3. Enclose a cover letter containing the following:

    Your name

    Your mailing address

    Your home phone number with area code

    Your credit card number and expiration date (or a check made payable to Gonyea & Associates in the amount of $39.95)

The following statement:

Please enter my resume (see file on diskette) into the Worldwide Resume/Talent Bank service. I understand the cost is $39.95 for a one-year posting.

4. Mail your diskette and cover letter to:

Gonyea & Associates, Inc.
ATTN: Worldwide Resume/Talent Bank
1151 Maravista Drive
New Port Richey, Florida 34655

You will receive confirmation via first class mail from Gonyea & Associates when your resume is received and posted into the Worldwide Resume/Talent Bank.

B
Traditional Resume Resources

As much as we like electronic resources, sometimes a good old-fashioned book can come in handy. Many books on the market today deal with job hunting and resume preparation—far too many to list in this resource section. However, we have selected a few of our favorites that we believe you will find helpful in preparing your resume or in conducting a job search, especially an electronic job search. You should be able to find copies at your local bookstore or library.

200 Letters for Job Hunters. William S. Frank, Ten Speed Press ($17.95, 330 pgs.).

Applying for Federal Jobs: A Guide to Writing Successful Applications & Resumes for the Job You Want in Government. Patricia B. Wood, Bookhaven Press ($17.95, 222 pgs.).

Career Opportunities Available ONLINE. Pam Dixon and Sylvia Tiersten, Random House Electronic Publishing ($16.00, 400 pgs.).

Dynamite Resumes, 2nd ed. Ronald L. Krannich and Caryl Rae Krannich, PhDs, Impact Publications ($11.95, 184 pgs.).

Electronic Job Search Revolution. Joyce Lain Kennedy, John Wiley & Sons, Inc. ($12.95, 205 pgs.).

Electronic Resume Revolution. Joyce Lain Kennedy, John Wiley & Sons, Inc. ($12.95).

Guide for Occupational Exploration (GOE). U.S. Department of Labor, Employment and Training Division (available from JIST Works, Inc., 800-648-5478).

Hook Up, Get Hired! Joyce Lain Kennedy, John Wiley & Sons, Inc. ($12.95, 240 pgs.).

In Search of the Perfect Job. Clyde C. Lowstuter and David P. Robertson, McGraw-Hill, Inc. (316 pgs.).

Job Search Letters That Get Results. Ronald L. Krannich and Caryl Rae Krannich, PhDs, Impact Publications ($12.95, 239 pgs.).

Networking Your Way to Your Next Job ... Fast. Clyde C. Lowstuter and David P. Robertson, McGraw-Hill, Inc. ($14.95, 224 pgs.).

Perfect Resume Strategies. Tom Jackson and Ellen Jackson, Doubleday ($10.95, 220 pgs.).

Resumes Don't Get Jobs: The Realities and Myths of Job Hunting. Bob Weinstein, McGraw-Hill, Inc. ($10.95, 247 pgs.).

Resumes Express. Tom Jackson, New York Times Books ($9.50, 110 pgs.).

Resumes That Knock 'Em Dead. Martin John Yate, Bob Adams, Inc., Publishers ($7.95, 214 pgs.).

The Book of U.S. Government Jobs: Where They Are, What's Available and How to Get One, 6th ed. **Highly recommended!** Dennis V. Damp, Bookhaven Press ($18.95, 254 pgs.).

The Edge Resume & Job Search Strategy. Bill Corbin and Shelbi Wright, Beckett-Highland Publishing ($23.95, 167 pgs.).

The 5 Secrets to Finding a Job. Barbara L. Siegel with Robert S. Siegel, Impact Publications ($12.95, 149 pgs.; $29.95, 2 cassettes).

The Guide to Basic Cover Letter Writing. Steven Provenzano, VGM Career Horizons ($7.95, 87 pgs.).

The On-Line Job Search Companion: A Complete Guide to Hundreds of Career Planning and Job Hunting Resources Available Via Your Computer. James C. Gonyea, McGraw-Hill, Inc. ($14.95, 252 pgs), includes free copy of America Online software.

The Perfect Cover Letter. Richard H. Beatty, John Wiley & Sons, Inc. ($9.95, 173 pgs.).

The Perfect Job Search. **Highly recommended!** Tom Jackson, Doubleday ($12.50, 198 pgs.).

The Perfect Resume. **Highly recommended!** Tom Jackson, Doubleday ($10.95, 209 pgs.).

Staying on Top When the World's Upside Down: 1000 Ways to Be Successful in Your Life and Your Work. Joe Tye, Paradox 21 Publications ($14.95, 275 pgs.).

Top Secret Resumes for the '90s! Steven Provenzano, Advanced Resume Service, Inc. ($10.95, 212 pgs.).

C

Electronic Resume Resources

This appendix contains selected information regarding *electronic* resume resources including:

❏ *BBS resume posting services* where you can post your resume or view the resumes of other job seekers (see page 234).

❏ *Commercial computer online services* that offer career and employment information, including the option for posting your resume or of viewing the resumes of other job seekers (see page 234).

❏ *Computer software programs* to help you prepare a standard (nonelectronic) resume (see page 235).

❏ *Internet online resume database services* where you can post your resume on the Internet or view resumes posted by other job seekers (see page 236).

❏ *Internet Web sites* that offer career and employment information (see page 242).

❏ *Private resume posting services* not found on commercial online network services, BBS services, or the Internet (see page 245).

❏ *A graphic scanning service* to turn your photographs and artwork into graphic (*.bmp) images for use with your *Resumaker* program (see page 247).

BBS Resume Posting Services

Identifying BBS services where you can post your resume, or where you can view and download the resumes of job seekers, is often a difficult thing to do in spite of the fact that there are tens of thousands of BBS services in this country.

This situation exists for several reasons. First, in most cases, BBS services are owned by private individuals or small companies and, as such, they do not or cannot afford to advertise nationally. Second, most BBS services are accessed by local computer users, and therefore BBS owners in general do not advertise outside their local area. Third, BBS services, due to the ease with which they can be started and discontinued, typically come and go daily! Services you see today may not be here tomorrow. What you can't find today may be online tomorrow.

Several directories of BBS services are available, but tend to become obsolete and outdated quickly. However, *Boardwatch*, a major magazine devoted to BBS services, publishes a list of boards on its own BBS service and a list of List Keepers (people who maintain lists of BBS services) for access by the general public. Thousands of boards are listed with *Boardwatch*'s BBS service. If you're serious about finding and using BBS services to post your resume, subscribing to *Boardwatch* and the use of their BBS service is highly recommended.

Copies of *Boardwatch* may be obtained in most bookstores and magazine stores. For more information, contact *Boardwatch* at 800-933-6038. To reach their BBS, dial 303-973-4222.

Commercial Computer Online Services

Millions of employers and employment recruiters already use commercial computer online network services, such as:

❑ America Online.
❑ CompuServe.
❑ Delphi.
❑ GEnie.
❑ Prodigy.

They advertise career and employment opportunities and/or communicate with job seekers via email or online chat. As a result, millions of job seekers are also logging online to find employment, often finding job ads that appear only online. If you're not using online services to find employment, you're likely missing out on many appropriate opportunities. Of the services listed, America Online and CompuServe offer the majority of the online employment-related services. America Online offers far more employment services than the other networks combined.

While there are a variety of what might be considered employment-related services on each network, we have listed the main area or areas online for each service where you can either post or review resumes.

America Online

Location online:	Career Center
How to get there:	use keywords = career center
Service:	Talent Bank (to access/post resumes)
Service:	Help Wanted-USA (to view help wanted ads)
To order service:	800-827-6364

CompuServe

Location online:	Career Management+ Forum
How to get there:	use go = career
Service:	Resume Library
To order service:	800-848-8199

To subscribe to any of these services, you first need to obtain access software from the service or services you wish to join. Once this software is installed on your computer, you will be able to connect directly to the service using your personal computer and a modem. Access to each service is available for a low monthly fee, plus reasonable hourly useage rates. Check with each service for more information regarding membership fees. Access software may be obtained at most computer software stores, via various mail order software companies, or from the services directly (see the preceding phone numbers).

Computer Software Programs

More and more career guidance and job seeking assistance is becoming available in the form of computer software. Many of the following programs are designed to help you produce a standard, printed resume. You should be able to find these programs in your local software store, or by calling the publisher or distributor listed.

Achieving Your Career: Job Search Software for the Whole Human Being (Up Software, Inc., 415-921-4691, suggested retail: $69.95, format: Macintosh and Windows).

Building Your Jobsearch Foundation: A Three Step Process Toward Building Your Future (Up Software, Inc., 415-921-4691, suggested retail: $45.95, format: Macintosh and Windows).

Career Design (Career Design Software, 212-889-8500, suggested retail: $49.00, format: DOS).

JobHunt 6-in-1 (listing of 12,000 employers nationwide) (Scope International, Inc., 704-535-0614, suggested retail: $39.95, format: Windows). An optional CD-ROM disk containing 100,000 employers is available for $69.95 for use with the Job Hunt 6-in-1 program.

Job Power Source: Job Finding Skills for the 90's (INFOBusiness, 801-657-5300, suggested retail: $49.95, format: CD-ROM and Windows).

Jumpstart Your Job Skills (Up Software, Inc., 415-921-4691, suggested retail: $69.95, format: Macintosh and Windows).

PFS Resume and Job Search Pro (Softkey, 800-227-5609, suggested retail: $49.95, format: Windows and DOS).

The Perfect Resume (Davidson Software, 310-793-0600, suggested retail: $49.95, format: Windows and CD-ROM).

The Ultimate Job Finder (secrets of finding job vacancies, internships, and grant opportunities the classifieds don't advertise) (Daniel Lauber, INFOBusiness, 800-657-5300, suggested retail: $49.95, format: DOS).

WinWay Resume (WinWay Corporation, 800-4winway, suggested retail: $39.95, format: Windows and CD-ROM).

Internet Online Resume Database Services

As of the writing of this book, the following Internet sites were available for posting your electronic resume and/or accessing (online or via download) resumes posted by other individuals. Because the Internet is in constant flux, some of these sites may not be operational when you attempt to access them. Also, new sites may spring up at any time. Use your favorite Internet search program, such as Yahoo, to find the sites that are available at the time you need assistance. If the service listed is a Web site, then its URL address is provided. If it is a Gopher site, then its Gopher address is listed.

123 Careers. A database of resumes that are uploaded at no cost; search is restricted to participating recruiters.
(URL) http://www.webplaza.com/pages/Careers/123Careers/123Careers.html

A+ On-line Resumes. A small compilation of resumes presented in HTML at no cost to the job seeker; no cost for search.
(URL) http://www.hway.com/olresume

AAA RESUME. A highly advertised service offering to upload resumes to an unidentified database for a minimal cost.
(URL) http://www.infi.net/~resume/upload.html

ACP On-line. An Australian database for computer affiliated jobseekers. No charge for upload; search by membership.
(URL) http:// www.ozjobs.com

Actors Pavilion. A database of actors is provided at no cost for either upload or search.
(URL) http://www.seal.com

ArtsNet. A no-cost resume upload and search service provided for the arts and entertainment industry.
(URL) http://artsnet.heinz.cmu.edu/career/career.html

BAMTA Job Bank Directory. A service provided by the Bay Area Multimedia Technology Alliance (BAMTA) at no cost for either upload or search.
(URL) http://mlds-www.arc.nasa.gov/form/BAMTA

Cal Poly MBA Association. A database of resumes of Cal Poly MBA grads; contains color photos of candidates; no cost to search.
(URL) http://www.calpoly.edu/~mgt/mbaa/resumes.html

Canadian Business Advertising Network. World Wide Job Seekers is a database of resumes provided by the CBAN at no cost to either upload or search.
(URL) http://www.calpoly.edu/~mgt/mbaa/resumes.html

Career Magazine. The World Wide Web Resume Bank is provided at no cost for either upload or search.
(URL) http://www.careermag.com/careermag/

Careersite. A restricted resume database available by membership at cost for search; no cost for upload.
(URL) http://www.careersite.com/

Computer Register. A limited database of computer associated professionals. Cost, if any, to upload, is not available; no cost to search.
(URL) http://www.computerregister.com

Cyberdyne/CVCentral. A resume processing center in the United Kingdom that uploads the resume interactively and then sends it to selected agencies. No cost for upload or search.
(URL) http://www.demon.co.uk/cyberdyne/cvcenter.html

Direct Marketing World Job Center. Provided as a free service to the Internet community; job seekers can post full resumes.
(URL) http://mainsail.com/jobs.htm

E-span Resume Database. A resume database acccessible to client companies; upload at no cost.
(URL) http://www.espan.com/resinfo.html

Float Your Resume. A small database of resumes in webpage form; fee for upload; no cost for search.
(URL) http://www.wwma.com/hr/

Franklin Search Group. A resume database for the biotechnical and medical industries; upload and search at no cost.
(URL) http://www.gate.net/biotech-jobs/c-menu.html

Future Access. A database of resumes provided as a service of *Employment Digest.* Upload at no (or modest) cost; search at no (or modest) cost.
(URL) http://futureaccess.com/

Get A Job! A database of resumes for Hypermedia Professionals. Upload and search at no cost.
(URL) http://sensemedia.net/getajob

Global Job Net. A database of resumes designed to provide some level of confidentiality. No cost for upload or search.
(URL) http://www.globaljobnet.com

Global Net's Latin American Career Center. A database of resumes posted in Spanish and made available to the Latin American community from all over the world.
(URL) http://www.globalnt.com/bolsa

Graphiti Printing & Graphics' Online Resume Service. A database of resumes provided at no cost for either upload or search.
(URL) http://www.careermag.com/careermag/

Hyper-Media Resumes. A resume database allowing for interactive resume uploads and search. Minimal cost for upload; no cost for search.
(URL) http://www.webcom.com/~resumes/

IntelliMatch. A database of resumes that are entered using a structured process and are then matched to job openings. No cost for upload at the basic level; moderate cost at enhanced level. Search by paid membership.
(URL) http://www.intellimatch.com

Internet Career Connection. Here is the Internet's central source of career and employment services and information. If you want to know what's available on the Internet related to the subject of careers, employment, and self-employment, stop into the ICC first. The online searchable employment ads and candidate resume databases are the largest databases of their kind on the Internet.
(URL) http://iccweb.com

Internet Professional Association. A database of resumes for the use of its employment industry professional members. No cost for upload.
(URL) http://www.onramp.net:80/ron/

Internet Resume Registry. A new database provided by Career and Resume Management for the 21st Century! Modest cost for upload; no cost for search.
(URL) http://crm21.com

Internet Stage and Screen Resources. A database consisting of resumes from Directors and Producers, Actors and Designers, Technical trades and Technical Crafts people, Pre- and Post-Production personnel.
(URL) http://www.stagenet.com/stagenet/

ITC Employment Agency. A modest database provided by the International Telecommunications Center for the no-cost upload and search of resumes from telecommunications personnel.
(URL) http://www.telematrix.com/employment/employment.html

JapanNet Resume Book. A compilation of printed resumes distributed to businesses seeking individuals with Japanese skills. No cost for upload or book.
(URL) http://www.asia-net.com/resume.html

JobTailor. A database of resumes compiled as portfolios. No cost for upload; search by fee paid contract.
(URL) http://www.jobtailor.com

Media Concepts Headshot Homepage. A database of resumes and headshots of New England actors and actresses. Upload for a fee; search without cost.
(URL) http://www.tiac.net/users/joegold/acting.html

MedSearch. A database of resumes for jobseekers in the medical field. No cost for upload; search at no cost; search with identity provided by membership only.
(URL) http://www.medsearch.com/

Monster Board Resume City. Resumes can be created and upload online for search by participating employers. No cost for upload; search by membership only.
(URL) http://www.monster.com/online.html

National Technical Employment Services (NTES) Resume Central. A database of resumes for contract professionals only. Various pricing plans for upload; search is without cost.
(URL) http://iquest.com/~ntes/

NetJobs. A Canadian database of resumes that are uploaded for modest fees; search without cost.
(URL) http://www.netjobs.com:8000/JWresume.html

Online Career Center. Contains the resumes of job seekers; minimal cost to upload; no cost to search.
(URL) http://occ.com/occ/

Online Employment Services. A searchable database provided by Online Employment Service to help people in the scientific and engineering fields. Search and upload free to anyone in a field related to optics.
(URL) http://www.spie.org/web/employment/employ_home.html

People Bank. A database of resumes of people interested in working in the United Kingdom, Ireland, and Australia. Upload at no cost; search by membership.
(URL) http://www.peoplebank.co.uk/ten/2reg.htm

PursuitNet. A database of resumes maintained for professional, technical, and management-level individuals qualified to seek jobs in the $30,000 to

$150,000 range. No cost to upload; no cost for search, except when placement is made.
(URL) http://www.tiac.net/users/jobs/index.html

Resume Net. A database of resumes provided by the Silicon Valley Computer Industry available for viewing at no cost. Upload is available at a modest cost.
(URL) http://www.resume-net.com/

Resume Publishing Company. Resumes can be posted in HTML format for a modest fee. Search is by URL provided by the job seeker; no open search capability.
(URL) http://www.webcom.com/~cha

Resumes Online. A database of resumes for job seekers from various disciplines provided at cost for the upload. Search without cost.
(URL) http://www.crocker.com:80/resumes/

Saludos Hispanos Resume Pool. A database of resumes for Hispanic people looking for work. No cost to upload; no cost to search.
(URL) http://www.calpoly.edu/~mgt/mbaa/resumes.html

Skill Search. A database of resumes developed from highly structured resumes that are then searched and matched to existing job openings. Cost for upload; cost for search.
(URL) http://www.internet-is.com/skillsearch/in-iis.html

Sports Related Job Listings and Resume Bank. A no-cost upload and search database of resumes of people interested in jobs in the sports and recreation industries.
(URL) http://www.onlinesports.com/pages/CareerCenter.html

Talent Hunter. A restricted database provided to the CGI industry. No cost for upload or for search.
(URL) http://www.lightside.com/~dani/ism/resumes/cgi-bin/talent-hunter.cgi

Taos Mountain Software. A database of software-related professionals provided at no cost to either job seeker or employer/recruiter.
(URL) http://www.taos.com/

Technology Registry. An online employment database for the technologies industries. No cost for upload; search by membership.
(URL) http://www.batnet.com:80/techreg/

TeleJob. An electronic job exchange board provided by the Swiss Federal Institute of Technology in Zurich. Resumes in the form of advertisements are free to individuals.
(URL) http://ezinfo.ethz.ch/ETH/TELEJOB/tjb_home_e.html

Transaction Information Systems. Resumes are uploaded to a database provided by Transaction Information Systems. No cost for upload. Search access restricted.
(URL) http://www.tisny.com/tis/tis_form.html

Top Jobs in Asia. Resumes are submitted by mail to a database utilized by Asian recruiting firm. No cost to upload.
(URL) http://www.hk.net/~eal/index.html

Trilogy Enterprises, Inc. Resumes are uploaded into a database utilized in-house only; no cost for upload.
(URL) http://www.teinc.com/trilogy/home.html

Tuscon Resume Pool. A database of resumes for job seekers associated with Tuscon, Arizona. Upload at a modest cost; search online without cost.
(URL) http://tuscon.com/resumes/

Virtual Africa/Headhunters International. A database of resumes submitted by job seekers at a modest cost. Search without cost.
(URL) http://www.africa.com/headhunt/

Virtual Headbook (Actors). A free resource for casting agents and talent scouts. Actor's headshots and resumes online are provided at a moderate cost.
(URL) http://www.xmission.com/~wintrnx/virtual.html

The Virtual Job Fair Resume Database. A service of Westech Career Expo; upload without cost.
(URL) http://www.careerexpo.com/pub/Rsubmit.html

Web Consultants Showcase. A directory of web publishing consultants. Upload and search provided at no cost.
(URL) http://infotique.lm.com/webcon.html

Web India. A database of resumes from professionals associated with India. Resume uploads are provided at a low cost; search free.
(URL) http://www.webindia.com/cust/us/resumes.html

Western Technical Resources. No-cost resume upload to database provided and utilized by Western Technical Contracting and Recruiting Services.
(URL) http://www.webcom.com/~wtr/

Internet Web Sites

The Internet is a large and constantly growing medium for the exchange of information. Many Web sites already offer cyberspace visitors various kinds of career and/or employment related information, other than or in addition to resume posting services. A search of the Web conducted by the authors revealed the following Web sites. To access these sites, you first need access to the Internet itself, plus a Web browser to view Web sites. Various commercial Internet access services exist; check your favorite computer software outlet. In addition to providing access to the Internet, each access service will normally provide you with the necessary software (i.e., Web browser) with which to access the Internet, including the most popular part of the Internet—Web sites! For each of the following sites, the appropriate URL Web site address is provided. Enjoy the trip!

In addition to accessing the Internet by using a commercial Internet access service, you can also reach the Information Superhighway by joining America Online, CompuServe, or Prodigy. These commercial network services now offer a Web browser and Internet access.

Our favorite commercial Internet access service is NetCom. By joining this service you will receive a copy of their NetCruiser software program, which makes traveling the Internet as easy as pointing and clicking your mouse. To become a member of NetCom, call 800-353-6600.

Academe This Week—Job Openings. Job openings in and out of academe are job openings acquired from the weekly issues of *The Chronicle of Higher Education.*
(URL) http://chronicle.merit.edu/.ads/.links.html

America's Job Bank. America's Job Bank links by computer the 1800 state employment service offices in the United States, thus providing rapid, national exposure for the more than 100,000 jobs listed by the local offices.
(URL) http://www.ajb.dni.us

American Employment Weekly. This is a 48-page tabloid containing help wanted advertising culled from ads reproduced from the Sunday editions of 50 leading newspapers across the country and selected firms.
(URL) http://branch.com/aew/aew.html

ASAE—Employment List. This site is a site or hypertext link to other employment resources. At the time of this writing, there were 120 of them. Mark this site as a valuable resource.
(URL) http://asae.org/jobs

Avotek Publishing—Headhunters' Address Guides and Employment Contact Worldwide. Avotek Publishing, located in the Netherlands, has established a multifaceted and extensive resource center for jobseekers, employers, and recruiters who are involved in the international scene.
(URL) http://www.universal.nl/jobhunt

Career and Resume Management for the 21st Century! CRM21 has rapidly become a destination for jobseekers, employers and recruiters who have discovered the vast resources provided by the more than 50 career-related businesses including career centers for women, diversity, military and contract/temp services.
(URL) http://crm21.com

Career Mosaic. A production of Bernard Hodes Advertising, this site provides an array of career-related services, including a database of jobs, a listing of career fairs, a College Connection, and employer profiles.
(URL) http://www.careermosaic.com

CareerNet—Career Resource Center. CareerNet is a website dedicated to providing easy access to other career-related sites. CareerNet provides a significant career related resource on the Net.
(URL) http://www.careers.org

CareerWeb. CareerWeb is an interactive online service that offers employers, franchisers, and career-related companies the opportunity to reach qualified candidates worldwide, at the same time offering qualified candidates the opportunity to browse career opportunities.
(URL) http://www.cweb.com

CC-Lite. Career Counseling—Lite provides career-related services in a friendly and professional manner, while geared toward helping people collect information about themselves and the world of work.
(URL) http://www.execpc.com/~cclite

CyberDyne CS Limited. This is an electronic job center based in the United Kingdom. In addition to a vast number of links to career-related resources, CyberDyne presents an extensive listing of recruiters worldwide.
(URL) http://www.demon.co.uk/cyberdyne/cyber.html

Contract Employment Weekly Services. C. E. Weekly, published by C. E. Publications, is designed to provide subscribers with information about immediate and anticipated job openings in the United States, Canada, and overseas. The focus is on temporary technical jobs.
(URL) http://www.ceweekly.wa.com/cew/ce_intro.html

Employment Edge. Employment Edge specializes in professional career placement throughout the United States. Their site is noted as a resource for other career-related resources with links to other websites.
(URL) http://www.employmentedge.com/employment.edge

FedWorld JOBS Library. This website lists all the files available from the JOBS Library of the FedWorld Information Network. The page is updated daily.
(URL) ftp://fwux.fedworld.gov/pub/jobs/jobs.htm

HiTech Careers. High Technology Careers WWW Publication provides career management and development information, technology trends, and future outlooks. Also provided are various other resources for jobseekers and employers.
(URL) http://careerexpo.com/pub/htc/htchome.html

Internet Career Connection. Here is the Internet's central source of career and employment services and information. If you want to know what's available on the Internet related to the subject of careers, employment, and self-employment, stop into the ICC first. The online searchable employment ads and candidate resume databases are the largest databases of their kind on the Internet.
(URL) http://iccweb.com

IEG—International Employment Gazette. IEG is a 64-page publication containing over 400 current job openings every two weeks from the international scene.
(URL) http://amsquare.com/america/gazette.html

IPA—Internet Professional Association. IPA is the online association for the employment industry which provides employment professionals and

those looking for contacts an opportunity for a one-stop solution to their employment-based needs.
(URL) http://www.onramp.net/ron

JAN (Job Accommodation Network) on the Web. JAN is an international toll-free consulting service that provides information about job accommodations and the employability of people with functional limitations; information about the Americans with Disabilities Act (ADA).
(URL) http://janweb.icdi.wvu.edu

JobSearch. JobSearch maintains an exclusive database of 40,000 companies and provides access to the hidden job market for anyone seeking employment in Southern California.
(URL) http://www.adnetsol.com/jsearch/jshome1.html

JobWeb. This is a service of the National Association of Colleges and Employers. Offers access to employment classifieds, candidate resumes, and other information for recent grads and alumni.
(URL) http://www.jobweb.org

MedSearch America. The website MedSearch America provides an opportunity to search jobs, search resumes, view employer profiles, and obtain valuable employment and industry information.
(URL) http://www.medsearch.com

Monster Board. This full-service career-related website provides viewers with career search, resume search, and employer profile viewing opportunities. Also available is a list of upcoming career fairs.
(URL) http://www.monster.com/home.html

NAS—The National Ad Search. This is an employment weekly that contains over 2500 employment opportunities each week.
(URL) http://amsquare.com/america/nas.html

NetJobs. In this Canadian-based full-service career center, viewers can post and search resumes, post and search jobs, obtain career information, and peruse listings of upcoming events. A list of participating employers is also provided.
(URL) http://www.netjobs.com:8000/index.html

Online Career Center. This is a full-service nonprofit career center. Attention should be given to the extensive and well utilized databases of job ads.
(URL) http://occ.com/occ

On Line Design. This website is dedicated to providing contract employment services for engineers, drafting, electronics, and desktop publishing/technical writing.
(URL) http://

Rensselaer Career Resource Homepage. This is an extensive list of online job databases and other employment related information that is found on the Internet.
(URL) http://www.rpi.edu/dept/cdc/

TKO Personnel, Inc. Founded in 1983, TKO has specialized since 1986 in Japanese recruitment for the semiconductor and software markets. Since1993, TKO added other Asia/Pacific, specifically China- and Korea-related positions for semiconductor and software markets.
(URL) http://www.internet-is.com/tko/in-yahoo.html

Private Resume Posting Services

Career Database
PO Box 626
Provincetown, MA 02657
Voice: 508-487-2238
Fax: 508-487-0371
Contact: Allan Wimer, Managing Director
Cost: $50/year; individual prices for inclusion in database
Career Database is a computer database containing several thousand resumes. The computer selects relevant data from the database and formats it into a career profile, which is then supplied to recruiters and employers worldwide. The service is available to job seekers in all career fields.

Career Search
Career Finders, Inc.
21 Highland Circle
Needham, MA 02194-3275
Voice: 617-449-0312
Fax: 617-449-4657
Contact: Tim Kelley, Sales Manager
Cost: Available upon request
Career Search provides an extensive database service whereby companies matching a job seeker's career objective may be identified. This national employment search system provides a database search service CD-ROM with the option of downloading search results to a client's computer.

American Chemical Society
1155 16th Street NW
Washington, DC 20036
Voice: 202-872-6208
Voice: 202-872-6213
Fax: 202-872-4529
Contact: Louis Carille, Program Assistant, or Lynn Bagorazzi, Program Assistant
Cost: Available upon request
American Chemical Society provides an online database of members. Members may enter their resumes, and employers may list announcements regarding job openings. The database may be searched and matches sent to prospective employers.

IFMA Job Referral Service
International Facility Management Association
1 East Greenway Plaza, Suite 1100
Houston, TX 77046-0194
Voice: 713-623-4362
Voice: 800-359-4362
Fax: 713-623-6124
Contact: Research Specialist
Cost: No cost to job seekers; $295 per search requested by employers
IFMA maintains a database of resumes of facility managers. The database may be searched according to criteria established by the employers who wish to find appropriate candidates.

North Coast Meridian
Route 52 and Maple Avenue
Pine Bush, NY 12566
Voice: 914-744-3061
Fax: 914-744-3961
Contact: Thomas F. Thomaschek
Cost: Free to job seekers and career planners
North Coast Meridian maintains a large database that contains specific information and resumes of candidates. The company conducts searches of its own database in order to match candidates and jobs.

PowerMatch (also available on the Internet)
625 Ellis St., Suite 303
Mt. View, CA 94043
Voice: 415-962-1425
Fax: 415-962-2682
Contact: Jen Whitmer, Marketing Coordinator
Cost: Site license of $54,000
PowerMatch is a fully integrated employment management system that includes a database of resumes of prospective candidates.

Restrac
1 Dedham Place
Dedham, MA 02026
Voice: 617-320-5600
Fax: 617-320-5630
Contact: Christie Currie (voice: 617-320-5322)
Gregory Morse (voice: 617-320-5351)
Cost: Furnished upon request
Restrac is a staffing system for companies with over 1000 employees. It contains a database of resumes that can be searched by recruiters or employers.

Roster, Inc.
6333 Constitution Drive
Fort Wayne, IN 46804

Voice: 219-436-6330
Fax: 219-432-7126
Email: roster@ix.netcom.com
Contact: Steve Trimarchi
Roster maintains a current database of over 10,000 individuals with managerial, technical, engineering, professional, sales, and other experience in a broad variety of industries that are located in, and seeking positions in, all geographic regions of the United States.

University ProNet
2445 Faber Place, Suite 200
Palo Alto, CA 94303
Voice: 800-726-0280
Contact: Director, University ProNet
Cost: Alumni, $35 for lifetime membership; employers, varies with subscription size.
University ProNet is a private database of alumni resumes representing the following 16 universities: Stanford, UC-Berkeley, MIT, UCLA, University of Michigan, Carnegie Mellon, Caltech, University of Texas, Ohio State University, University of Chicago, Columbia, University of Wisconsin, Cornell, University of Illinois, Yale and University of Pennsylvania.

Resumaker Graphic Scanning Service

If you have a 35-mm color photograph or any graphic illustration or artwork that you would like to display within your *Resumaker* multimedia resume, and if you are unable to convert the photograph or artwork into a bitmap format (*.bmp) as required by the *Resumaker* program, you are invited to contact OnLine Solutions, Inc. You may mail your artwork to OnLine Solutions, who will then scan your artwork and produce a *.bmp file. OnLine Solutions will then mail or email you back your bitmap file. For further information regarding cost, please contact:

OnLine Solutions, Inc.
Wayne Gonyea, President
1584 Route 22B Beckwith
Morrisonville, NY 12962
518-643-2873

D
Online Employment Advertising Services

Boot up, Get Online, Find a New Employee or Job Fast!

Employers and employment recruiters wishing to find new candidates to fill available positions have discovered that online advertising can publicize their job opening announcements to millions of job seekers worldwide—faster, easier, and at a lower cost than traditional means of employment advertising. Reaching a wider audience, getting instantaneous responses from job seekers, and saving money are just some of the reasons employers and recruiters are turning to online advertising to satisfy their personnel needs.

As a result, job seekers are flocking by the millions to online services to access the thousands of employment ads that now appear online daily. By knowing how to job hunt electronically, job seekers can access more than 100,000 employment listings online on any given day! Never before could job seekers access such a volume of job opening announcements, from employers worldwide, and through the ease and convenience of their personal computer.

If you're an employer, employment recruiter, or job seeker interested in using electronic advertising, you should explore three leading service providers:

Help Wanted-USA

This service, offered by Gonyea & Associates, Inc., maintains the largest single collection of help wanted ads available online of any commercial network service. Each week, Help Wanted-USA posts more than 15,000 current help wanted ads for professional positions from A to Z, from companies nationwide and around the world.

For employers and employment recruiters, advertising online is available at the rate of $75 per ad for an unlimited length listing, which will be posted for a two-week period. Volume discounts are available.

For job seekers, Help Wanted-USA ads may be accessed on America Online and the Internet at the following Web site location:

Internet Career Connection URL = http://iccweb.com

In addition, access may be obtained by CompuServe, Prodigy, GEnie, and Delphi members using their service's Web browser and by connecting to the above Internet Web site.

For further information, contact:

Gonyea & Associates, Inc.
1151 Maravista Drive
New Port Richey, Florida 34655
813-372-1333

America's Job Bank

Sponsored by the United States State Employment Service, this Internet Web site location lists employment announcements gathered from state employment offices nationwide. On any given day, America's Job Bank may contain 100,000 help wanted ads for various level positions (blue collar, clerical, trade, professional, etc.) from employers nationwide. Ads appearing on this Internet site are not available on any commercial network service.

To reach America's Job Bank on the Internet, use URL http://www.ajb.dni.us/

For employers wishing to post help wanted notices, contact your local state employment service.

E-Span

Similar in its objective to Help Wanted-USA, E-Span publishes help wanted notices collected from employers nationwide. While fewer in number, E-Span's position announcements include professional and nonprofessional positions.

Access may be obtained by job seekers on America Online and CompuServe, as well as via the Internet at the following Web site location: http://www.espan.com

For additional information, contact:

E-Span
8440 Woodfield Crossing
Suite 170
Indianapolis, IN 46240
800-682-2901

E
Glossary

Antivirus   A special computer software program that can detect viruses and destroy them. *See* Virus.

ASCII   A generic file format that can be generated by word processing and text editing programs. Documents formatted as ASCII (aka text) are universally understood and can be read by any word processing or text editing program.

Baud   A measure of speed for computer modems governing how fast data can be transferred via a phone connection. Speeds range from slow (2400 or less) to higher speeds including 9600, 14,400, and 28,800.

BBS (Bulletin Board System)   A communications system created by combining special software programs, a computer, a modem, and a telephone line. BBSs are most often used by individuals or companies to exchange information, files, programs, data, and email, as well as to chat online.

CD-ROM   A medium for storing information for access with the use of a computer. Currently one of the largest storage options available beyond 3.5-inch disk and hard drive storage options. Similar in design and use to music CDs.

Cyberspace   A term, coined by William Gibson in his novel *Neuromancer,* that refers to the invisible place in the universe where people can connect and communicate through the use of computers and computer network services.

Document A generic term used to describe letters, memos, reports, or other items created by a word processing program.

Download The processing of transferring data or information from a remote computer (usually a commercial network service, BBS, or a site on the Internet) to your own computer.

Electronic Job Hunting The process of looking for employment notices on computer online network services.

Electronic Resume A resume that is not in print format, but one that is available and can be transmitted as a computer-generated document.

Email address A word or phrase, often one you select, that identifies your electronic mailing address, where email can be sent and received.

Email Messages, such as notes, letters, reports, etc., that are sent from your computer to another individual (computer) via a commercial or private network, and vice versa. Information may be sent via email or as an attached file to an email message.

File Transfer Protocol (FTP) The process of sending files via a computer network.

Information Superhighway The anticipated electronic communications network envisioned by the Clinton/Gore administration that will connect all U.S. citizens via computers. Often confused with the Internet, which is the prototype of the Information Superhighway.

Internet Currently the world's largest network of connected computers. Originally created by the U.S. government, the Internet now connects government agencies, the military, commercial businesses, organizations, educational facilities, and private individuals worldwide.

Login The process of connecting to a computer network service using a personal computer. The actual process of dialing in and identifying yourself to the network's host computer.

Logout The process of disconnecting from the network.

Modem A device that connects to your computer and your phone outlet, allowing you to communicate via the phone line with other computer users worldwide.

Multimedia Computer software programs that contain more than one of the following elements: video, animation, sound, text, or graphics.

Network A group of computers connected for the purpose of sharing data and information. A network could be small, connecting only two computers, or large, connecting millions of computers.

Offline The opposite of online. When you are offline, you are disconnected from a computer network and unable to transmit or access information that is normally available via the network.

Online The state of being connected to a computer network, either commercial or private. When you are online, you are capable of transmitting and accessing information via the network.

Post The act of leaving information on some online network service, BBS, or site on the Internet. An example is to post your resume online.

Searchable database A collection of information found online or via a computer that may be accessed using keywords.

Shareware Computer software that you may try before purchasing. Depending on the preferences of the author of the program, you may use the program and, if you wish to keep it, must pay the author the required fee.

"Shine Your Light" A term often used by job seekers when stressing that people should take active steps to let others know about their employment value and qualifications.

Surfing Going online and roaming or looking indiscriminately for information in a wide number of places.

SysOp (system operator) The person who manages a bulletin board system.

Teleconferencing (aka online conferencing) Meeting online with other individuals for the purpose of discussing personal or business matters.

Upload The process of transferring data or information from your computer to a remote computer (usually a commercial network service, a BBS, or a site on the Internet).

URL (uniform resource locator) An addressing system used on the Internet to indicate the location of Web sites. An example is http://iccweb.com.

Virus A special computer software program that, if allowed to enter your computer, may cause damage to your computer files. *See* Antivirus.

Web site (aka World Wide Web or WWW) A location on the Internet that is graphical in design and appearance, and that may contain data, information, video, sound, and text. The most popular access medium on the Internet today.

Index

America Online, 4, 37, 234
Ames, Gary, xiii, 201

Bakos, John, xiii, 201, 224
BBS services, 234
Blind resume, 41
Bulletin Boards, 42

Career and Resume Management for
    the 21st Century! 242
Chronological resumes, 115
Combination resumes, 116
Compressing files, 112
CompuServe, 4, 37, 234
Computer:
    baud, 37
    CD-ROM drive, 38
    fax card, 38
    memory, 37
    monitors, 37
    mouse, 37
    printer, 38
    sound card, 38
Credit cards, 42
Cyberspace, 1

Delphi, 37, 234

Electronic resume:
    advantages, 21
    formats, 5
    purpose, 5
Email, 28
    address, 29
    attached file, 29

File Transfer Protocol (FTP), 28
Functional resumes, 115

GEnie, 37, 234
Gibson, Timothy, xiii, 202
Gonyea & Associates, Inc., 47, 227-230

Help Wanted-USA, 248

Information Superhighway, 1, 4
Internet, 1, 4
    address, 30

Internet Career Connection, 238, 243
Internet Resume Registry, 238

Jackson, Tom, xiv, 3, 202
Jordan, Kathryn, xiv, 201, 224

Keywords, 16, 62

Multimedia resume, 7, 18

Online file library, 28
Online Job Search Companion, 9, 232
Online resume database, 27
OnLine Solutions, 247

PKZIP, 113
Prodigy, 4, 37, 234
Provenzano, Steven, xi, 201, 224

Resumaker:
  description, 7, 19, 90

installation, 92
starting/use, 92
Resumes Online:
  description, 7, 45, 46
  exporting as a text file, 88
  installation, 47
  Run Resume Wizard, 50
  starting/using, 48

Special keyboard commands, 52

Targeted resumes, 116
Techno-Marketing, Inc., 91
Text document (file), 6

Virus infection, 43

Wilson, Debarah, xiv, 202
Worldwide Resume/Talent Bank Service, 46,
  227

Ziffnet, 37

About the Authors

James C. Gonyea, President of Gonyea & Associates, Inc., is recognized as an expert in career and employment guidance, especially in the use of online resources for effective career planning and job placement. In his 25 years of practice, James Gonyea has counseled thousands of clients.

James Gonyea created the nation's first electronic career and employment guidance agency, called the Career Center, available on the America Online computer network service, and an Internet sister service known as the Internet Career Connection.

James Gonyea also created *Help Wanted-USA* and *Worldwide Resume/Talent Bank*, two of the nation's premier employment services.

Wayne M. Gonyea established OnLine Solutions, Inc. to specialize in the management and uploading of electronic resumes and in the development of Web sites, and to provide merchants with a means of selling electronically on the Internet.